M&A FROM PLANNING TO INTEGRATION

M&A FROM PLANNING TO INTEGRATION

**Executing Acquisitions
and Increasing Shareholder Value**

**Robert J. Borghese
Paul F. Borgese**

**Association for
Financial Professionals**

McGraw-Hill
New York   Chicago   San Francisco   Lisbon   London   Madrid   Mexico City
Milan   New Delhi   San Juan   Seoul   Singapore   Sydney   Toronto

Library of Congress Cataloging-in-Publication Data

Borghese, Robert J.
    M&A from planning to integration: executing acquisitions and increasing shareholder
value / Robert J. Borghese, Paul F. Borgese.
        p. cm.
    ISBN 0-07-137521-X
    1. Consolidation and merger of corporations—United States—Management 2.
Corporations—Valuation—United States. 3. Consolidation and merger of
corporations—Law and legislation—United States. I. Title: M and A from planning to
integration. II. Borgese, Paul. III. Title.

HG40′:8.M4 B67 2001
658.1′:—dc21   2001044003

McGraw-Hill

A Division of The *McGraw·Hill* Companies

1 2 3 4 5 6 7 8 9 0   AGM/AGM   0 9 8 7 6 5 4 3 2 1

ISBN 0-07-137521-X

Printed and bound by Quebecor/Martinsburg.

This publication is designed to provide accurate and authoritative information in regard to the subject
matter covered. It is sold with the understanding that the publisher is not engaged in rendering legal,
accounting or other professional service. If legal advice or other expert assistance is required, the services of a competent professional person should be sought.

> —*From a declaration of principles jointly adopted by a Committee*
> *of the American Bar Association and a Committee of Publishers.*

McGraw-Hill books are available at special quantity discounts to use as premiums and sales promotions,
or for use in corporate training programs. For more information, please write to the Director of Special
Sales, Professional Publishing, McGraw-Hill, Two Penn Plaza, New York, NY 10121-2298. Or contact
your local bookstore.

This book is printed on recycled, acid-free paper containing a minimum of 50 percent recycled, de-inked
fiber.

CONTENTS

ACKNOWLEDGMENTS

Like any viable M&A effort, the development of this book has been an exercise in teamwork. First, we would like to thank Jim Kaitz, Reese Nank, Courtney Gentleman, Kraig Conrad, Lucretia Boyer, and the many others at the Association for Financial Professionals who worked with us through many versions of this manuscript. Second, we would like extend gratitude to writer Thomas P. Fitch for his research and substantial editorial contribution to several sections of the initial manuscript. Finally, we would like to thank our editors at McGraw-Hill, including Kelli Christiansen and Maureen B. Walker, who provided us with invaluable advice on how to make this book a more useful tool for corporate executives.

Although this book is a good introductory text on the M&A process, it is not meant to be purely for academic study (e.g., read once for an end-of-semester exam and then used as a paperweight, if it makes it onto an executive's desk at all). Rather, it was developed as a step-by-step tool that can be referred to again and again in a multitude of M&A–related situations. What makes the book different from many of the more theoretical books already published on this popular topic is that it includes a plethora of actionable insights from practicing M&A professionals, especially Joseph Connolly, Steve Sammut, and Fred Militello. We would especially like to thank Paul Morin for substantial contributions to several sections of this book, including performing due diligence, managing integration, and developing an acquisition scorecard.

We also are significantly indebted to the many management thinkers whose work is referenced throughout this book. For certain specific sections of our *M&A Strategy Guide,* (Part II of this volume), our objective was not to reinvent any wheels, but rather to put new, insightful spins on well-tested ones that are relevant to some aspect of the M&A process. To this end, we included many frameworks, checklists, and perspectives developed by influential business writers on a variety of topics, including leadership, strategy, and scorecarding.

Also, this book would not have been completed without the ever-present support of our friends and colleagues. We particularly would like to acknowledge Jovanka Ciares, Michael Bertoline, Peter Briscoe, Daryl Capuano, Jim Cardillo, Brian Corbett, Henry Hsia, Jason Kaplan, Zuhair Khan, Ian MacMillan, Gary Miller, Joel Port, John Quinn, Eric Raimo, Vicky Schwartz, Richard Shell, Eric Siegel, Leslie Smith, James Spady, and Robert Thompson, all of whom have shaped our thinking over the years.

Finally, we would like to thank our family for providing us with fantastic opportunities to grow and educate ourselves. We especially need to thank our parents, Helene and Salvatore Borgese, who have provided us with a shining example of one of the most important types of mergers that any of us will ever experience.

THE TREASURY'S ROLE IN MERGERS AND ACQUISITIONS

The treasury's role in corporate finance activities over the years has grown from one of managing cash and treasury transactions to one of providing strategic financial advice and guidance. Although technology and process improvements have helped to foster this evolution, the recognition of treasury's value to the success of the organization is a key component of the transformation. That recognition comes from the company's most senior leadership, analysts, and shareholders, as treasury professionals exercise skills such as strategic planning, technology consulting, leadership of self-directed work teams, and management of cross-functional economic efficiency projects.

In the case of mergers and acquisitions (M&A), the dismal track record of many value-destroying integrations has prompted a greater involvement of operational functions in the due diligence process. Traditionally, due diligence was handled by an investment banker, attorney, or M&A specialist—the treasurer would become involved only at the integration phase. Today, most organizations realize that the groundwork for a successful integration is laid well before the transaction is completed. Tight resources and a drive to achieve stated performance targets has led senior management to rely on internal resources to ensure that transactions are completed smoothly. As such, more and more frequently treasury is charged with validating the deal's potential value and confirming the representations made by the acquisition target. Frequently, treasury also is instrumental in investor relations activities, dilution recovery, and operational integration.

As the role of financial professionals continues to expand, the practical experience and strategic vision treasury brings to the table in a merger is vital. Appendix G, "The Due Diligence Process in Mergers and Acquisitions: Treasury's Role," is a summary of a presentation made at the AFP 21st annual conference in 2000. The discussion focuses on the role treasury can play in the M&A process and the issues that are imperative to deriving value from the transaction and achieving the desired results from the integration.

INTRODUCTION

Every day it seems there is a new merger and acquisition (M&A) deal splashed across the headlines. All are portrayed as glamorous, bold solutions, which will lead to fantastic increases in shareholder value. Unfortunately, the glad-handing and backslapping at the press conference where the deal is announced usually fade to a more somber scene, which often ends in downsizing, culture clashes, and destruction of shareholder value.

Decades of corporate experience coupled with extensive academic research from as far back as the 1960s indicate that such value destruction is the norm and not the exception (see Figure I-1). Value destruction can only be avoided if corporate executives who are planning and executing corporate acquisition programs are armed with a structured program that will guide them through the M&A process and force them to think clearly and critically about that process.

And the need for M&A guidance is on the rise. At the time of this writing, preliminary data released by Thompson Financial Securities Data indicates that U.S. companies executed acquisitions valued in excess of $1.84 trillion in 2000, which is an increase of nearly 18 percent from the approxi-

FIGURE I-1 How Mergers* Affect Shareholder Value.[1]

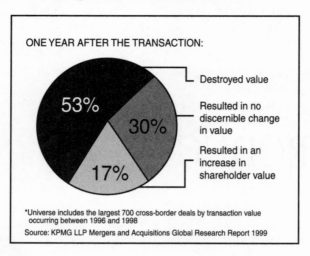

ONE YEAR AFTER THE TRANSACTION:

53%

30%

17%

— Destroyed value

Resulted in no discernible change in value

Resulted in an increase in shareholder value

*Universe includes the largest 700 cross-border deals by transaction value occurring between 1996 and 1998

Source: KPMG LLP Mergers and Acquisitions Global Research Report 1999

mately $1.56 trillion worth of deals completed the year before. As the volume and pace of M&A activity have increased, so too has the number of corporate executives who are thrust into the role of managing some aspect of an acquisition. Corporate executives at these combining companies, who may be very competent in their respective functional areas, suddenly must execute merger and acquisition transactions with little or no training. *M&A from Planning to Integration* provides such corporate executives with the structured framework that will guide them through the M&A process and force them to think clearly and critically as they proceed through each step in a transaction.

To rationalize the process of a merger and acquisition transaction it is necessary to reduce it to a series of discrete steps. Virtually all merger and acquisition transactions should proceed through the following steps:

Step 1: Thinking Through Strategic Objectives

Step 2: Assessing Structural Capacity

Step 3: Identifying and Screening Potential Acquisition Targets

Step 4: Performing Due Diligence

Step 5: Valuing the Acquisition Target

Step 6: Selecting the Appropriate Legal and Tax Structures for the Transaction

[1]Unlocking Shareholder Value: The Keys to Success—Mergers and Acquisitions. A Global Research Report, 1999. Reprinted with permission from KPMG.

Step 7: Managing Integration

Step 8: Monitoring Progress through Acquisition Scorecarding

Step 9: Implementing an Acquisition Feedback Loop

While each of these steps takes on a different level of importance, depending on the particular transaction at hand, together they form the basis of a structured framework for thinking about merger and acquisition transactions. These nine steps form the basis for the structured framework that is referred to as *The M&A Strategy Guide.*

As an aside it is important to note that throughout this book the term "M&A" is intended to cover both mergers and acquisitions, even though these two forms of transactions differ significantly in their legal and tax implications. Moreover these terms are often used interchangeably. A more precise definition of each is included in *Step 6: Selecting the Appropriate Legal and Tax Structures for the Transaction.* Also, for the sake of convenience, the book refers to "acquiring" and "target" or "acquired" companies. Although many transactions are portrayed as "mergers-of-equals," one company's management team usually dominates—if not during the transaction, then at some point afterward. By "acquiring" a company, what is meant is this dominant entity.

OVERVIEW OF THE M&A STRATEGY GUIDE

At the core of *M&A from Planning to Integration* is the nine-step *M&A Strategy Guide* (Part II of this volume), which outlines a methodology designed to assist the corporate executive in formulating, structuring, and executing a transaction. *The M&A Strategy Guide* rationalizes the acquisition process by dividing it into a series of discrete steps and outlining the basic issues that arise as each step is taken.

A STRATEGY-LEVEL TOOL

The value of *The M&A Strategy Guide* to the corporate executive is the discrete yet organic approach it brings to the acquisition process. Too often, executives become overly focused on the details of the transaction. Time after time, corporate executives experienced in M&A advise focusing on the big issues. *The M&A Strategy Guide* therefore should be thought of as a strategy-level tool that will keep executives on track and force them to think clearly and critically about the transaction.

Step 1: Thinking Through Strategic Objectives

As with any endeavor, *defining strategic objectives* should be the first step. Therefore, the *Guide* begins with the step entitled "Thinking Through Strategic Objectives." The management of an acquiring company must be able to clearly articulate the reasoning behind its growth strategy. Some of the most common reasons for pursuing merger and acquisition transactions include: increasing geographic reach, expanding product and service offerings, providing liquidity for company founders, and acquiring promising new technologies. Step 1 forces corporate executives to clearly articulate their reasons for pursuing growth through M&A. This first step is crucial, because all of the remaining steps flow from the strategic decisions made at this early stage.

Step 2: Assessing Structural Capacity

The second step in *The M&A Strategy Guide* is *Assessing Structural Capacity*. Many companies skip this self-assessment step, focusing rather on defining criteria for prospective targets and performing due diligence on identified targets. The acquiring company, however, must first assess its own readiness and capacity to embark upon an acquisition strategy before assessing the target company. This step outlines the issues that should be considered by a potential acquirer prior to embarking upon such a strategy.

Step 2: Assessing Structural Capacity, identifies the areas that should be the focus of such a self-evaluation program, including: (a) readiness of the acquisition team to tackle strategic, legal, financial, and operational aspects of the acquisition program; (b) assessment of the financial strength of the acquiring company; (c) analysis of the value of the acquiring company; and (d) assessment of the ability of the acquiring company to use pooling-of-interests accounting or purchase accounting in consummating a transaction.

Step 3: Identifying and Screening Potential Acquisition Targets

The third step is *Identifying and Screening Potential Acquisition Targets.* This section of the *Guide* offers practical guidelines for selecting potential acquisition targets and covers such factors as the composition of the search team, the definition of acquisition criteria, the sourcing and screening of appropriate targets, and the initial contact.

Step 4: Performing Due Diligence

The fourth step is to *performing due diligence* on the potential acquisition target. This section of the guide reviews the four main areas of due diligence, namely strategic, financial, legal and operational.

Step 5: Valuing the Acquisition Target

The fifth step is *Valuing the Acquisition Target.* Many books have been written on corporate valuation, however, these books usually delve into the financial underpinnings of the valuation models without providing the reader with a clear understanding of strategic concepts, which ultimately determine whether the acquisition will increase shareholder value. This section of the *Guide* reviews and discusses two core concepts in valuation: (1) *intrinsic* value and (2) *synergistic* value. It then provides a brief overview of two of the most common methods of determining intrinsic value: (1) *discounted cash flow methodology* and (2) the *market-multiple method.*

Step 6: Selecting the Appropriate Legal and Tax Structures for the Transaction

The sixth step is *Selecting the Appropriate Legal and Tax Structures* for the transaction. This is a complex task, requiring a thorough understanding of the acquiring company, the target company, each of their respective objectives, and the legal, tax, and accounting treatment of each transaction structure. These issues are complicated and constantly evolving, and can only be navigated with the assistance of expert legal and tax counsel. The purpose of this step is to provide corporate executives with a basic understanding of the various transaction structures so that they are at least conversant in these issues.

Step 7: Managing Integration

The seventh step is *Managing Integration.* Recent research indicates that poorly planned and executed integration is one of the main causes of failed acquisitions. Managing the integration of acquired companies is a complicated task, requiring close attention to a number of variables. The *Managing Integration* section provides suggestions on leadership in the context of M&A; taking advantage of M&A restructuring to instill good management philosophies in the newly combined organization; and the key variables that executives must address during the integration process. These include: (a) effective communication; (b) human resource issues; (c) legacy relationship issues; and (d) optimization of cross-selling to the customer base.

Step 8: Monitoring Progress through Acquisition Scorecarding

The eighth step is *Monitoring Progress through Acquisition Scorecarding*. The Acquisition Scorecard should provide the decision maker with a holistic view of the enterprise without overwhelming him or her with too much information. This is accomplished by selecting and monitoring a few key business metrics, including: (a) financial; (b) innovation; (c) customer; (d) internal operations; and (e) human resources.

Step 9: Implementing an Acquisition Feedback Loop

The ninth and final step is *Implementing an Acquisition Feedback Loop,* which demonstrates how the acquiring company can take lessons learned from one acquisition and use them to better plan and execute subsequent transactions.

These steps also incorporate conceptual frameworks (such as those developed by Professors Michael Porter, John Kotter, and others), which have been adapted and expanded to illustrate their relevance in the broader framework of *The M&A Strategy Guide*. Originally, these tools were developed to help executives address management problems not necessarily related to an acquisition strategy. The purpose of including these tools in the *Guide* is to demonstrate how these tools may be relevant in planning and executing an acquisition.

M&A FROM PLANNING TO INTEGRATION

M&A Basics

1

M&A HISTORY AND CURRENT TRENDS

BACKGROUND

A historical perspective on M&A activity contributes to an understanding of the strategic drivers of successful transactions. The following overview, drawn in part from Patrick A. Gaughan's *Mergers, Acquisitions, and Corporate Restructurings,*[1] reveals that M&A activity over the past century has been driven by a wide range of forces, including technological innovations, economic conditions, regulatory developments, and innovations in financial products.

We currently are experiencing the fifth wave of significant M&A activity in U.S. economic history. The first great wave of consolidation in the United States took place at the turn of the last century and was characterized by consolidations in several industries through horizontal mergers. The second wave took place from the mid-1910s until the stock market crash of October 1929. This wave was fueled by the post-World War I economic boom. Horizontal mergers continued to be the norm, yet vertical deals also played a

---

[1]*Mergers, Acquisitions and Corporate Restructurings,* Patrick A. Gaughan, John Wiley & Sons, August 1999.

significant role during this wave. The third wave ran from the mid-1960s until the end of that decade, which is often referred to as the "Go-Go Years" in reference to the booming stock market at the time. This wave ushered in the conglomerate era in which companies made acquisitions outside of their core industries. The fourth M&A wave, which occurred during the 1980s introduced the terms *corporate raider, junk bonds,* and *hostile takeover* to our vocabularies. Corporate raiders relied on significant debt financing to buy companies, break them up, and sell the pieces for a quick profit.

THE FIRST WAVE OF M&A: LATE 1890s TO EARLY 1900s

The first wave of mergers and acquisitions, which began at the turn of the last century, was concentrated in mining (primary metals, petroleum products, chemicals) and manufacturing (transportation equipment and fabricated metal products). This M&A activity was characterized by horizontal mergers, which were an attempt to achieve economies of scale. It was thought that growing the sheer size of one's company through M&A would lead to lower per-unit costs and thus greater efficiency. The landmark transaction of this era was the billion-dollar merger that formed USX Corporation by joining U.S. Steel, Carnegie Steel, and nearly 800 smaller steel companies. Other of today's household names that were formed during this wave include E.I. du Pont, Eastman Kodak, and General Electric.

Approximately 300 major combinations took place during this period despite the enactment of the Sherman Antitrust Act. This Act declared that the formation of monopolies and other attempts to restrain trade were unlawful and punishable as criminal offenses under federal law. However, the Justice Department simply did not have the resources to enforce the Act.

Business historians note that several factors beyond this lax enforcement of federal antitrust laws contributed considerably to the rampant M&A activity of the period. Most notable was the development of the U.S. railway system in the aftermath of the Civil War. Linking the country's regional markets through a web of transcontinental steel tracks created one national market. With this transportation system in place, companies could deliver their products to distant markets at less cost. This gave companies the impetus to strive for greater economies of scale through acquisitions. The majority of the corporate combinations of the time, however, failed to achieve the anticipated increases in efficiency.

Known as the "trustbuster" because of his pro-competitive stance, President Theodore Roosevelt, who occupied the Oval Office from 1901 to 1909, was largely unsuccessful in curbing this first wave of horizontal (or what was thought of at the time as "monopolistic") mergers. It was not until the end of Roosevelt's tenure in office that the government began having greater success with its antitrust cases. It was not government action, but rather the stock market crash of 1904, followed by the banking panic of 1907, that brought an end to the M&A activity of the first wave.

THE SECOND WAVE OF M&A: MID-1910s TO LATE 1920s
The second wave of merger and acquisition activity was sparked by the post–World War I boom economy. However, this wave was met with considerable resistance due to renewed interest in antitrust legislation within Congress. In 1914, Congress passed the Clayton Act, which strengthened the earlier Sherman Antitrust Act by prohibiting specific business practices. Also, in 1914 Congress passed the Federal Trade Commission Act, thus establishing the Federal Trade Commission (FTC). Unlike the earlier Sherman Act, the Federal Trade Commission Act and the Clayton Act were given teeth through the creation of this new enforcement agency. The FTC was granted the authority to investigate antitrust violations and enforce the laws.

In this stricter antitrust environment, fewer horizontal mergers were consummated. Instead companies began to explore vertical mergers (buying companies at different points on their supply and/or distribution chains) as well as conglomerates (merging firms in unrelated industries.) Such conglomerations were not as radical as those of the third wave, which put together companies in extremely disparate industries; however, there was some experimentation in the name of growth.

The industries affected by M&A activity in this wave echoed those of the first wave: primary metals, petroleum products, chemicals, and transportation equipment. As in the first wave, this second period of M&A activity saw the genesis of many of today's household names including General Motors, IBM, and John Deere. The second wave ended with the stock market crash of October 1929 and the Depression that followed.

THE THIRD WAVE OF M&A: MID- TO LATE 1960s
In the mid-1960s, a rise in consumer confidence added fuel to a booming economy, which in turn, created a bull market in stocks. With this optimism as a backdrop, the third wave of M&A made an entrance.

This third wave of M&A activity revolved around a movement toward conglomeration. Companies seeking to expand again had to face a more stringent antitrust environment. The Celler-Kefauver Act of 1950 strengthened the antitrust laws further by closing loopholes that had been found in the Clayton Act and were being exploited by companies hungry for growth. With horizontal and vertical mergers being thwarted by this stricter law, companies had no choice but to expand by acquiring companies in industries unrelated to their own.

The industrial titans of the era, like Harold Geneen, the chief executive of ITT, acquired companies simply to grow in size, with little thought as to whether the acquired companies could work together synergistically. Many major corporations of the 1960s expanded into so many different industries that they almost rival today's mutual funds in terms of their diversity.

This regulatory pressure to grow through diversification was accompanied by the rise of management science. The prevailing view of this new discipline was that professional managers could manage any business in any industry. This academic concept was disseminated into the business world as more and more corporate executives sought the credential of masters of business administration (MBA) from the prominent universities that were now offering that degree. Therefore, it was thought that a generic business degree prepared executives to run any big company, and the bigger, the better.

One of the best-known examples of a conglomerate created during this third wave is ITT. This conglomerate was made up of wildly unrelated businesses that included Avis Rent-A-Car, Continental Baking, and Sheraton Hotels as well as restaurant chains, consumer credit agencies, and home-building companies.

This wave peaked in 1969 and then declined in part due to the drop in the stock market in that same year. Many of the cross-industry acquisitions of this period were sold off in the decades that followed, mainly due to the fact that the acquirers had overpaid for the companies they bought. Academic research in finance since that time indicates that the stock market punishes, rather than rewards, corporate diversification. The generally accepted thinking in this regard today is that there is significant value in management expertise and concentration of attention on highly focused businesses.

THE FOURTH WAVE OF M&A: THE 1980s

The "Go-Go Years" of the 1960s were followed by the high-inflation, stagnant growth economy of the 1970s, which was caused in part by the Arab oil embargo of 1973. Significant M&A activity was rekindled in 1981, however.

The M&A catchphrase of this period was "hostile takeover." A hostile takeover was an attempt, unwelcome by the board and management of the takeover target, to buy a corporation usually by making what is known as a *tender offer*—an offer directly to a company's shareholders—to purchase the outstanding stock of that company. Such buyers were usually what would be called *financial* buyers, as opposed to *strategic* buyers. Instead of buying a company with plans to absorb it for long-term strategic growth reasons, as would a strategic buyer, a financial buyer is more interested in the pure financial results of the transaction. Usually this strategy involves purchasing a company with the intention of quickly breaking it into pieces and selling those pieces to the highest bidders. In some cases, takeover attempts were merely ploys by corporate raiders to sell the target companies' shares at significantly higher prices than what had been paid for them a short time earlier. Very profitable premiums (known as "greenmail") were paid in order to avoid the threat of a takeover by hostile shareholders.

Relatively few (yet extremely large) hostile takeovers dominated the M&A headlines of the 1980s. No one felt safe as even the country's largest companies were threatened with takeover attempts. Corporate management had never been so openly challenged, and in response they resorted to an arsenal of antitakeover defenses. Devices such as staggered boards, "golden parachutes," and "poison pills" were designed to either dissuade unwanted acquirers by making the transaction prohibitively expensive or else by compensating target companies' boards, management, and shareholders, should these unwelcome acquirers force themselves on them.

In order to execute these huge deals, corporate raiders had to rely on significant amounts of debt financing; hence the rise of the *leveraged buyout* (LBO). In an LBO, a public company is taken private when its outstanding shares are purchased, usually by means of debt capital. The innovative development of the "junk bond" market—the low-quality, high-yield corporate bond market—by Michael Milken of the investment bank of Drexel Burnham Lambert funded many a takeover.

Leveraged buy-out firms became wildly successful, yet many of the corporations that they left in their wakes were crippled by the hasty deals that had been made without sound corporate strategy in mind. To add to the chaos, Japanese companies were buying high-profile American businesses, and U.K. institutions quietly bought up a sizable piece of corporate America.

In the face of all of this activity, M&A became a defensive play for many American management teams. It was a scramble to acquire in order to avoid being acquired, which led to a rash of hastily executed deals that were doomed to fail. The relatively high cost of capital in the 1980s, coupled with poor acquisition planning and execution, resulted in many unsuccessful M&A deals. Such failures would become obvious in the early 1990s when a flurry of bankruptcies resulted from the inability of many companies to pay the exorbitant interest costs sustained in the high-leverage debt deals of the 1980s.

The M&A party came to an end on a few frenzied days of trading in October 1987 when the Dow Jones Industrials dropped 508 points, or

22.6 percent. Then came the savings & loans scandal, which required nearly a half-trillion dollars' worth of federal intervention during a time of explosive federal deficits. The M&A market slowed down in response, waiting for the dust to settle.

The largest M&A deals of this fourth wave include the Kohlberg, Kravis, and Roberts (KKR) purchase of RJR Nabisco; Chevron's purchase of Gulf Oil; Philip Morris' absorption of Kraft; Bristol Myers' merger with Squibb; Texaco's purchase of Getty Oil; and du Pont's acquisition of Conoco.

THE FIFTH WAVE OF M&A: THE 1990s AND BEYOND

There was relatively little M&A activity at the beginning of the 1990s. As the economy came out of the 1990–1991 recession, however, M&A activity was on the rise once more. By the mid-1990s, M&A records were being broken again. For example, in the record year of 1995, over $400 billion in deals were announced. Several high-profile deals signaled the beginning of a new wave. Disney acquired Capital Cities for $19 billion and Chemical Bank merged with Chase Manhattan in a $10 billion transaction.

The millennium ended with a string of record transactions with never-before-seen valuations. Some of the notable deals include the Citicorp-Travelers merger, the Daimler-Chrysler merger, and the AOL Time Warner merger.

The merger and acquisition activity at the turn of the millennium had no single set of characteristics or drivers—every industry appeared to have motivations of its own, and the vibrancy of the capital markets, the availability of cash, and the currency of inflated public securities provided the fuel for such activity. However, there was one notable distinction from the frenzy of the previous decade. While announcements and prices were up, the attention to integration issues was noticeably more deliberate. The actual results of this activity will not be known for several more years, but a number of good practices emerged which are highlighted in this book.

There are several trends that may lead to an extension of this fifth wave of M&A. With the bursting of the Internet bubble on Wall Street, the valuations of all companies are beginning to return to more realistic levels. M&A activity may continue unabated for the next several years as venture capitalists force distressed companies in their portfolios to liquidate by being acquired. Established companies that have faltered over the past few years also may have to put themselves on the block in order to satisfy impatient shareholders. Companies that have spent millions on building their brand names over the last several years can be had at bargain-basement prices; and so, bricks-and-mortar companies envious of these Internet rivals may buy the viable ones to jump-start their online presence.)

Understanding the history of merger and acquisition activity of the past century is helpful in understanding the reasons why corporations have pursued such programs and what has generally worked and what has not.

CATEGORIES OF M&A TRANSACTIONS

The motivations for corporate M&A activity are complex and varied (see Figure 1-1). To illustrate this point we describe various categories of corporate acquisitions in the following section. These categories help set the stage for broader strategic thinking, which will take place in Step 1.

Although corporate acquisitions can be evaluated by how much shareholder value has been created, one also must take into account the deal's original strategic objective. For example, in some cases an acquisition may be necessary in order for a company to remain competitive. Although such a move might not generate significant shareholder value, it might save an otherwise distressed company. In such a case, even a loss in shareholder value in the short term may prove to be necessary for long-term success.

FIGURE 1-1   Different reasons for seeking growth through acquisitions.[2]

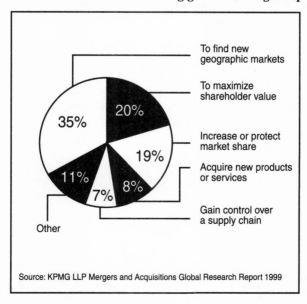

Source: KPMG LLP Mergers and Acquisitions Global Research Report 1999

[2]Unlocking Shareholder Value: the Keys to Success—Mergers and Acquisitions, a Global Research Report, 1999. Reprinted with permission from KPMG.

Financial Buyers versus Strategic Buyers

The buyout firms of the 1980s are examples of *financial buyers*. Buyout firms are in the business of acquiring companies with underutilized assets that are leverageable, improvable, and ultimately salable. Generally speaking, financial buyers do not acquire companies for the very long run. Their methods involve the divestiture of product lines and businesses, and the constant restructuring of the acquired company's finances in order to ready the acquired company for resale.

Although companies today can learn from the discipline of financial buyers, the trend is against making acquisitions in order to break up and sell off pieces of the target. Currently there is a move toward acquisitions that have more of a strategic fit with the buyer. Such buyers are called *strategic buyers*. *The M&A Strategy Guide* has been prepared with the strategic buyer in mind.

Integration within and across Industries

Horizontal Integration   A company that is seeking to strengthen its current link or links in the value chain by acquiring competitors or similar businesses in a different geographic area is undertaking a strategy of *horizontal* integration. Many of Cisco Systems' acquisitions involve niche companies whose technology and core business fill Cisco's strategy of providing a comprehensive end-to-end networking solution.

Vertical Integration   A company that remains in the same industry but seeks to participate in other links in the value chain by, for example, acquiring suppliers or production technology, or acquiring sales or distribution capacity, is undertaking a strategy of *vertical* integration. The acquisition by the drug company Merck of the pharmaceutical benefits management company Medco is representative of this strategy.

Diagonal Integration   A company that pursues an acquisition that involves both horizontal and vertical elements is undertaking a strategy of *diagonal* integration. The AOL Time Warner deal is an example of diagonal integration. It is a merger that combines content and intellectual property ownership, with distribution technology and infrastructure. The marriage may define an entirely new media industry.

Conglomeration   Companies like ITT, which make acquisitions across disparate industries, undertake a *conglomerate strategy*. As will be discussed later in this book, the stock market values focus over diversification, and so the trend is away from conglomeration.

2

OVERVIEW OF COMMON ACQUISITION PITFALLS, AND TACTICS FOR AVOIDING THEM

Recent research indicates that despite a generation's worth of experience with growth through acquisition strategies, mergers and acquisitions of the past decade have not been any more successful in creating shareholder value than did the transactions of the 1960s, 1970s, or 1980s.

As a prelude to delving into the details of the *Guide,* the following table (Figure 2-1) reviews some of the common pitfalls of M&A planning and execution. Along with each of the pitfalls are suggestions on how these pitfalls can be avoided or how any adverse impact can be minimized.

FIGURE 2-1   Acquisition pitfalls and how they can be avoided or any adverse impact minimized.

Corporate Acquisition Program Pitfalls	Proactive Steps
Pitfall 1 — Poorly planned corporate strategy: The top executives in an acquiring company must understand and agree upon their overall corporate strategy before embarking upon the risky growth strategy of M&A.	**Suggestion:** Executives must develop a corporate strategy based on assessments of the strengths and weaknesses of their companies as well as the external environment in which they must operate. *Step 1: Thinking Through Strategic Objectives*, offers a series of frameworks that can be used to develop an effective corporate strategy.
Pitfall 2 — Overpayment for acquisition targets: Synergy estimates are overoptimistic. Expectations regarding rapid cost savings and cross-selling are unrealistic. These and other potential benefits always take more time than expected to materialize and when they do materialize are often less significant than anticipated.	**Suggestion:** *Step 5: Valuing the Acquisition Target,* focuses on the elusive components of synergistic value, which drives M&A deals. As is mentioned in the step, executives experienced in M&A sometimes discount or even completely ignore the value attributable to synergies when determining an appropriate price for a target company.
Pitfall 3 — Cultural issues are ignored: Culture clashes have proven to be at the root of many failed acquisitions. Usually, decision makers spend their time poring over financial and legal documents while ignoring significant management and human resource issues.	**Suggestion:** Executives on an acquisition team must closely scrutinize the compatibility of company cultures and norms. While a study of culture is never exact, and is best done over time, it should never be neglected. Operational and financial integration, while crucial, are not enough to ensure a good fit. *Step 7: Managing the Integration*, provides frameworks for dealing with the "softer" side of integration.
Pitfall 4 — Rushed due diligence: Typically, financial and legal due diligence are adequately performed (due in part to the retention of outside experts), but strategic and operational due diligence are often insufficient.	**Suggestion:** Thorough due diligence should be performed. This includes in-depth investigations in all four key areas covered in *Step 4: Performing Due Diligence* — strategic, financial, legal, and operational.
Pitfall 5 — Unclear acquisition criteria: When the acquisition criteria are unclear, acquisitions tend to be opportunistic rather than strategic.	**Suggestion:** As is explained in *Step 3: Identifying and Screening Potential Acquisition Targets*, detailed acquisition criteria should be developed and adhered to throughout the selection process. This acquisition criterion will flow from the corporate strategy, which is developed in *Step 1: Thinking Through Strategic Objectives*.
Pitfall 6 — Failure to monitor the integration progress appropriately: M&A integrations are notoriously complex. Often, executives are too busy "putting out fires" to plan next steps or ensure that necessary activities have been performed properly.	**Suggestion:** *The M&A Strategy Guide* is meant to reduce the complex process of M&A into discrete steps that are clear and actionable. This same strategy must be employed at the tactical level as well. Milestones with accompanying timelines must be established and adhered to. *Step 8: Monitoring Progress Through Acquisition Scorecarding*, provides general guidelines on implementing this process.

3

CORPORATE STRATEGIC PLANNING AND THE M&A PROCESS

Corporate strategic planning has fallen in and out of favor over the past several decades. Many equate strategic planning with Soviet-style multiyear plans and argue that the business environment moves too quickly to benefit from such planning. In many cases, it seems that strategic planning is waved off due to simple laziness or an intellectual inability to grasp what may be a multitude of complex issues. *The M&A Strategy Guide* rejects such perspectives. This multistep tool and the overall framework outlined in this book were developed to force disciplined thinking, which is a necessity in all business planning and especially in the complex realm of M&A planning and execution. Of course, the business environment is in constant flux, but this only means that planning time horizons must be shortened and strategic plans must be revisited constantly.

In the 1980s, influential Harvard professor, Michael Porter, focused attention on the subject of corporate strategic planning through his classic books, *Competitive Advantage* (Free Press, 1985) and *Competitive Strategy* (Free Press, 1980), along with a series of articles that were published in the *Harvard Business Review* (HBR).

In his HBR article, "From Competitive Advantage to Corporate Strategy" (HBR, May–June 1987), Porter defines "corporate strategy" as "the overall plan for a diversified company," as opposed to the competitive strategy that is pursued at the business unit level. "Corporate strategy," he writes, "is what makes the corporate whole add up to more than the sum of its business unit parts." According to Porter, corporate strategy should answer two questions: first, what businesses should the corporation be in? and second, how should these business units be managed?

Porter defines strategy developed at the business unit level as *competitive strategy*. Examples of competitive strategy include pursuing a low-cost provider strategy or a product-differentiation strategy. In this context, pursuing a horizontal acquisition in order to create economies of scale is a competitive rather than a corporate strategy. For practical purposes, this book's definition of strategy includes both corporate strategy and competitive strategy as defined by Porter.

THE DISMAL TRACK RECORD OF CORPORATE STRATEGIC PLANNING

Porter argues that flaws in strategic thinking are the root cause of many corporate strategic blunders. He rejects studies that focus on changes in merged entities' short-term market values as indications of strategic success. He indicates that such short-term market reactions are highly imperfect measures of the long-term success of acquisition activity.

Porter also rejects the use of shareholder value to judge performance since, to have a controlled experiment, one would have to compare the actual shareholder value change *with* the M&A activity to the shareholder value change that would have resulted *without* this same activity. This clearly is impossible.

He therefore suggests another method for testing successful implementation of corporate strategy through M&A activity. He uses the number of companies or business units retained by the acquiring company as an indicator of successful corporate planning and execution.

Porter studied 33 well-known U.S. companies over the period from 1950 to 1986 to test this hypothesis. The study included: Allied Corp., Borden, du

Pont, Exxon, General Electric, IBM, ITT, Johnson & Johnson, Mobil, Procter & Gamble, Tenneco, 3M, Westinghouse, and Xerox. The results of this study indicated that the track record of corporate strategic planning is very poor. He found that on average the corporations in the study divested more than half of their acquisitions in new industries during the period studied. Furthermore, 14 of the 33 companies divested more than 70 percent of the acquisitions they made in new fields. He specifically notes that even a well-regarded company like General Electric divested "a very high percentage of its acquisitions, particularly those in new fields."

The results of Porter's study emphasize the importance of well-thought-out strategic planning. *The M&A Strategy Guide* begins with this lesson in mind. Determining a corporation's overall strategy, be it corporate strategy and/or competitive strategy, will drive the rest of the merger and acquisition process. Step 1 of *The M&A Strategy Guide* outlines several frameworks for thinking about corporate strategy in the M&A context. Once the strategy has been defined, the remaining steps in the *Guide* map out a plan for executing on that strategy.

However, before proceeding to the first step of the *Guide* it is instructive to understand that a merger and acquisition strategy is only one of a number of growth strategies that a corporation may pursue. In order to set the context for a detailed discussion of merger and acquisition planning and execution, we proceed with a discussion of the alternative corporate growth strategies that may emerge from the corporate strategic planning process.

OVERVIEW OF THE MAJOR CORPORATE GROWTH STRATEGIES

Corporate growth can be achieved through a range of strategies. The five most basic strategies are *organic growth, corporate venturing, strategic alliances, corporate private equity investment,* and *mergers and acquisitions.* These strategies are not mutually exclusive; in fact, many successful growth companies employ a mix of them at any given time. Obviously, this book assumes that growth will be achieved at least in part through M&A. Even executives who have already made the decision to grow through M&A should review this section before proceeding, as there are many valuable lessons that can be learned from the other growth strategies, which may influence their strategic thinking. An overview of each strategy follows.

Organic Growth

This approach to corporate growth pursues growth through innovation of existing product and service lines and penetration of new markets. One of the challenges of this approach to growth, particularly for public companies, is that investors often do not reward a company for pursuing such a strategy, as the expected rate of earnings growth is perceived to be too slow. Another challenge is the fast pace of change in many industries and the inability to generate and support adequate exploitation of market opportunities purely on the basis of internal resources. For these and other reasons, one of the other four approaches to growth is often used to augment the organic growth approach. For example, strategic alliances may be formed to overcome the lack of sufficient internal resources and distribution channels.

Corporate Venturing
In the corporate venturing approach, growth is achieved through the use of internal resources to start and run new ventures, often outside existing product and service lines and markets.

Corporate ventures are new businesses that are internally generated and funded by the sponsoring company. They have several common characteristics regardless of the venture undertaken: They are start-up activities managed within the funding company; represent an activity new to the organization; and are undertaken with the goal of increasing sales, profits, productivity or quality. Technology companies often launch corporate ventures as a response to a perceived competitive threat.

There has been a surge in corporate venturing activity over the past decade, partly in response to an increased emphasis on "entrepreneurial thinking"—a mindset that embraces change, innovation, and growth (see Figure 3-1). Key challenges in corporate venturing include finding qualified "intrapreneurs" (corporate entrepreneurs) and overcoming internal political challenges to external searches for the right project champion. In many cases, outsiders with less of a political track record in the company are brought in to run intrapreneurial ventures. Regardless of who runs the new venture, however, it is critical that they have strong support from the company's senior management; otherwise the likelihood of failure is high.

Strategic Alliances
As the Internet opens up new sales channels, competition is intensifying and the pace of business is accelerating. In this new environment, knowledge and relationships are key strategic assets, and in order to tap into these assets, companies are increasingly looking outside of their organizations. Strategic alliances are often seen as a less risky way to leverage the assets of two or more organizations without entering into a costly, complex merger.

FIGURE 3-1   Corporations with venturing programs.
Source: The Corporate Venturing Report/Asset Alternatives Inc.

1996 — 49 companies
1997 — 70 companies
1998 — 108 companies
1999 — 203 companies

Companies form alliances for many different strategic reasons: (1) to speed entry into new markets; (2) to acquire new skills and technologies; and (3) to share fixed costs. Alliances also enable an acquisition-minded company to perform a more complete and less rushed due diligence of a potential takeover target than could be had with a straightforward acquisition.

Many corporate executives believe that alliances can provide them with the benefits of acquisitions without the risks and costs involved in M&A. A PricewaterhouseCoopers survey of CEOs at 425 of the fastest-growing companies in the United States over the past five years reveals that two-thirds are involved in an average of 4.8 strategic alliances.[1] According to a 1997 study by the consulting firm, Booz, Allen & Hamilton, the average return on strategic alliances is 17 percent.[2] This study, however, also found that the failure rate for strategic alliances is fairly substantial. Also, the media has seemingly lost interest in strategic alliances, believing that many of them are nothing more than marketing hype.

Like mergers and acquisitions, successful alliances flow from good self-assessment, insightful strategic planning, and a thorough selection process. Although some of the steps outlined in *The M&A Strategy Guide* are not necessary in a partnering situation, executives who wish to pursue strategic alliances would do well to follow the *Guide*'s relevant steps. Briefly, one should (1) think through strategic objectives by way of thorough self- and external analyses; (2) create strategic alliance criteria to assist in partner selection; (3) plan an alliance operating strategy; (4) monitor success; and (5) prepare contingencies for exiting or extending the relationship. Obviously, this last step is much more complex if one enters into an M&A arrangement rather than a strategic alliance. This consideration should not be taken

[1]Reported in the online version of *The Deal,* January 2, 2001.

[2]J. Harbison and P. Pekar, Institutionalizing Alliance Skills: Secrets of Repeatable Success (Booz, Allen & Hamilton, 1997).

lightly. For this reason, dating first with a strategic alliance may be preferable to going straight to the chapel with an M&A deal.

Bertelsmann and Napster Form an Alliance

In October 2000, PRNewswire reported that the international media company Bertelsmann had formed a strategic alliance to further develop Napster's person-to-person online file-sharing service. Napster had startled the record industry in 1999 with a software application that enables users to locate and share music files. This development was very controversial since consumers could obtain high-quality music online without compensating the recording companies that held copyrights on this music.

Through their strategic alliance, the two companies are developing a new business model for distribution of entertainment content over the Internet. They will offer a secure membership-based service that will provide the Napster online community with high-quality file sharing while still compensating music copyright owners, such as recording artists, songwriters, and recording companies. In effect, Napster is providing Bertelsmann with access to its online community of over 38 million music fans, while Bertelsmann will provide content by making its music catalog available.

What makes this alliance unique is that before the announcement, Bertelsmann (along with others in the music industry) was suing Napster over copyright infringement issues. Under the terms of this new agreement, Bertelsmann will drop its suit and provide a loan to Napster to help develop the new service. Bertelsmann also will hold a warrant to acquire a portion of Napster's equity.

Corporate Private Equity (CPE)

In this approach growth is achieved by investing in ventures (usually early stage) in key markets and technologies. These investments typically are minority stakes in young companies and sometimes turn into acquisitions of those companies as they mature. Corporate private equity has increased significantly in popularity in recent years as the need for rapid innovation has intensified and as private venture capital firms have achieved exceptional financial returns.

Corporate private equity investment is essentially a corporate development function, which makes minority investments in privately held companies that have strategic significance to the corporation. It is focused on augmenting or accelerating the corporation's own business development function by finding better, cheaper, and faster ways of achieving operational and growth objectives. A corporate private equity investment can be seen as a precursor to a full acquisition deal. Making such an investment may enable a company intent on pursuing an acquisition strategy to gain a valuable perspective and "inside information" on a potential acquisition candidate. Gathering information in this fashion greatly diminishes the possibility of making the common mistakes that hamper a typical M&A due diligence process, which is often hasty and incomplete.

In recent years, corporate private equity investment has been transformed into a core component in the growth strategies of many corporations. The growth of corporate private equity is due to several factors, including the phenomenal growth and financial success of the private venture capital industry, corporate outsourcing and spin-offs, the rationalization of R&D portfolios, changes in the nature of relationships with suppliers, and, most significantly, the upsurge in entrepreneurial culture. Corporations have participated in the surge in venture capital activity by making substantial investments in venture capital funds, increasing the level of direct investment in private equity transactions, and, in some cases, forming their own strategic venture capital subsidiaries.

CPE programs have appealed to corporations for a variety of reasons:

- They offer a means of identifying and partnering with companies whose products and technologies might play important roles in the development of the corporation's business.

- They offer an inside perspective on possible acquisition targets.

- They offer an opportunity to outsource product design and development in a cost-efficient manner.

- They offer the prospect of creating reliable suppliers of materials and components, and of "outsourcing" selected operations.

- They provide access to new and emerging technologies.

- They provide a means of realizing value from internal R&D programs, which are no longer relevant to the corporation's core mission.

Intel Corporation: An Example of a Corporate Private Equity Program

Since the mid-1990s, Intel has invested more than $2 billion in over 200 companies, usually in the very early stages of development. Its investments are relatively small, on the order of $1 million to $2 million in each company. Private venture capital funds with as much capital to deploy as Intel would probably not consider investments of that size. But Intel's strategy is to invest not only for financial return but also, perhaps more important, for strategic reasons.

Leslie Vadasz, an Intel senior vice president, director of corporate business development, and a member of Intel's board of directors, heads Intel's private equity investment program. He was the third employee at Intel, back in the late 1960s, and has been a major contributor to the company's extraordinary growth. Vadasz' mission is quite clear given Intel's position as a dominant supplier of semiconductors: feed the demand for ever-more-powerful microprocessors.

To accomplish this objective, Intel must not just produce faster chips, but also ensure that applications are being developed that will continue to demand more powerful microprocessors. As a result, Intel has invested in everything from content developers to bandwidth expanders to facilitators of e-commerce. Any company that will help to feed Intel's core mission is a potential investment target.

In many cases, Intel invests alongside traditional venture capitalists and other strategic investors. Intel prefers this approach as it does not want to be in the "business of managing other people's businesses." Sometimes it will request observation rights at board meetings, but rarely will it exercise voting power. In reality, however, like many other strategic investors, Intel still has extensive influence over its portfolio companies, as the leverage of being affiliated with Intel can often make or break a company in the marketplace.

Corporate Mergers and Acquisitions

This approach pursues growth through the acquisition of other companies. A *horizontal acquisition* is an acquisition of a company that offers products or services similar to those of the acquiring company. When the acquisition is of a supplier, distributor, or other company along the value chain it is termed a *vertical acquisition.* Presently, such phenomena as globalization, the Internet (and other major technology shifts), deregulation, and privatization have created a competitive environment that mandates rapid change and growth. Many companies are choosing to make acquisitions an important ingredient in their quest to grow rapidly and meet the challenges of dynamic markets. The focus of this book is on planning and executing a strategy of growth through acquisition. As is explained in a later chapter, such a growth strategy carries with it significant risk and requires the mastery of several interrelated processes.

Horizontal acquisitions typically are "core," as they involve the acquisition of a competitor. In vertical acquisitions and acquisitions outside the industry of the acquiring company, the answer to the "core" question becomes much less clear. Factors to be considered include the similarity of competencies required to deliver the product or service and the use of the same or similar distribution channels. If effectively running the acquired company involves development of a largely new set of operating competencies, then typically the acquisition would not be considered core. Justification of the acquisition would therefore need to be based on other factors, which, given the current investment mindset, would present more difficulties.

Buy, Build, or Ally

Another way to look at growth strategies is to divide them into three general categories: *buy, build,* or *ally.* An acquisition strategy is of course classified as a buy strategy. Corporate private equity may also be considered another form of a buy strategy in that it involves the purchase of a stake in an outside company. The strategies of organic growth and corporate venturing are examples of build strategies. Growth is termed *organic* when it is achieved without the help of alliances with or purchases of other companies. Finally, companies ally with one another with the expectation that mutual benefits will accrue from the relationship.

Nortel Chooses to Buy Rather than Build

Nortel Networks Corp., a manufacturer of digital networking systems, has successfully pursued a growth-through-acquisition strategy, acquiring more than a dozen companies in 1999. Like Cisco Systems, Nortel set its sights on niche market companies that own critical pieces of information technology, thereby shortening its own research and development cycle.

One of Nortel's major acquisitions was its purchase of Bay Networks, a data management firm acquired for $9.1 billion in 1998. Bay Networks, which became a wholly owned subsidiary of Nortel, gave Nortel access to the Internet provider (IP) market for voice, data, and video transmission across a wide range of networks.

Nortel made the decision in the fall of 1997 to focus on technologies based on Internet protocols, which by then were becoming an industry standard. The company also decided that data networks like Nortel's would have to migrate from standard telephone technology to Internet technology to survive. Instead of developing these technologies internally, Nortel sought to pursue an acquisition strategy of targeting companies that are developing such technologies.

The strategy appears to have been successful. According to CEO John Roth, it was not unusual for internal Nortel R&D projects to continue for five years or more without achieving measurable results. Consequently Nortel would not be able to compete in emerging technologies if it could not accelerate its R&D cycle. In circumstances such as these, a buy strategy may be much more preferable than a build strategy.

The M&A Strategy Guide

C H A P T E R 4

STEP 1: THINKING THROUGH STRATEGIC OBJECTIVES

The foundation of the entire merger and acquisition process is predicated on the clear articulation of the company's underlying corporate strategy. Accordingly, the strategy formulated in Step 1 will significantly impact each subsequent step in the acquisition process.

Due to the importance of defining corporate strategy, the *Guide* reviews two frameworks that will assist the corporate executive in formulating corporate strategy. These frameworks include: (1) Porter's "essential tests" for corporate strategy development, and (2) SWOT analysis. These different frameworks enable corporate executives to examine their strategic thinking through a variety of different lenses.

THE NUTS AND BOLTS OF STEP 1
Porter's Industry Analysis
The three essential tests that make up Porter's industry analysis are drawn from earlier work, which has come to be known widely as *Porter's Five*

Forces. According to this framework, a significant part of the explanation for differential profit-making across industries lies in the differences in industry structure. Industries are more or less attractive based on five characteristics: (1) *degree of rivalry* in the industry; (2) the *threat of substitutes;* (3) *barriers to entry;* (4) *supplier power;* and (5) *buyer power* (see Figure 4-1). A brief explanation of these forces follows:

Degree of Rivalry   More competitors drive down prices, therefore an industry with a high degree of rivalry is less attractive.

Threat of Substitutes   If consumers can easily substitute one product for a competing product, the industry is less attractive. For example, makers of alu-

FIGURE 4-1   Porter's five forces.[1]

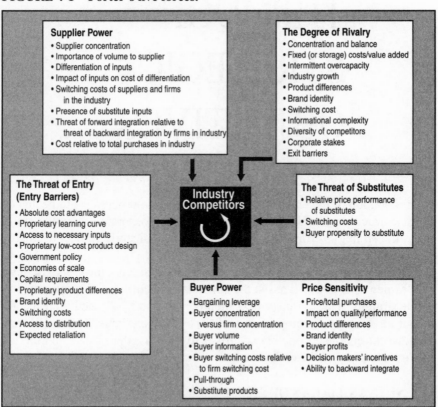

[1]Based on "The Five Competitive Forces that Determine Industry Profitability" from *Competitive Advantage: Creating and Sustaining Superior Performance,* Michael Porter, Free Press, June 1998. Reprinted with permission from Simon and Schuster, Inc.

minum cans are constrained from raising their prices by manufacturers of glass bottles.

Barriers to Entry   Although any company can theoretically enter any industry in a free-market environment, there are certain barriers to entry that make such a move very costly and perhaps, in reality, impossible. Such barriers to entry include: *excessive start-up costs; patents or other proprietary knowledge;* and *government regulation.*

Supplier Power   Manufacturers are reliant on raw materials to create products. In some cases, if a supplier dominates its industry, it may be able to limit the profits that can be made by a manufacturer that buys its raw materials. Such a supplier could exert force by raising its prices since there is little competition in the supply of this raw material. Because of this supplier's power, the manufacturer is forced to buy the raw material at these high prices, which in turn affects its margins.

Buyer Power   In this case, the buyer can set the price because there are many suppliers of the same product.

Industry Analysis
Porter's first two tests focus on industry analysis, and so they are based on these five forces discussed in the preceding text:

1.   **The attractiveness test.** The industries that a company is considering diversifying into must be attractive from the perspective of these five forces. For example, attractive industries will have: high barriers to entry; suppliers and buyers with limited bargaining power; few substitutes; and limited rivalry. One must remember that these forces are very dynamic, however. An industry may be unattractive before a company enters it through a merger or acquisition, yet, by entering the industry, the company may make that industry more attractive by realigning these forces.

2.   **The cost-of-entry test.** This test focuses on the barriers-to-entry force. Porter's emphasis on this force is interesting in that much of the academic research on why M&A deals fail—subsequent to the publication of his books and articles on the five forces—points to the fact that companies often overpay to acquire their targets. If the cost to buy a new company exceeds the returns of such a move, then obviously shareholder value is destroyed rather than created. Costs-of-entry here refer not only to the "hard costs" represented by the price of the

acquisition, however. Executives also must take into account the time, energy, and sometimes political capital that must be expended in order to enter a new industry. Such a move is not unlike a start-up situation, in which enormous resources are required to build momentum.

The major components of the costs-of-entry are addressed in *Step 5: Valuing the Acquisition Target.* The hope of corporate executives intent on an acquisition strategy is that the synergies achieved by combining the entities will outweigh the total costs involved. However, very often the expected returns calculated to justify paying high premiums are not realized, either because (1) the synergistic value created by merging the entities is unrealistic, or else (2) the expectations are realistic but the combined entity could not achieve them because of faulty integration planning and execution. These issues are explored in further steps in *The M&A Strategy Guide;* however, corporate executives should be cognizant of the importance of cost-of-entry issues at this early stage.

Porter's third and final test focuses on company-specific issues:

3.   **The better-off test.** Much like the cost-of-entry test, the better-off test is not a simple calculation with a clear answer. Basically, before an acquisition is made, the acquirer should determine with a high degree of certainty that the benefits of operating the combined entity will outweigh the costs involved in buying and integrating the acquired company. The valuation section of this book introduces this same concept in more depth through what is termed "synergistic value," which is the value created through the combination of the two entities.

At this stage, however, this third test is intended to trigger thinking on this crucial issue. Basically, according to this test, diversification through M&A must bring some new competitive advantage that the two entities did not have access to on an individual basis. Porter believes that this test is the one which is most ignored by executives. He believes that too often company size is confused with shareholder value, and that revenues are too often pursued instead of earnings. Again, it is important to begin thinking in these terms for, as obvious as this may seem, research has shown that this analysis is not done as thoroughly as it should be.

DEVELOPING ACQUISITION CRITERIA THROUGH SWOT ANALYSIS

Keeping in mind corporate objectives and current product-market strategies, executives should next consider multiple strategic alternatives. Each strategic alternative should be analyzed thoroughly in the context of a typical SWOT analysis (i.e., Strengths, Weaknesses, Opportunities, Threats).

This concept of the SWOT analysis was popularized by the management consulting firm McKinsey & Company and is used in a wide variety of business planning situations. Admittedly, this simple tool may not prove as useful to huge conglomerates which must take into consideration various strategies among a large number of business units; however, it is mentioned here because it is a good starting point, which is often skipped over to the detriment of the acquiring company.

An honest self-evaluation is necessary to fully understand all relevant corporate strengths and weaknesses, while an environmental analysis is necessary to assess opportunities in the marketplace and threats from market trends and competitors. This environmental analysis should include a review of social, economic, political, regulatory, and technological issues.

Acquisition criteria will flow from a review of the results of this SWOT analysis. It may be appropriate to play to strengths and downplay weaknesses, or it may be necessary to fill in weaknesses with acquisitions so as to remain competitive based on threats in the environment.

The acquisition criteria that result from this analysis will be revisited in *Step 3: Identifying and Screening Potential Acquisition Targets.* At this point, the team performing this analysis should agree on which acquisition criteria are the most important given the strategic objectives of the company. The team members should force themselves to write out these specific criteria, along with the reasoning behind them.

Although it is tempting to approach this analysis with actual candidates in mind, it is best to focus on the desired criteria independent of any companies that may fulfill such requirements. At this point in the process, it is best to remain open-minded. Step 3 will force the acquisition team to face the reality of available candidates, but it is best (at least at this stage) to avoid force-fitting actual candidates into criteria. Too many M&A deals have started off flawed because acquiring companies skipped this step by choosing their target company first and justifying its suitability after the fact.

Depending on the strategy pursued, the acquisition team may have to generate acquisition criteria with regard to industries as well as companies. Industry criteria may include parameters such as projected market growth rates, regulatory issues, barriers to entry, and capital versus labor intensity. Some common acquisition criteria are management quality, share of market, profitability, size, and capital structure.

GE: CHANGING CORPORATE STRATEGY IN
RESPONSE TO EXTERNAL THREATS

Over the past few decades, General Electric has been held up as a model company whose best practices are worthy of emulation. With its legendary CEO Jack Welch at the helm, GE grew into a massive company with a market capitalization in excess of $400 billion at the time of this writing. Perhaps more impressive than its size, however, is the diversity of products and services offered under the GE umbrella: power generators, light bulbs, locomotives, dishwashers, refrigerators, aircraft engines, as well as financial services (housed under GE's subsidiary GE Capital) such as equipment leasing, reinsurance, and credit cards. Incredibly, in an era when the market usually discounts diversified companies and pays premiums for pure-plays, GE is bucking the trend.

Unlike other conglomerates like ITT before it, GE's portfolio of businesses sprang from a carefully crafted strategy. Welch became CEO in 1981 and was soon causing controversy when he decided to sell off GE's housewares business, which was viewed as part of the company's heritage. In developing his corporate strategy, Welch first looked externally to see what threats and opportunities were on the horizon. Starting in the early 1980s, manufacturing in the United States was becoming increasingly less profitable due to the advent of new Asian competitors who could quickly manufacture knock-off products at much lower costs than their U.S. rivals. Welch saw this threat to GE's product line coming. In response, he decided to focus on developing more innovative products such as CAT scanners, while getting out of businesses such as manufacturing toasters. He did not stop with housewares, however. He shed other divisions of the company that had had long traditions and had to withstand much criticism for doing so. He initiated massive downsizing and restructuring programs at GE well ahead of the trend in corporate America.

While GE was divesting low-margin manufacturing divisions, it began acquiring higher-margin businesses such as financial service firms. Welch's strategy was to migrate to more service-oriented businesses such as those that would make up GE's highly profitable subsidiary, GE Capital. All of this reshuffling of the GE portfolio was aimed at achieving the goal of being first or second in very profitable markets. Welch knew that double-digit growth could not come from the portfolio of low-margin manufacturing businesses that GE was in at the time. Not only did Welch clearly understand the implications of the threats and opportunities around him, but also more important, he had the ability to implement a new strategy that would exploit the new market conditions..

C H A P T E R 5

STEP 2: ASSESSING STRUCTURAL CAPACITY

BACKGROUND

In Step 1, corporate executives are provided with tools that will assist them in articulating an overall corporate strategy. One of the frameworks suggested to help in this process, the SWOT analysis, focuses attention on external factors (opportunities and threats) as well as a self-assessment of the company's own strengths and weaknesses. This internal analysis, however, is performed at a strategic level during this initial step. *Step 2: Assessing Structural Capacity* extends this process down to a more operational level. This step is basically a due diligence investigation that a potential acquiring company should perform on itself.

The second step in *The M&A Strategy Guide* involves an assessment of the company's readiness and capacity to embark upon a merger or acquisition. This step is referred to as *assessing structural capacity*. It is based on the premise that a company must first look inward and evaluate its own strengths and weaknesses. Only then will it know if it has the ability and capacity to pursue a strategy of corporate growth through acquisition.

A program of corporate self-evaluation offers a number of other advantages as well:

- It prepares the company to respond quickly and judiciously to takeover attempts by other companies.

- It helps to identify strategic investment and divestment opportunities.

- It assists the company in structuring a potential acquisition on a cash versus stock basis.

Step 2: Assessing Structural Capacity points out those areas that should be the focus of such a self-evaluation program (see Figure 5-1). It first begins with an assessment of the acquisition team. Many of today's emerging companies may not have the resources that larger companies have at their disposal to retain outside advisors to assist in the acquisition process. Nonetheless, the acquisition team must be ready, in terms of experience and resources, to tackle strategic, legal, financial, and operational aspects of the acquisition program.

The second area for scrutiny is the financial strength of the acquiring company: what level of financial resources can it bring to bear upon a merger and acquisition program?

Third, the financial value of the acquiring company itself is assessed, since such a determination will often impact the structure of a transaction, especially in circumstances where the transaction will involve an exchange of stock between the acquiring company and the target or its shareholders.

Finally, this step evaluates the ability of the acquiring company to use pooling-of-interests accounting or purchase accounting in effectuating a

FIGURE 5-1   Assessing structural capacity.

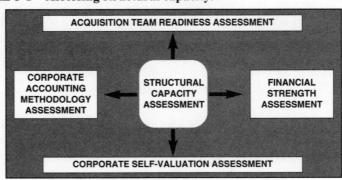

transaction. While this analysis may not be relevant going f
changes in accounting treatment currently being proposed by
Accounting Standards Board (FASB), this analysis is included pending
final outcome of the decision with respect to the elimination of pooling-of-
interests accounting and any modification to purchase accounting which
may be enacted to make up for the loss of pooling.

THE NUTS AND BOLTS OF STEP 2
The Acquisition Team Readiness Assessment

The first step in *assessing structural capacity* is to evaluate the readiness
of the acquisition team. The merger and acquisition process can be divided
into three major stages: (1) *planning,* (2) *execution,* and (3) *implementation.*
Each stage is characterized by certain key activities, and these activities must
be overseen by the acquiring company's senior management and the team
responsible for the corporate acquisition program.

The concept of "readiness" applies to each of the three phases of the
acquisition process, and it is critical to develop an internal team that is
competent to take the lead in all three. For a broader perspective on aspects
of these phases, see Figure 5-2. Such a team should be composed of senior
and junior level persons from the following areas: (a) corporate strategy;
(b) finance and accounting; (c) legal; and (d) operations. Since persons
assigned to the acquisition team typically will need to continue performing their day-to-day corporate functions as well, it is also important to
recruit outside advisors, or an outside team, to augment both the expertise
and the availability of the internal team. Again, due to financial constraints, many of today's emerging companies may have to make do with

FIGURE 5-2 Managing the phases of the merger and acquisition process.

Planning	Execution	Implementation
Team Selection	Initiate Discussion	Integration
Mission, Vision, and Values	Due Diligence	Communication Program
Growth Strategy	Terms of the Transaction	Compensation
Acquisition Criteria	Deal Closing	Titles
Surveillance Program	Develop Integration Plan	Norms
		Scorecarding
		Feedback Loop

their internal resources and only recruit outside assistance on an as-required basis.

Readiness requires that an entire team is ready for deployment. Senior management should periodically make a thorough assessment of the experience and strengths of the staff, as well as the experience and capacity of intermediaries, investment banks, accounting firms, law firms, and other outside professionals engaged in the acquisition transaction. Gaps should be filled with appropriate additional training and the identification of skilled outside sources with a solid understanding of the company and its industry. Many acquiring companies find it useful, even critical, to set up a space (often called the "war room") in which to hold regular meetings of the team and to house confidential documents. The war room environment facilitates communication and helps to maintain a feeling of common purpose and camaraderie during the very demanding acquisition process.

Gaps in the acquisition team should be identified early and a plan devised for filling them. Generally, skill gaps are easy to identify, using an inventory like the one in the figure below. But other common trouble spots on acquisition teams are more subtle, such as a lack of strategic perspective or inexperience at integrating a wide range of facts, with all their accounting and tax implications, and applying them to the proper structuring of an acquisition transaction.

Figure 5-3 provides an overview of the key aspects of team readiness. The criteria listed apply to all three phases of the merger and acquisition process.

FIGURE 5-3   Four key components of assessing structural capacity or criteria for team readiness for the merger and acquisition process.

Strategic
- Understand macro variables
- Understand market trends
- Understand competitors
- Understand target company positioning
- Ensure strategic fit

Financial
- Ensure target financial statement accuracy
- Perform sanity check projections
- Understand tax issues
- Value the target
- Recommend appropriate financing

Legal
- Consider antitrust issues
- Ensure tax compliance
- Review environmental liabilities
- Review key contracts
- Ensure intellectual property protection
- Review labor/employment issues

Operational
- Audit culture and morale
- Constantly review management team qualifications
- Review production/distribution processes
- Audit information management
- Audit research and development
- Audit regulatory compliance systems

CISCO SYSTEMS: MAKING GOOD USE OF INTERNAL TEAMS

Cisco Systems, arguably one of the most successful deal-makers in the 1990s, has done most of its acquisitions using internal resources. Cisco's finance staff and centralized business development team handle preacquisition negotiations. (The company shuns the use of investment bankers.) In most of its acquisitions as many as 35 full-time employees may become involved in some aspect of the transaction, from preacquisition due diligence to postacquisition integration. Between 15 and 25 employees are assigned to work with target company employees. Their job is to answer questions and handle employee benefits, salaries, and other operational issues.

One of the most important teams that must be assembled in anticipation of a transaction is the finance team. Figure 5-4 indicates four key activities that this team must perform during the process.

The second issue that must be addressed within *Step 2: Assessing Structural Capacity,* is assessing the financial strength of the acquiring company (see Figure 5-5). To assess a company's financial ability and capacity to undertake a corporate acquisition program, the financial statements of the company and other relevant operating data are analyzed with the aid of special interpretive tools.

The four tests that are relevant in determining financial strength in this context are:

- **Asset and Liability Quality Assessment,** which examines the strength of the company's existing assets and liabilities.

FIGURE 5-4   Four key activities the finance team must perform during the acquisition process.

Corporate Finance	Audit
• Review current capital structure	• Ensure accuracy of financial reporting
• Assess fit of capital structure and strategic objectives	• Assess competence of target's financial management team
• Develop appropriate financing approach	• Monitor financial due diligence
• Manage relationship with financial institutions	• Assess adequacy of financial controls
Tax Strategy	**Cash Management**
• Ensure local, state, and federal tax compliance	• Analyze cash requirements of deal
• Develop tax optimization strategy for deal structure	• Assess adequacy of cash reserves
• Ensure effective use of NOLs, if any exist	• Manage investment of excess cash
	• Assess adequacy of target's treasury management systems

FIGURE 5-5   The financial strength assessment.

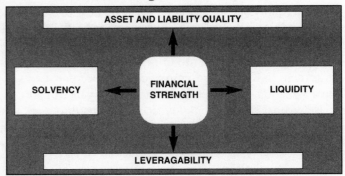

- **Liquidity Assessment,** which measures the company's ability to meet its current obligations using its cash and current assets.
- **Solvency Assessment,** which determines the company's ability to meet long-term debt obligations.
- **Leveragability Assessment,** which determines the company's capacity for leverage as part of a corporate acquisition strategy.

The use of these tools should not be a rigid process but rather a flexible approach tailored to the needs of a specific company in a specific industry.

Asset and Liability Quality Assessment
The first test is to assess the quality of the assets and liabilities of the acquiring company. Four measures are used to assess asset quality, and three measures are used to assess liability quality (see Figure 5-6).

Liquidity Assessment
Liquidity is assessed by reference to three liquidity ratios. These ratios indicate a company's ability to convert noncash assets to cash or to obtain cash to meet its financial obligations (see Figure 5-7).

Liquidity will also be affected by a company's ability to obtain financing as discussed is the leveragability assessment.

Solvency Assessment
A company's solvency depends on the company's earnings power because it will not be able to meet its financial obligations unless it is profitable. Solvency is assessed by reference to the three ratios in Figure 5-8.

FIGURE 5-6   Components of the asset and liability quality assessments.

Components of the Asset Quality Assessment

- **Cash.** How much of a cash balance is available for use?

- **Accounts Receivable Turnover** $= \dfrac{\text{Credit Sales}}{\text{Average Accounts Receivable}}$

- **Inventory Turnover** $= \dfrac{\text{Cost of Goods Sold}}{\text{Average Inventory}}$

- **Fixed Assets** $=$ Is there sufficient maintenance of productive assets to assure the current and future earnings power?

Components of the Liability Quality Assessment

- **Current Liabilities to Total Liabilities** $= \dfrac{\text{Current Liabilities}}{\text{Total Liabilities}}$

- **Current Liabilities to Shareholder Equity** $= \dfrac{\text{Current Liabilities}}{\text{Shareholder Equity}}$

- **Current Liabilities to Sales** $= \dfrac{\text{Current Liabilities}}{\text{Sales}}$

FIGURE 5-7   Liquidity Ratios.

- **Current Ratio** $= \dfrac{\text{Current Assets}}{\text{Current Liabilities}}$

- **Quick Ratio** $= \dfrac{\text{Cash + Marketable Securities + Accounts Receivable}}{\text{Current Liabilities}}$

- **Working Capital** $=$ Current Assets $-$ Current Liabilities

The results of the solvency ratio analysis must be compared with industry norms and standards to reveal the company's capacity to protect creditors should it sustain losses.

Leveragability Assessment

Leveragability is assessed by reference to the four financial leverage ratios in Figure 5-9. These ratios indicate the degree of leverage a firm has assumed.

The results of the financial leverage ratio analysis must be compared with industry norms and standards to reveal the company's capacity to deploy leverage in its corporate acquisition program.

FIGURE 5-8   Solvency assessment ratios.

- **Long-Term Debt to Net Worth** = $\dfrac{\text{Long-Term Debt}}{\text{Net Worth}}$

- **Cash Flow from Operations to Long-Term Debt** =

  $\dfrac{\text{Cash Flow from Operations}}{\text{Long-Term Debt}}$

- **Interest Coverage** = $\dfrac{\text{Net Income + Interest + Taxes}}{\text{Interest}}$

FIGURE 5-9   Financial leverage ratios.

- **Debt** = $\dfrac{\text{Total Debt}}{\text{Total Assets}}$

- **Debt to Equity** = $\dfrac{\text{Long-Term Debt}}{\text{Total Equity}}$

- **Debt to Total Capitalization Ratio** = $\dfrac{\text{Long-Term Debt}}{\text{Long-Term Debt + Shareholders' Equity}}$

- **Times Interest Earned** = $\dfrac{\text{EBIT (Earnings before Interest and Taxes)}}{\text{Long-Term Debt Interest Charges}}$

GUIDELINES IN THE USE OF FINANCIAL RATIOS FOR THE FINANCIAL STRENGTH ASSESSMENT

- Ratios should be calculated for several past periods as well as for the current period, in order to determine trends.

- Results of the analysis should be compared with the applicable standards, such as industry averages over time or lender requirements.

- Focus should be placed on all major variations from the applicable standard, particularly if there is a consistent trend over a significant period of time.

- The causes of the deviations from the applicable standard should be investigated by cross-checking with other ratios and raw data.

THE CORPORATE SELF-VALUATION ASSESSMENT

The third step in *assessing structural capacity* is the assessment of the value of the acquiring company. Assessing a company's ability to engage in a corporate acquisition program necessarily involves a valuation of the acquiring company as well as the target company. This valuation is necessary because acquisitions often involve an exchange of stock between the acquiring company and the target, in which case the purchase price will be determined by the value each company places on the shares of its own stock. The financial analysis of an acquisition in which shares of the acquiring company are being exchanged in whole or in part for the shares of the target necessarily requires sound valuations of the acquiring company as well as the target company.

If the acquiring company's management believes that the market is undervaluing its shares, then setting the purchase price by market valuations may result in overpaying for the acquisition. The acquiring company would then earn less than the target rate of return on its investment. Conversely, if management believes that the market is overvaluing its shares, then setting the purchase price at the market valuation may obscure an opportunity for offering the target's shareholders additional shares of the acquiring company while still achieving the desired rate of return.

To assess its own value, the acquiring company can use a number of different techniques including the two most commonly used, the *discounted cash flow method,* and the *market multiple method.* A more detailed discussion of these valuation methodologies is including in Step 5.

THE CORPORATE ACCOUNTING METHODOLOGY ASSESSMENT

The fourth and final step in *assessing structural capacity* is evaluating the ability of the acquiring company to engage in a pooling-of-interests transaction. On April 21, 1999, FASB voted unanimously to eliminate pooling of interests as an acceptable method of accounting for business combinations. The prospect of its elimination aroused fierce opposition from many businesses which argued that the elimination of pooling of interests would make it much more difficult for companies pursuing merger and acquisition strategies.

On December 6, 2000, in light of its intention to eliminate pooling-of-interests accounting, FASB voted unanimously that goodwill need not be written off over any particular period of time. Instead, goodwill would be allowed to remain on a company's books indefinitely until the company determines that the operations of the acquired company are performing so poorly that a write-off is required. On December 20, 2000, FASB announced that its proposal should be retroactive, meaning that companies currently amortizing goodwill would no longer have to do so. These two recent announcements are intended to make purchase accounting much more palatable in light of the proposed elimination of pooling. Therefore, much of this step may not be relevant if pooling has actually eliminated as appears to be the case as of this writing. However, this step has been retained in *The M&A Strategy Guide* pending the final fate of pooling-of-interests accounting.

Background on Pooling versus Purchase Accounting

Accounting Principles Board Opinion No. 16, *Accounting for Business Combinations* ("APB No. 16") is the principal authoritative accounting pronouncement for merger and acquisition transactions. APB No. 16 outlines two accepted methods of accounting for merger and acquisition transactions: the *purchase* method[1] and the *pooling-of-interests* method.[2]

The structure of the business combination will dictate which of the two accounting methodologies must be used. If the business combination meets 12 specific criteria outlined in APB No. 16, it must be accounted for as a pooling-of-interests. Those criteria are listed in Figure 5-10.

These criteria fall into three broad categories: (1) the attributes of the combining companies, (2) the manner in which the companies are combined, and (3) the absence of planned transactions. The purchase method of accounting must be used for any business combination that does not meet all of the 12 criteria for a pooling-of-interests transaction.

CNET Networks, Inc., Acquires Ziff-Davis:
An Example of Purchase Accounting

Companies with solid balance sheets and prospects for continued growth in earnings have financed acquisitions under purchase accounting rules.

CNET Networks, Inc., the Internet media company, bought the online businesses of Ziff-Davis, Inc., for $1.6 billion in stock in July 2000, using purchase accounting. CNET announced it would finance the transaction by issuing 50 million new shares of stock, and exchange CNET common stock for outstanding shares of Ziff-Davis and ZDNet, the tracking stock created by Ziff-Davis in 1999 for its online businesses.

---

[1]Under the purchase method, the purchase price and costs of the business combination are allocated among all of the assets acquired and liabilities assumed on the basis of their fair market value. If the purchase price exceeds the fair market value of the underlying assets, the buyer must account for the excess as goodwill. The profits and losses of the target company are included in the acquiring company's financial statements from the closing date of the acquisition.

[2]Under pooling method, the assets and liabilities of the target company are transferred to the buyer's balance sheet at the same carrying amounts as on the target's balance sheet. The current year earnings of the target are combined with those of the buyer and the book value of the target company's balance sheet is combined with the book value of the buyer's balance sheet.

FIGURE 5-10   Pooling of interests criteria.

Criterion No. 1: Autonomy. Both the acquiring company and the target must be autonomous, meaning that neither can have been a subsidiary or division of another entity within two years prior to initiation of the plan of combination.

Criterion No. 2: Intercorporate Ownership. Each of the combining companies must be independent, meaning that prior to the combination neither combining company owns ten percent or more of another combining company's stock at the initiation or consummation dates.

Criterion No. 3: Single Transaction. The combination must be effected in a single transaction or completed in accordance with a specific plan within one year after the plan is initiated.

Criterion No. 4: Voting Stock as the Principal Consideration. The acquiring company must offer and issue only common stock with rights identical to those of the majority of its outstanding voting common stock in exchange for substantially all of the voting common stock interest of the target company at the date the plan of combination is consummated.

Criterion No. 5: No Change in Equity Interest. None of the combining companies change the equity interest of voting common stock in contemplation of the business combination within two years prior to the initiation date or between the initiation date and the consummation date.

Criterion No. 6: Reacquisition of Stock. Each of the combining companies may reacquire shares of voting stock only for a purpose other than the business combination, and no combining company may acquire more than a normal number of shares between the initiation date and the consummation date.

(continued)

FIGURE 5-10 *(Continued)*

Criterion No. 7: No Change in Ratio of Ownership. The ratio of the interest of an individual common stockholder to that of other common stockholders must remain the same as a result of the exchange of stock to effect the business combination.

Criterion No. 8: No Restriction on Rights. The voting rights to which the common stockholders in the combined entity are entitled must be exercisable by the stockholders. The stockholders may neither be deprived of nor restricted in exercising those rights for any period.

Criterion No. 9: Combination Resolved at Consummation. The combination must be resolved at the consummation date, and no provisions of the consummation plan relating to the issuance of securities or other conditions may be pending.

Criterion No. 10: Redemptions. The combining companies do not agree directly or indirectly to retire or reacquire all or part of the common stock issued to effect the combination.

Criterion No. 11: Financial Arrangements. The acquiring company may not agree to reacquire any of the common stock issued to the target's former shareholders, nor may the acquiring company enter into other financial arrangements for the benefit of the target's former shareholders.

Criterion No. 12: Intended Asset Dispositions. The acquiring company must not intend to dispose of any significant portion of its or the target's assets within two years after the combination, other than in the ordinary course of business or to eliminate duplicate facilities or excess capacity.

CNET is the owner of one of the most frequently visited Internet sites—its Web site averaged 16.5 million daily page views in the first quarter of 2000. The company acquired rival Ziff-Davis to strengthen its position with advertisers and extend its market to 25 international markets, including China and Japan. The deal puts CNET in the top 10 sites based on monthly users.

CNET's better-than-expected earnings—$200 million in 2000, according to company projections—and ample cash reserves helped push through its purchase of Ziff-Davis, a onetime computer magazine publisher turned Internet media company. CNET also pledged to buy back $100 million in outstanding common stock

POOLING-OF-INTERESTS ACCOUNTING
When to Use Pooling-of-Interests Accounting
Pooling-of-interests accounting is often preferred if the focus of the acquiring company will be on the combined entity's income statement after the close of the transaction. Income statements for periods after the close of the transaction are not subject to the depreciation, goodwill amortization, or other charges that would be attributable to a purchase price in excess of book value. In a pooling-of-interests transaction, there are no uncertainties regarding valuation and the determination of the purchase price. Financial statements for prior years are restated to reflect the new business combination, so that the ability to compare financial statements on a year-to-year basis is maintained.

Disadvantages of Pooling-of-Interests Accounting
However, since the target company's assets are not restated at fair market value, certain common measures of financial performance may not be comparable with those of other companies in the same industry. In addition, any positive earnings trend during periods prior to the combination may be reversed as a result of restating the prior years' earnings to include those of the target company.

PURCHASE ACCOUNTING
When to Use Purchase Accounting
Purchase accounting often is preferred if the focus of the acquiring company will be on the combined entity's balance sheet after the close of the transaction. The balance sheet after the acquisition will record the target company's assets and liabilities at their fair market values instead of at their historical costs. Therefore the balance sheet of the combined entity after the acquisition appears stronger under the purchase method than under the

pooling-of-interests method. In addition, since the restatement of prior years' financial statements is not required under the purchase accounting method, reported sales and earnings trends may show an improvement due to the combination of the two entities' results.

Disadvantages of Purchase Accounting

However, there are a number of disadvantages to the purchase accounting method. The income of the combined entity is subject to additional depreciation, goodwill amortization, and other charges that may adversely affect reported earnings. The purchase accounting method also is subject to uncertainty regarding the determination of the purchase price and the valuation of assets and liabilities. Finally, since prior years' financial statements are not restated as they are under the pooling method, they cannot be meaningfully compared to financial statements for the combined entity.

POOLING-OF-INTERESTS ACCOUNTING: THE END

As previously indicated, on April 21, 1999, FASB voted unanimously to eliminate pooling of interests as an acceptable method of accounting for business combinations. FASB argued that the purchase method of accounting gives investors a better idea of the initial cost of the transaction and the investment's performance over time. The prospect of the elimination of pooling-of-interests accounting aroused fierce opposition in the M&A community. In response to this opposition FASB has proposed to eliminate one of the most troublesome aspects of purchase accounting, namely, the charge to earnings caused by the amortization of goodwill, in order to ease the pain of forcing companies to use purchase accounting.

On December 6, 2000, FASB voted unanimously that goodwill need not be written off over any particular period of time. Instead, goodwill would be allowed to remain on a company's books indefinitely until the company determines that the operations of the acquired company are performing so poorly that a write-off is required. The argument supporting this ruling is that some intangible assets such as goodwill do not depreciate in value over time and therefore should not be required to be written off until it has been determined that its value has been impaired.

On December 20, 2000, FASB extended this ruling by announcing that its proposal should be retroactive, meaning that companies currently amortizing goodwill would no longer be required to do so. These two recent announcements are intended to make purchase accounting much more palatable in light of the proposed elimination of pooling. A final rule is not expected from FASB before the spring of 2001 and the effective date of the ruling has yet to be disclosed.

However, despite the controversy surrounding the decision to ban pooling, the overall impact on merger and acquisition activity (outside of megatransactions) may be limited. Information from the Securities Data Corporation's *Merger & Corporate Transaction Database* indicates that only a small percentage of transactions in the past five years have used the pooling method. But while these transactions may be relatively few in number, they account for a disproportionately large share of the value of merger and acquisition transactions during that period. For example, in 1998, only 517 of 9734 completed transactions were treated as a pooling of interests, but the value of those transactions, $580.6 billion, accounted for nearly 45 percent of the total $133 trillion in deal volume.

While the elimination of pooling-of-interests treatment may adversely affect certain segments of the merger and acquisition marketplace (given the potential of purchase accounting for diluting earnings), the change may force market analysts to evaluate companies on the basis of cash flow instead of fixating, as they presently do, on net income. Since the value of a company is cash flow driven, companies will be forced to more critically assess whether the quantitative measures of the success of a business combination match the qualitative measures that are touted in order to justify the transaction.

For more detail on the issues surrounding the FASB ruling, see Appendix I, "FASB's Rule on Accounting for Business Combinations: Resolution of an Important Controversy."

STEP 3: IDENTIFYING AND SCREENING POTENTIAL ACQUISITION TARGETS

BACKGROUND

The third step in *The M&A Strategy Guide* is *Identifying and Screening Potential Acquisition Targets.* This section offers guidelines for establishing a practical search and screen program to uncover acquisition opportunities.

THE NUTS AND BOLTS OF STEP 3

Definition of Acquisition Criteria

Any search and screen program begins with a broad set of acquisition criteria that fit the strategic and financial goals of the corporate acquisition program.

This exercise is an extension of the corporate strategic planning process. The following are some of the factors to be considered:

- Characteristics of the target company and its industry
- Size and growth rate of the target company's market(s)
- Market share and competitive position of the target company within its market(s)
- Defensible position of the target company within its market(s)
- Revenue, earnings, and cash flow history of the target company
- Balance sheet strength of the target company
- Strength of the target company's intellectual property
- Investment to be made in the target company and required rates of return

Organization of the Search Team

The next step in the search and screen program is to organize a search team. The search team should include an "inside team"—the individuals within the acquiring company who will spearhead the search and screen program—and, when appropriate, a supporting "outside team" composed of intermediaries, investment bankers, attorneys, accountants, and consultants.

The inside team should consist of a core group of multidisciplinary professionals from within the acquiring company with backgrounds in business development, finance, operations, law, and accounting. In a larger company, the inside team is typically based out of the corporate development department, which maintains various internal technical models for evaluating and structuring acquisitions and has access to external databases which may be useful in identifying possible target companies.

The challenge is not to obtain data on target companies but rather to organize the vast amounts of data that are available through online databases and other Internet resources. The inside team should have the ability to source and assimilate vast amounts of information and to perform the kinds of sophisticated analyses that will reveal whether, and to what extent, the potential targets meet the acquiring company's acquisition criteria and its strategic and financial objectives.

The inside team is often best equipped to identify potential acquisition targets because its members have industry contacts, familiarity with industry dynamics, knowledge of customers and suppliers, and understanding of the competitive strengths and weaknesses of potential targets.

An outside team of intermediaries, investment bankers, attorneys, accountants, and consultants can supplement the inside team by helping to identify candidates for acquisition and by bringing a range of professional expertise to bear on the investigation and evaluation of a potential target.

√ Identification of Potential Acquisition Targets

The third phase of the search and screen process is the identification of potential acquisition targets based on the defined acquisition criteria. The search process should be approached in at least two different ways. The acquiring company should, as is traditional, circulate among the outside search team its set of acquisition criteria and solicit suggestions for appropriate acquisition targets. While this "mass market" approach usually is successful in identifying acquisition targets, it is essentially reactive: it depends on opportunities to present themselves. Most of the information on potential acquisition targets acquired in this manner is already public, and an attractive target will have already garnered the attention of a host of other acquiring companies.

In addition, acquiring companies committed to a serious long-term acquisition program must use a proactive approach in their search and screen program—an approach that identifies a potential target well in advance of the target's willingness or readiness to engage in an acquisition. Often the acquiring company can develop strategic alliances with the target company for research and development, marketing, or sales. These alliances will, to a certain extent, tie the target company to the acquiring company and will allow the acquiring company to cultivate a relationship with the target until such time as the target is willing or ready to be acquired.

The inside search team should conduct database searches for potential acquisition targets based on the acquisition criteria outlined in the first step of the search and screen process and should review acquisition candidates identified by the outside team. This process (see Figure 6-1) will likely result in a host of potential acquisition targets.

√ Ranking of Potential Acquisition Targets

Having identified potential acquisition targets, the inside team must then assess how well and to what extent the potential targets fit the underlying acquisition criteria, and should rank the targets by the degree of fit. Some acquiring companies use detailed fit charts and point systems to aid in the process of ranking target companies. These methodologies will eliminate a vast majority of the potential targets as inadequate fits.

√ Contacting Potential Acquisition Targets

The fifth phase of the search and screen process is to develop a strategy for contacting the potential acquisition targets. The contact should be made by an intermediary or a representative of the buyer through a letter addressed to

FIGURE 6-1   Acquisition search and screen model.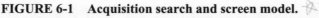

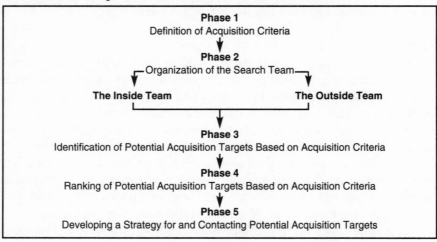

the management of the target company. The letter should present a thought-
ful and clear articulation of the strategic goals of the acquiring company and
demonstrate how the target company, in particular, can contribute to the realization of those goals. The letter should be followed up with a telephone call
in which the representative or intermediary explains the inquiry, confirms
certain basic nonconfidential information in the acquiring company's possession, and seeks to schedule a meeting where the parties can discuss, on a
preliminary basis, a potential transaction.

Once first contact is established and both parties agree to move forward
in principle, it is important to ensure a confidentiality agreement is in place
before proceeding with the exchange of sensitive information. A properly
structured confidentiality agreement will protect both parties during the disclosure of sensitive organizational information that is part of the next step in
The M&A Strategy Guide, Step 4: Performing Due Diligence. A sample confidentiality agreement is included as Appendix A.

7

STEP 4:
PERFORMING DUE
DILIGENCE

BACKGROUND

The fourth step in *The M&A Strategy Guide* is *Performing Due Diligence* on the potential acquisition target. The objective of performing due diligence is to uncover and analyze all issues that are likely to impact the success and cost of the acquisition.

These issues range from the highly objective, such as whether the accounting statements of the target company are accurate, to the highly subjective, such as whether the organizational cultures of the acquiring and target companies can be successfully integrated. The results of the due diligence investigation are critical in assessing the value of the target company and the potential viability of the merger. A sample due diligence checklist is included as Appendix D.

The four main areas of due diligence in an acquisition are: (1) strategic, (2) financial, (3) legal, and (4) operational. The key aspects of each of these areas of due diligence are explored in detail on the following pages.

THE NUTS AND BOLTS OF STEP 4
Key Elements of Strategic Due Diligence

Effective strategic due diligence requires forecasting the future through a delicate blend of rigorous quantitative analysis and intuition/experience. Given the typical tight timeline in an acquisition, it is not always possible to perform as much analysis as may be ideal, so intuition and experience tend to play key roles in decision making. Strategic due diligence typically is performed to understand the characteristics and trends of the markets in which the target company operates. The objective is to determine how the target is positioned in the current market and, given where the market is going, how well the target is likely to be positioned in the future.

The task of assessing the market position of a target company can be divided into several steps. The order of the steps is not as critical as the quality and the completeness of the data collected and the analysis performed. The following is a method for rationalizing the process of strategic due diligence. Listed are some of the key characteristics of the target company's market that should be considered. *Note:* The elements listed should be reviewed for each market and market segment in which the target operates. It is also important to keep in mind that this represents a high-level view; each area should be explored in greater detail, based on its level of significance and the time constraints of the due diligence process.

Key elements of the target's market include the following:

- **Structure:** What is the level of concentration of key players in the market? For example, the American automobile manufacturing industry is an oligopoly, whereas the auto repair business has a very large number of competitors. Whether the industry is highly concentrated or highly fragmented has important implications for the target's ability to significantly change its position in current market segments, or in the industry as a whole.

- **Size:** If the target is not selling into a large market, expectations for expansion of market share and for profit margins must be realistically adjusted.

- **Growth:** Is the market growing rapidly? If it is not growing, or if the target does not already have a large, relatively protectable market share, or a compelling plan for winning customers from competitors, the desirability of the acquisition is questionable.

- **Market Leaders:** Who are the market/segment leaders? Are their positions so strong as to be unassailable? Does the target company have a new technology or new business model to win customers from entrenched market leaders?

- **Key Subsegments:** In most markets, there are a few subsegments that produce a large percentage of the overall profitability. What are those subsegments in the target's market? What is the current activity and what are the future prospects of the target company in these key subsegments? The target should either itself be strong in these subsegments or should provide an opportunity for the acquiring company to become stronger in them.

- **Key Customers:** Who are the key customers in the target's market or market segment? How is the target positioned to sell to the key customers in its markets or in the existing/future markets of the acquiring company? Access to key customers is often one of the most attractive attributes of potential acquisition targets.

- **Key Differentiators:** Most markets and market segments have a small set of differentiating product or service attributes that have an inordinate impact on competitive success or failure. What are the key differentiators in each market and segment? If the target is not strong in key areas of differentiation, how costly would it be to make it stronger?

- **Substitutes:** Given the pace of advances in technology, many product and service markets previously assumed stable have seen an influx of less expensive, better-quality substitutes. Such "paradigm shifts" can radically change an entire industry in a short period of time. What substitutes are at issue currently in the target's markets and what substitutes can be seen on the horizon?

- **Profitability:** What is the profitability of each of the markets and segments into which the target sells? Profitability can be characterized by typical gross margins and operating margins or by whatever metrics are most relevant in the industry.

- **Relationship Sell:** How much of the target's business depends on the relationships of key employees with customers? In some cases, the relationships will be with the current owners of the target; in other cases, with key salespersons. (Usually, the size of the company determines where these key relationships will be formed.) If employee relationships with key customers are a major driver of sales at the target company, there is significant risk inherent in the acquisition. In such a case, it is extremely important to structure incentive programs to encourage retention and performance of key employees.

- **Other:** There may be several other key areas of strategic due diligence to be analyzed. The nature of such areas typically is industry- and situation-specific. An industry-knowledgeable acquisition team is critical in identifying and assessing such areas.

Key Elements of Financial Due Diligence

Effective financial due diligence begins with analysis of the target's audited financial statements and if the target is publicly held, Forms 10-K and 10-Q. If the target can provide only unaudited financial statements, the acquiring company must exercise even more than the usual care to ensure their accuracy.

First Union Buys The Money Store: The Importance of Financial Due Diligence

First Union's bold move into the risky subprime lending market is a good example of an acquisition that failed due to inadequate financial due diligence. The company's acquisition of The Money Store ended in June 2000, nearly two years after acquiring the company for $2.1 billion. The Money Store's focus was on loans to consumers with bad credit. First Union, after admitting that the home-equity lender would probably not turn a profit for another three years, took a $2.8 billion charge to close the Money Store operation a few days before the second anniversary of the purchase of the chain. The Money Store had branch offices in all 50 states.

First Union paid a rich price for the acquisition, buying The Money Store at the peak of the subprime lending market. The purchase price included $1.8 billion in goodwill. First Union failed to carefully check out the loan portfolios of The Money Store, a leader in the subprime lending market, a business notorious for a high charge-off rate.

Further, the acquiring company must perform ratio analysis to understand how the target has performed financially over time and in relation to industry benchmarks. The ratios used in the *Assessing Structural Capacity* step may be useful for such an analysis. It is critical that the acquiring company develop a solid understanding of how the target has performed, and combine this with the results of the strategic due diligence in order to assess the target's prospects for improved performance in the future. The financial data also must be viewed in light of broader industry trends they are to contribute in a meaningful way to an assessment of the target.

The financial due diligence team should analyze trends in various ratios: profitability, liquidity, leverage and market value (if public) for the target and its industry. Historical as well as trend data for the company and the industry should be used to develop pro forma earnings and cash flow statements. The financial due diligence team should find out whether and to what extent the target will be able to generate revenues and earnings growth internally. Earnings and cash flow are usually the determinants of the value of the target company and therefore should be carefully considered in assessing the initial attractiveness of the target and determining the price to be offered for it.

Sales Projections   Often, a company preparing itself for sale will manage its revenues and earnings in a way that makes it more attractive to potential suitors and increases its valuation. If the company has shown extraordinary revenues and earnings in recent periods, what are its prospects for sustaining such levels of growth in the future? An in-depth analysis of the sales pipeline is one approach to understanding the top-line prospects for the target. Depending on the length and predictability of sales cycles in the target's industry, a sales pipeline analysis will be more or less helpful in assessing the company's short- and medium-term prospects for revenue growth. Typically, such an analysis will not be particularly helpful for predicting the longer-term growth prospects of the target: too many factors can intervene in the long term. To the extent possible, the due diligence team should seek out confidential conversations with major customers, both current and prospective, for these can provide insight into the revenue growth potential of the firm.

Accounts Receivable   An analysis of the target's accounts receivable would include verification of the collectability of outstanding invoices. If the company has undergone periodic audits conducted by an outside firm, then the focus of investigation should be on significant invoices sent out to customers after the effective date of the most recent audit. The acquiring company should also inquire into the status of any major accounts receivable, even if covered by the most recent audit. Beyond major receivables outstanding, it is also important to get a sense of overall receivables aging and the target company's collection practices. What does the typical collection cycle look like at the target company, as compared with the industry average?

Returns and Allowances   Analyzing the target's returns and allowances over time and as compared to industry averages can be a reliable indicator of potential quality problems. But trends in returns and allowances provide only part of the picture. If deteriorating trends are detected, these findings should be compared to those obtained from the operational due diligence. Such problems with quality of product or service delivery can be not only very costly in the short term but a lead indicator of more fundamental problems that can quickly erode the target's profitability.

Customer/Product Profitability   Some experts see the ability to report profitability by customer and by product as the ultimate objective of management accounting systems. The ability to report information in this way is dependent upon a well-conceived and executed management information system. The reality is that most companies, even very large ones, with sophisticated management teams and management information systems, are unable to report profitability at such a granular level. But if profitability is not reported at this level, the management team is poorly equipped to make fact-based decisions. The acquiring company's due diligence as it relates to profitability reporting is relevant to the contemplated transaction in two important respects: first, it reveals how well the target's reporting system will integrate with that of the acquiring company; and second (if the target's system is unsatisfactory) gives an indication of how much time and money will be required to raise the target's reporting capabilities to an acceptable level. Time and care should be invested up front in the financial due diligence process to understand the strengths and limitations of the target's reporting systems for profitability as well as other financial management information.

Analysis of Goodwill   Goodwill is defined as the amount by which the acquisition cost exceeds the fair market value of the assets acquired less the present value of the liabilities assumed. Generally accepted accounting principles (GAAP) require that goodwill be amortized over future periods, not to exceed 40 years. In some cases, regulatory agencies such as the Securities and Exchange Commission may require that goodwill be amortized over a much shorter period. Although goodwill may seem to be largely a postacquisition accounting issue, it is important for the acquiring company to realize that the amortization of goodwill will impact the income statement of the combined companies for many years to come. In the case that the target has previously recorded goodwill from earlier acquisitions, this goodwill should be eliminated upon applying fair value to the target company.

As was discussed earlier in *Step 2: Assessing Structural Capacity,* FASB has recently eliminated one of the two methods allowed for accounting of goodwill: pooling of interest. In a pooling, combining companies simply add together the book values of assets and liabilities to create their new balance sheet. FASB will now require that all business combinations be accounted for by using the remaining method, purchase accounting. Under this method an enterprise is identified as the acquirer in the combination and is required to record the firm it bought at the cost it actually paid. The excess of the purchase price over the fair value of the acquired company's net worth is recorded as goodwill. For more detail on the issues surrounding the FASB ruling, see Appendix I, "FASB's Rule on Accounting for Business Combinations: Resolution of an Important Controversy."

Tax Contingencies Since most companies tend to be very aggressive in their efforts to minimize current period taxes, tax contingencies can be problematic in acquisitions. It is therefore critical to make a thorough analysis of a target's potential tax liabilities. Relevant issues for review include any audits or investigations that may be pending with the IRS or other tax authorities, reconciliation of taxable income to book income, and the tax basis of the company's assets. Federal, state and local tax laws and regulations are very complex and constantly changing, requiring the attention of tax experts throughout the due diligence process.

Unrecorded Liabilities Unrecorded liabilities include items that represent significant current and future exposure for the target, and therefore, for the acquiring company. Significant issues warranting review include: pension liabilities, employment benefits, customer allowances/discounts, and product and service warranties.

Inventory In certain businesses, inventory is a significant item on the company's balance sheet. Management of this asset can have a profound effect on the operating results of the company. In addition to the standard ratio analyses, including inventory turnover, the acquiring company should examine trends in inventory levels over time and from season to season. It is important to understand how fluctuations in inventory levels affect the cash flow of the target company and to determine whether there are opportunities to better manage this asset. Additionally, it is important to understand whether the current inventory is fairly valued and whether significant write-offs are likely to be required.

Net Operating Losses (NOLs) Since the existence of NOLs in a target company can, depending on the structure of the acquisition, enhance its attractiveness as an acquisition candidate, it is important to fully understand them. Specifically, it is critical that the acquiring company understand the amounts and expiration dates of existing NOLs. It also is important to determine whether the acquisition will impact the status of existing NOLs. Review of NOLs as a tax matter warrants the services of tax accountants and attorneys.

Key Elements of Legal Due Diligence

The legal due diligence review typically is performed by a combination of internal and outside legal counsel. The main objective in this review is to verify disclosures made by the target company and to ensure that the acquiring company is not assuming any major undisclosed liabilities. The objective of legal due diligence is to afford the acquiring company an opportunity to factor all findings of existing and contingent liabilities into its evaluation of the target company. The following list, though not exhaustive, covers the key areas that a legal due diligence review should investigate: corporate/shareholder documentation; antitrust laws; labor/employment; litigation; contracts; intellectual property; real/personal property; tax liabilities; insurance; and environmental issues. These key areas of legal due diligence are described in more detail in the paragraphs that follow.

Corporate/Shareholder Documentation   First and foremost, it is necessary to confirm that the corporate records of the target have been properly maintained and that the entity is in good standing in those jurisdictions in which it was formed and in which it is doing business. Review of the formation and organizational documents such as articles of incorporation, corporate minutes, and corporate bylaws also should reveal the target's procedures in key areas such as shareholder and director voting, election of directors and officers, and approval of fundamental transactions. These documents, along with other corporate records, also will confirm the proper issuance of corporate securities and other instruments.

Antitrust Laws   Antitrust considerations can have a significant impact on a corporate acquisition. Any pending or overtly threatened actions by third parties or governmental entities with respect to antitrust issues must be weighed for likely impact on the future form and viability of the target. The acquiring company also should review the pricing and sourcing policies of the target to evaluate the risk of future antitrust actions.

Premerger Reviews

The U.S. Department of Justice requires companies involved in a merger to get prior approval if an acquiring company has annual sales of $100 million or more, or if the acquirer would get a controlling interest (more than 50 percent of the voting securities) in a target company. The Hart-Scott-Rodino Act of 1976 imposes a 30-day waiting period (15 days for cash tender offers) after the filing of a premerger notification with the federal government. In most mergers, the Hart-Scott-Rodino filing is a formality; the government routinely waives the full 30-day waiting period and approves a merger if the transaction is not seen as anticompetitive.

Mergers of competing firms with significant market share in the same industry are likely to get closer scrutiny by government lawyers, who may try to block them on the grounds that they violate federal antitrust laws. In 1994, when Microsoft attempted to buy Intuit, the largest vendor of personal financial accounting software, the Justice Department filed suit to stop the acquisition. It claimed that a Microsoft-Intuit merger would stifle innovation and lead to higher prices. The Justice Department action came only months after Microsoft had voluntarily agreed to cease certain restrictive business practices with its dealers, following a government investigation.

Had the Intuit acquisition gone through, it would have combined the number one vendor (Intuit, developer of the "Quicken" personal financial software, with a 69 percent market share), with the number two vendor (Microsoft, with a 22 percent share) in the personal financial software market. The all-stock acquisition was valued at about $2.0 billion. Microsoft, in attempting to counter government antitrust charges, said it planned to sell its own personal financial software package, "Microsoft Money," to software developer Novell Inc. After months of legal wrangling, Microsoft said it was abandoning its planned acquisition of Intuit to avoid a prolonged legal skirmish with the government.

In hindsight, the issues raised by the Microsoft-Intuit merger extended far beyond the market in personal financial software. According to some legal experts, the Justice Department's real interest in the case centered on maintaining open competition in the then-nascent online commerce market. By 1999, Microsoft and Justice Department lawyers were back in court again, taking opposing sides in a landmark antitrust case in which the government sought to declare Microsoft a monopoly and break up the giant software vendor into smaller, independently managed companies.

Labor/Employment In recent years employment litigation has become more common and costly and is therefore a key risk to be assessed in the legal due diligence process. The acquiring company and its legal counsel must review any collective bargaining agreements, employee handbooks, employment agreements, restrictive covenants and confidentiality agreements, and the target's general employment practices. Other key issues include obligations under employee benefit programs, retirement plans, stock-related compensation, and responsiveness to allegations of harassment and discrimination.

Litigation   Legal due diligence should include a review of all pending litigation including copies of complaints, answers, motions, and discovery. In addition such due diligence should include a review of all matters in which litigation is being overtly threatened.

Contracts   Legal due diligence should include a review of all material contracts which the target has entered into or by which it is bound. Such agreements include those with officers, directors, and shareholders, those related to commitments to customers and suppliers, and those related to other fundamental transactions in which the target has engaged.

Intellectual Property   In many cases, much of the value of a target company comes from its intellectual property. The acquiring company must review the target's intellectual property rights and ensure that all required documentation for patents, trademarks, copyrights, and Internet domain names has been properly filed and maintained. The acquiring company also must gain a full understanding of any existing licensing agreements and documentation related to any infringement claims in which the target is involved. Finally, it is critical to confirm that the target's nonpatented trade secrets are adequately protected.

   Since intellectual property assets, such as trademarks, copyrights, patents, and trade secrets are becoming increasingly important in assessing a business' overall value, an acquiring company must understand thoroughly the different types of intellectual property and the extent of the legal protections afforded to each. An overview of intellectual property considerations in merger and acquisition transactions is included as Appendix F.

Real/Personal Property   All documentation related to significant real and personal property must be reviewed for accuracy and adequacy. Compliance with building codes and zoning ordinances must be confirmed. Terms of significant leases must be reviewed for fairness, and title to significant owned properties must be confirmed to be unencumbered.

Tax Liabilities   The target's compliance with tax laws in all relevant jurisdictions must be confirmed. The acquiring company should review tax returns for the previous five years and any correspondence with the IRS or state tax authorities regarding alleged violations or audits. Tax issues are another area of potential land mines that must be carefully navigated with the assistance of experienced tax and legal counsel, particularly given that tax strategies are a significant driver of the acquisition process.

Insurance The acquiring company must examine current insurance policies, and in some industries, depending on the nature of the potential liabilities, prior insurance policies. The acquiring company should focus on such issues as the extent to which the target is self-insured, key policy exclusions, unresolved claims, and coverage gaps. Risk management personnel and legal counsel with experience in insurance matters should lead the effort to understand the scope of the target's coverage. As many companies, particularly those in financial services, have found in recent years, uninsured risks can render even a sizable company insolvent overnight.

Environmental The potential exposure to environmental claims has risen dramatically in the past decade. Due diligence in this area should reveal the environmental implications and inherent liability in the target's business operations. Some industries are of course more prone to environmental liabilities than others, but no industry is exempt. Careful review of potential issues in this area will lower the probability of unexpected postacquisition claims.

Key Elements of Operational Due Diligence

Operational due diligence often fails to get the attention needed to make a truly informed acquisition decision. Time pressure and the desire to maintain confidentiality are the two main reasons that operational due diligence is often brushed over. In the case of horizontal mergers, operational due diligence should just be the extension of any well-implemented competitor intelligence program. In the case of vertical mergers, operational due diligence can be couched in terms of prospecting for new customers or suppliers, or gaining a better understanding of existing ones. As for time constraints, a proactive policy with respect to horizontal and vertical intelligence can minimize the amount of time that needs to be spent on "real-time" operational due diligence. It is not possible to gather intelligence on all industry players on an ongoing basis of course, but it is possible to follow the key players and to develop a permanent framework for such data gathering.

Potentially good sources of information include former target company employees that now work for the acquiring company, other industry players, customers, news articles—in fact, any primary or secondary source that can be tapped with discretion. Several of the key areas of operational due diligence are covered in the following paragraphs.

Maintaining Good Employee Relations: The IBM-Rolm Example

Skilled employees are a technology company's most precious asset. Successful acquirers have learned from experience the importance of having good relations with employees of a target company. They need to resist the temptation to tell people how to run their operations.

IBM learned this lesson the hard way when it acquired telecommunications equipment maker Rolm in 1984 without first performing adequate operational due diligence. IBM, despite giving assurances it would respect Rolm's independence and its contribution to IBM's expansion into the telecommunications field, began interfering with management of its newly acquired subsidiary soon after completing the merger. Instead of providing administrative and sales support, IBM went too far. IBM managers required Rolm to fill open positions with IBM personnel. IBM even tried to get Rolm to adopt its mainframe-oriented business model, even though the two companies were far apart in management style and corporate culture.

Cultural differences may have contributed to Rolm's lackluster performance under IBM management, but declining sales eventually forced IBM to unload its Rolm unit. After four years of poor results, IBM sold Rolm in 1988 to Siemens AG for a substantially lower price than the $1.3 billion it paid to acquire the telecommunications equipment maker. Financial analysts said Rolm had disappointing financial performance even before the buyout, as niche market competitors began to appear, and by the time IBM sold the company, it was losing $100 million a year.

Culture/Morale   Consideration of potential culture clashes and morale degradation is one of the most critical—yet most frequently overlooked—issues in assessing the probability of acquisition/merger success. Since corporations are made up of individuals and groups of individuals, the human factor plays a very important role in the success or failure of any acquisition. Asking two organizations with different working styles to join forces and maintain or even increase productivity is a tricky proposition. Will the culture of one organization dominate that of the other? If so, what will be the impact on the productivity of the employees in the subordinated company?

While it may be difficult to obtain meaningful insights on the culture of a target company in advance of an acquisition, the effort must be made. Human resource departments are beginning to benchmark against competitors, so this may be a starting point for comparison. If it becomes clear that the cultures of the acquiring company and target are dramatically different, the acquiring company should consider this issue in the broader context of the acquisition decision. In some cases, it may be more prudent not to merge the companies, but rather to let them continue as separate operating entities. In other cases, it may be wiser to forego the acquisition altogether. Research and experience have proven that two companies significantly mismatched on the human level are highly unlikely to succeed.

AT&T's Purchase of NCR: Insufficient Cultural Due Diligence

The burden of operational due diligence intensifies when companies are under competitive pressure to make a quick decision. A good example of what can go wrong is AT&T's 1991 hostile takeover of NCR Corporation. AT&T's executives were searching for a new growth strategy following the 1984 breakup of AT&T and deregulation of long-distance telephone service. They believed that telecommunications technology and desktop computing were converging, and wanted to position AT&T as a player in the new market.

AT&T executives considered NCR Corporation a prime takeover candidate, since NCR manufactured personal computers as well as mainframe computers, and its personal computer line was thought to be profitable. Management also believed that NCR's computing prowess would reach its full potential under AT&T's direction. And they believed the two companies, both conservatively managed, were compatible in management style. AT&T launched its hostile takeover and paid a hefty premium to acquire NCR. A more thorough self-assessment and due diligence investigation would have uncovered serious technical and management differences between the two companies—differences that eventually proved insurmountable.

Engineers from AT&T's Bell Labs, examining NCR's PC technology only after the merger, discovered that AT&T's switching gear was incompatible with basic PC technology, reducing the expected synergies. Similarities in management style also turned out to be superficial. NCR's senior management ruled a company with highly centralized decision making, while AT&T was highly decentralized. Attempts to smooth out the cultural differences— doors and walls were replaced by glass partitions, for instance—all backfired. The management differences alone were probably enough to undermine the merger. Numerous attempts to salvage the deal by shuffling management staff also failed to produce results. (AT&T even changed the name of its computer manufacturing subsidiary for a few years, and then changed the name back to NCR.) After years of heavy losses and little to show for its investment, AT&T spun off NCR to AT&T shareholders in January 1997.

Management Team   The two key issues with respect to the management team are ego and competence. The acquiring company must structure the merger in such a way as to retain the competent players and elevate them to positions of authority in the combined entity. It is critical to map out on three organizational charts, the existing and anticipated formal and informal power structures of the acquiring company, the target, and the combined entity. Taking such a step in advance of the acquisition gives the acquiring company a sense of whether the situation is likely to be workable. If it is anticipated that a large number of the key players in the acquiring company and/or the target will leave as a result of the merger, this of course calls into question the wisdom of pursuing the transaction.

Production   The level of operational excellence in production is, of course, a key issue for both service and manufacturing firms. Understanding the production and service delivery systems that exist at the target company provides an important perspective on the need for capital expenditures and training in the future. Additionally, it provides a perspective on the work ethic and commitment to quality of the existing employee base. It takes many years of training, internal public relations, and effective management to generate a culture that focuses on effective delivery of quality products and service. If such efforts have not been made prior to the acquisition, the acquiring company must assess how important such a commitment will be to future success in the relevant industry. If it will be key to success in the future, this must be factored into the valuation and the anticipated competitiveness of the target in the short and long run.

Distribution   The distribution channels are critical to an understanding of the overall marketing plans of the target company. It is crucial to closely analyze the target company's current and future strength in key distribution channels. This analysis goes hand-in-hand with the research on distribution performed as part of strategic due diligence. As "bricks and mortar" competitors in many industries have discovered, it is possible to be leapfrogged almost overnight by new competitors that embrace cutting-edge technology. If the target is not bringing a progressive distribution approach to the table, then the acquiring company should begin the development of a plan to innovate in distribution to stay ahead of the curve.

Information Management   Like culture clashes, information technology (IT) management missteps are often at the root of acquisition failures. There are two key issues in this area. First, it is critically important to realize that merging legacy IT systems from two companies is extremely complex and usually takes much longer and costs a great deal more than normally anticipated. This reality should be taken into account by the acquiring company in valuing the target, particularly if the acquiring company is looking to the information management area for any cost or productivity synergies. Historically, such synergies have proven to be elusive. Second, there is a growing movement to assess the alignment of information management strategy with corporate strategy. The extent to which companies have achieved such alignment varies widely. The degree to which the target's information systems support its approach to managing the business can be a telling indicator of how sustainable the success of the company is. This gets back to the issue of how dependent the success of the target is on intellectual property contained in the heads of a few key employees. The more such intellectual property has been translated into information management systems that can be understood by the acquiring company, the higher the assumed probability of postacquisition success, even in the event of an exodus of key target company employees.

Harvard Pilgrim: Poor Technology Integration Planning

Harvard Pilgrim, a Massachusetts HMO, grew by acquiring other HMOs. In 1994, the Harvard Community Health Plan merged with Pilgrim to form Harvard Pilgrim Health Care. The two companies did not bring back-office data processing departments together, and they had different medical billing systems. They did not bill insurance companies or the government correctly (some claims were even paid twice because of incompatible medical billing systems). Harvard Pilgrim restated revenue and profit numbers, costing $22 million. Because of this blunder, the company filed for bankruptcy protection in 1999 under Massachusetts' HMO insolvency law.

Research and Development Gaining a solid understanding of the target's strength in research and development is more or less important, of course, depending on such factors as type of business (service or manufacturing) and speed of industry innovation. Access to new technology is often the motivation for acquisition activity, but even in the cases where the motivation is different, it is important that the acquiring company gain a solid understanding of the target's portfolio of proprietary technology/methodology. The key then is to map how the target's R&D capabilities match up with those of the acquiring company. In some cases this will not be an important due diligence factor, whereas in others, it will be the impetus for the transaction. Depending upon the capabilities and time constraints of the acquiring company's in-house R&D staff and also upon the sensitivity of the proprietary information, it may be necessary to have the target's portfolio assessed by outside experts.

Regulatory While compliance in all relevant areas will certainly be covered in the legal due diligence, this issue, from an operational due diligence perspective, is one of assessing existing compliance systems. The acquiring company must assess whether the target has in place adequate systems for monitoring compliance with key regulatory requirements. To the extent that the target does not have such systems in place, the acquiring company must assess the feasibility and cost of incorporating such monitoring into existing systems. If such incorporation is not deemed possible, the acquiring company must factor into its valuation of the target the cost of putting such systems in place. In the case of inadequate existing systems, the acquiring company may also want to ensure rigorous legal due diligence on the target. If the systems are inadequate, the chance of instances of noncompliance in the past (and future) is likely to be higher.

As discussions regarding the potential acquisition proceed and more sensitive information is requested, the parties will typically execute a confidentiality agreement to protect confidential and proprietary information being disclosed in the course of negotiations. A sample confidentiality agreement is included as Appendix A. The objective of these negotiations is typically to reach agreement on a *letter of intent*. The letter of intent will outline the basic terms of the transaction. A sample letter of intent for a stock purchase transaction is included as Appendix B. Once the letter of intent has been signed, the due diligence process, outlined in detail in Step 4, will commence. An outline of a sample work schedule in an asset purchase transaction from the point of the signing of the letter of intent, through the due diligence phase, to the closing of the transaction, is included as Appendix C.

C   H   A   P   T   E   R

STEP 5: VALUING THE ACQUISITION TARGET

BACKGROUND
Does the Stock Market Value Corporate Diversification?

There is a significant amount of empirical evidence that supports the theory that corporate diversification destroys value. A 1990 study by Morck, Shleifer, and Vishny found that companies in the 1980s that made unrelated acquisitions actually earned negative returns. In a 1995 study, Berger and Ofek compared the prices of U.S. conglomerates to portfolios of firms in the same industries. In other words, they compared the total price of business units "bundled" into a diversified firm to sets of individual companies in the same industries yet with each company focused on one industry. They found that the average price of the conglomerates was 15 percent less than the value of the portfolio of focused companies. Research published in 1997 by Shin and Stulz indicates that poorly performing business units in conglomerates are subsidized by better-performing business units. This would indicate that the managers of such conglomerates are not being efficient in allocating resources across their various business units. The implication is that the stock market does a better job of valuing business entities and allocating capital accordingly than managers sitting atop a diversified firm. The market therefore seems to put a greater value on focus than diversification.

The Hubris Hypothesis

Pride is considered the worst of the seven deadly sins, and many believe it is at the top of the list of M&A vices as well. Just as the fatal flaw of pride is the downfall of many a Greek and Shakespearean tragic figure, so too is it often cited as the cause of failure in M&A. So much so that Richard Roll's article, "The Hubris Hypothesis of Corporate Takeovers,"[1] is often cited in M&A literature. According to Roll, the personal motives of executives at acquiring firms sometimes play a more important role in M&A decisions than do shareholder value considerations. He believes that many M&A deals are executed because executives at acquiring companies want to build their reputations by growing their companies. Such personal ambitions drive acquisition-minded executives to submit bids beyond reasonable prices. At the end of the bidding process, the winner actually is left with an overvalued asset. The expected value of the combined entities' future earnings may not exceed the high premiums paid for these acquisitions, and so shareholder value will actually be lost.

Some researchers support Roll's claim, while others doubt it. The empirical evidence is not conclusive either way; however, Roll's hypothesis highlights the importance of the human factors in influencing what many people may believe is a strictly technical valuation process. Roll believes that the pride of executives clouds their thinking and makes them believe that they can value targets better than the market can. Regardless of whether Roll is correct in his analysis, executives at acquiring companies are wise to heed his warning.

THE VALUE TRANSPARENCY MOVEMENT

Although our main concern is mergers and acquisitions, it is important to note that over the last decade there has been an increase in corporate reorganizations designed to break up companies in the name of enhancing shareholder value. An understanding of the reasoning behind breakup strategies is important in giving executives involved in M&A a more complete perspective on how the market values the different strategies of corporate diversification and focus.

Corporate executives often note that they are frustrated with analysts who are assigning values to their companies at levels far below what these executives believe they are worth. In an attempt to make this value clear and understandable to the market, there has been a movement toward "value transparency." The thinking is that there exist pieces of diversified companies that

---

[1]"The Hubris Hypothesis of Corporate Takeovers," Richard Roll, *Journal of Business,* vol. 59, no. 2, April 1986, pp 197–216.

are not being valued highly enough because they are "hidden" in a bundle comprised of many companies. If these pieces were to stand alone, their value would become more obvious, and their prices as stand-alone entities would be bid up to reflect the more favorable values.

In order to achieve such "value transparency," corporations have been restructuring through a wide array of different transactions, including *divestitures, equity carve-outs,* and *spin-offs.*

A divestiture is the sale of a piece of a company (for example, a division) to another party. In this case, the piece's value will be easier to analyze since it can be viewed as a stand-alone entity. The hope of the selling company is that the price at which it can sell this piece will be greater than the value the market believes it adds as a part of the diversified company. An equity carve-out is a type of divestiture in which a parent company sells equity in one of its subsidiaries to the public through an initial public offering (IPO).

In a spin-off, a parent company divests a business unit or subsidiary, yet it is not sold for cash or securities. Instead, shares in the new company are distributed to the shareholders of the parent company on a pro-rata basis. Notable spin-offs include: Quaker Oats' spin-off of its toy manufacturing subsidiary, Fisher-Price; General Motors' spin-off of EDS; and Pacific Telesis' spin-off of Air Touch. The creation of Lucent Technologies out of AT&T was actually a combination of an equity carve-out and a spin-off of the parent company's remaining equity interest.

AT&T's Spin-Off of Lucent Technologies

In September 1995, AT&T announced that it would divide its operations into three publicly traded companies. In addition to AT&T, the communications services company, there would be a network systems company called Lucent Technologies and a computer company called NCR. With regard to the formation of Lucent, first there was an equity carve-out in which 17 percent of the new company was offered to the public through an IPO. The remaining 83 percent of the company was distributed tax-free to AT&T shareholders. The market reacted very favorably to the announcement as AT&T's stock quickly jumped 11 percent. These spin-offs were designed to leave AT&T as a "pure play" in communication services. "Pure play" is a term used to denote a company's concentration in one line of business as opposed to the diversification achieved through a conglomerate strategy.

Empirical Evidence Regarding Value Transparency Strategies

Empirical evidence clearly indicates that there are positive effects on shareholder value when companies engage in these types of transactions to increase "value transparency." The extensive research on these different types of divestitures involves what is known as *event studies,* which track daily stock return behavior around the time of the transaction announcement. One of the more recent event studies was conducted by J. P. Morgan in 1995. The study shows that there are sharp positive stock price reactions around announcement dates, and the bigger the spin-off, the greater the positive effect on share prices.

Again, this topic is discussed here in order to provide a better perspective on how the market values the various corporate strategies that companies pursue. One might conclude that divestitures, equity carve-outs, spin-offs, and other value transparency strategies are generally good for shareholders, while mergers and acquisitions are usually bad. Regardless of this general impression, however, there are many major companies such as Cisco Systems, Nortel Networks, and WorldCom, which clearly would not have succeeded as much as they actually have if not for their focus on M&A. Undoubtedly, growth through acquisition can generate enormous increases in shareholder value. One of the main questions, however, is how much should a company pay for growth? This is where *Step 5: Valuing the Acquisition Target,* comes in.

THE NUTS AND BOLTS OF STEP 5

Three decades of academic research and corporate experience with M&A have proven that the majority of mergers and acquisitions have destroyed rather than created shareholder value. There are several major causes of such failures. Step 1 addressed the main culprit, which is buying a business that is not a good strategic fit for the acquiring company. Running a close second after poor strategic fit is overpaying for the acquisition target.

The acquiring company usually must pay a premium over the current market value of the target company in order to win shareholder agreement. Often, the acquirers justify this premium by convincing themselves and their shareholders with the seemingly magical word "synergy." The thinking is that the potential cost savings of slashing redundant operations and the potential revenue increases generated through cross-selling opportunities will more than outweigh this acquisition premium. It seems, however, that management is more likely to lose focus and that the massive energies expended to overcome cultural mismatches end up turning one plus one into less than two rather than the fabled three.

To compound the problem, bidding wars may occur. Such a contest increases the acquisition premiums to even more dizzying heights. This often-frenzied activity not only forces acquiring companies to rush due diligence, but also raises the hurdle even higher so that the company that ends up winning the prized target must meet even greater performance expectations in order to justify the new, higher premium. The key therefore is not only to be realistic during the valuation phase, but also not to lose perspective of this valuation when challenged by a competing bidder.

M&A Start-Up Costs

Much of *Step 5: Valuing the Acquisition Target* emphasizes the need to determine a realistic value of the benefits that will accrue to the newly formed entity, which are attributable to what is called "synergistic value." It is hard enough to realistically analyze all the potential synergies that could be achieved in a particular M&A deal; however, one also must realize that in order to take advantage of those potential synergies, significant costs may be involved. These costs are above and beyond the actual cost of purchasing the acquired company.

From this perspective, it is beneficial to look at the newly combined entity as a brand-new company. Although many assets from each of the two stand-alone companies will be leveragable in the "new" company, many will not. For example, whole new technology purchases might need to be made in order to ensure proper information flow within the newly combined entity. Whether such costs are factored in at the valuation stage may change the success equation. The hope is that many of these hidden costs will be uncovered during the due diligence stage, so that expenditures that must be made to realize the synergy value of a merger can be incorporated into the valuation.

Paying Top Dollar for Snapple

When many deals are reviewed retrospectively, it becomes obvious that the acquiring company's projected revenues, profits, and cash flows prove to be wildly unrealistic. A good example of obvious overpayment driven by overly optimistic projections is the case of Quaker Oats' acquisition of Snapple in November 1994. Most industry analysts believe that the $1.7 billion price tag was $1 billion too much to pay for the beverage company, given the company's financial situation and the industry outlook at the time. Studies indicate, typically, that the acquiror's stock price falls when a new acquisition is announced and the target company's stock rises; however, in this case, the stock prices of both companies declined on the day the deal was announced. Most telling is that a little more than two years later, Quaker Oats sold Snapple to Triarc Companies, Inc., for less than 20 percent of what it had paid for the beverage company.

In this case, there were significant oversights during the due diligence step. Many believe that Quaker Oats purchased Snapple in a defensive move to avoid being taken over itself. It seems that in the rush to sign on the dotted line, the Quaker Oats management did not take the time to think through the true synergies that would result. They did not understand the target company as well as they should have. Supplier relationships were not fully explored—especially those with Snapples' bottling companies. But most fatal of all were the rosy projections that were made regarding continued growth in the beverage segments that Snapple served. Snapple was not a low-cost producer. Rather, it had succeeded based on its positioning as a premium product. Quaker Oats' sales projections, which were the basis for the offer price, did not take into consideration the possibility of future heavy competition by low-cost producers. The projected revenues, which were expected to more than justify the premium paid for Snapple, never materialized, and this led to Quaker Oats' sale of the division to Triarc. It is interesting to note that in September 2000, Triarc turned around and sold Snapple to Cadbury Schweppes plc for $1.45 billion, which is less than 10 percent of the price originally paid by Quaker Oats.

Sometimes It Is Better to Walk Away from a Deal

Companies sometimes get involved in bidding wars, which can prove disastrous. During the bidding process, the price for a target company may be bid up beyond realistic levels. The winner is then stuck with paying a premium that will never be recouped through future cash flows. Thus the winner, plagued by what is known as "the winner's curse," really ends up being the loser. Once a realistic valuation for the target company is determined, suitors should respect that valuation and refuse to bid significantly higher than that price.

Many companies who buy others at a peak in the market often find themselves wishing they had waited until prices had come down to more realistic levels. Such is the case with many who bought Internet companies at the exorbitant prices of the late 1990s. On the flip side, many of the so-called New Economy companies probably wish they had sold out before the market correction.

Walking Away from an Expensive Deal

In February 1999, USA Networks, operator of television shopping channel QVC and Ticketmaster Online City Search, attempted to buy Lycos, the Internet portal. The merger would have combined USA Networks' retail distribution channels with Lycos' brand name recognition as the third-largest Internet portal. However, merger talks broke off three months later after negotiators for the companies failed to agree on adequate valuation of Lycos. Lycos investors objected to terms of the $18 billion merger, saying that the premium per share offered by USA Networks was inadequate compared to what buyers were paying at the time to acquire other Internet companies.

Lycos investors had wanted a share of the combined company larger than the 30 percent ownership offered by USA Networks.

KEY CONCEPTS OF VALUATION

There are many books that focus on company valuation. The objective here is not to rehash common valuation methods but rather to give an overview of the major issues surrounding this crucial step in the M&A process. Whereas many valuation methodologies often do little more than confuse corporate practitioners by delving into mind-boggling detail, it seems appropriate in the context of *The M&A Strategy Guide* to focus attention on a high-level perspective of the process. Of course, this does not mean that valuation is a simple process. Indeed, it is often more of an elusive art than a disciplined science, as can be seen in the six predeal activities listed in Figure 8-1. The top three activities are very important to the success of a deal and the ultimate realization of value, but are rather difficult to quantify.

From a strategic perspective, there are two key valuation concepts that must be explored during the valuation process—*intrinsic value* and *synergistic value*. Intrinsic value refers to the basic value of a company independent of the acquisition. Several methodologies are currently used to determine intrinsic values. *The M&A Strategy Guide* provides an overview of two of the most common valuation methods: (1) *discounted cash flow* and (2) *market comparables*. There are two intrinsic values that must be calculated and considered—one for the acquiring company and one for the target company.

FIGURE 8-1   Six predeal activities that boost the odds of a successful merger.[2]

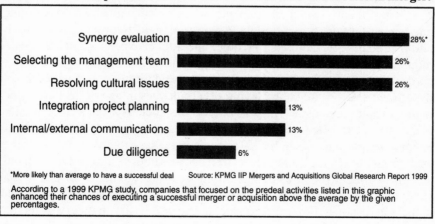

Synergy evaluation	28%*
Selecting the management team	26%
Resolving cultural issues	26%
Integration project planning	13%
Internal/external communications	13%
Due diligence	6%

*More likely than average to have a successful deal   Source: KPMG IIP Mergers and Acquisitions Global Research Report 1999

According to a 1999 KPMG study, companies that focused on the predeal activities listed in this graphic enhanced their chances of executing a successful merger or acquisition above the average by the given percentages.

[2]Unlocking Shareholder Value: the Keys to Success—Mergers and Acquisitions, a Global Research Report, 1999. Reprinted with permission from KPMG.

Calculating the Value Attributable to Synergy

The concept of synergy is often captured in the equation: $1 + 1 = 3$. The thinking is that by joining forces, two companies can perform significantly better than the simple sum of the performances achieved by each's efforts alone. Synergistic value refers to the value added as a result of the combining of the two entities. In the equation just cited, the synergistic value would be 1, which is arrived at by subtracting 2 (the value of the separate components on the left of the equation) from 3, the sum total on the right of the equation. Conceptually, this unit of 1, which makes the equation incorrect mathematically, is the main goal of all the hundreds of billions of dollars of M&A transactions executed each year.

Synergistic value addresses value improvements above and beyond those that each company would realize if the combination did not take place. Whereas calculating intrinsic values are fairly straightforward and at least somewhat formulaic, arriving at a synergistic value is a much more complicated process because of all the assumptions that must be made.

Certainly, there are many issues to be considered when trying to calculate the value of synergies, including tax benefits attributable to the combination and the value of information sharing between the entities. However, it seems that for long-term success, the two key drivers of synergistic value are benefits attributable to (1) *cost-cutting* and (2) *cross-selling*. Since they are of overriding importance, *The M&A Strategy Guide* focuses on these two critical success factors.

Cost-Cutting

The first of the two main components of synergistic value concerns savings due to cost-cutting. Synergies achieved through cost-cutting arise from the elimination of jobs, facilities, and other operational expenses that are deemed redundant due to the combining of the two entities. For example, once the two companies are combined, there is usually no need for two accounts receivable departments. Costs are cut by laying off employees in one of the two departments. Achieving cost savings in other areas such as a sales force are less clear-cut. If the M&A deal was conceived and executed in an attempt to expand geographic reach, the sales force necessary to cover the combined sales areas should logically at least remain the same, or it may even expand.

One of the difficulties of calculating cost savings in advance is that an individual's position on an organizational chart may not reflect his or her actual job responsibilities. Positions that may seem easy in theory to cut may prove to be crucial to the ongoing operations of the newly combined company. Therefore, although these costs may seem fairly straightforward to calculate, an understanding of positions at the operational level is necessary to determine what can be eliminated and what must be preserved.

Massive Cost-Cutting after the Citicorp-Travelers Merger

Banking is a slow-growth industry, characterized by overcapacity and declining margins. With the recent trends in deregulation and with thousands of banks in the United States alone, it is an industry ripe for consolidation. In April 1998, the banking giant Citicorp announced a merger with the insurance company Travelers Group, which created the world's largest financial services firm with nearly $700 billion in assets. Once the dust settled, the combined company's stock price had been slashed by more than half (see Figure 8-2). However, by October 2001, three years after its lows in October 1998, the stock had nearly tripled in value.

Increases in shareholder value were expected to come from cost-cutting and cross-selling initiatives. In December 1998, Citicorp announced that it would cut 10,400 jobs, which represented nearly 6 percent of its worldwide workforce. Big layoffs were expected, but this figure was much more than had been anticipated. Although Citicorp delivered on the cost-cutting that it promised, most analysts believe that it was not as successful as had been expected in terms of cross-selling different financial services to its customers.

Cross-Selling

The value attributable to cross-selling opportunities is the second major component of synergistic value. Cross-selling refers to the combining entities' abilities to sell their products and/or services to each other's customer bases.

Calculating the component of synergistic value derived from cross-selling opportunities is much more elusive than the relatively "hard" costs that can be calculated when forecasting cost-cutting opportunities. Unlike costs, which can be controlled quite closely by a company, projected revenues are difficult to predict. It is difficult enough to forecast the future

FIGURE 8-2   The synthetic Citigroup.[3]

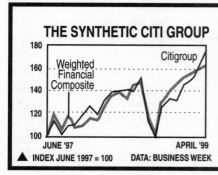

THE SYNTHETIC CITI GROUP

Reed is also gauging Citi's progress by matching the company against a "synthetic" competitor, a weighted composite of the stock prices of seven other financial services firms. The index was designed to approximate the same business mix as Citigroup. "And the proposition in my mind is: Do we do better?... We're a tad better than any synthetic right now, but not meaningfully. On the other hand, we're not worse."

[3]"Business Week Online," June 7, 1999. Reprinted with permission from *Business Week*.

sales of each stand-alone company, dependent as such forecasts are on market assumptions. Formulating sales forecasts for a combined entity is vastly more difficult, however, given that many more variables, such as customer reactions, must be taken into account.

In theory, cross-selling should lead to considerable increases in revenue. In reality, one company's customers may not be interested in the products of the second company. Moreover, adding more products to one's offerings might significantly change the company's positioning and perhaps turn off consumers who do not see the aggregated product mix as appropriate with respect to the company's brand image.

Sears' Failed Dreams of Cross-Selling

In the 1980s, Sears, Roebuck & Co. severely damaged its brand image in part because of M&A activity and in part because of the retailer's diversification strategy of being a one-stop shop for a wide variety of consumer products and services. On one side, Sears was faced by the rise of fashionable stores such as The Gap and The Limited. On the other side, it had to compete with the low-cost outlets like Kmart and Wal-Mart. The typical consumer could not see Sears as fashionable if it also sold products like bowling balls.

More specifically, with regard to cross-selling, in 1981, Sears added the real estate and brokerage services offered by Coldwell Banker and Dean Witter, respectively, to the insurance services it offered through its Allstate subsidiary. Faced with growing competition in the mature retailing industry, Sears sought to leverage its vast store of computerized data on the purchasing, payment, and demographic characteristics of its customer base by expanding into the financial services business. At the time, the financial service industry was experiencing significantly higher returns on equity than retailers. Furthermore, research on the buying habits of Sears' cardholders seemed to strongly indicate that their current customers would be inclined to purchase financial services through the company.

The strategy was successful initially. Soon after, however, competitors in financial services such as Fidelity Investments realized that time-constrained consumers were beginning to prefer shopping for financial services via phone and mail. Although its financial division was quite successful, Sears' dreams of cross-selling retail items and financial services to their customers were not realized in the long run. Its failed retail strategy incited shareholder activists, which forced a management shakeup in 1992. Coldwell Banker was sold in its entirety, Dean Witter was spun off, and even a 20 percent stake in Allstate was sold. The market reacted positively to the restructuring. When the restructuring was announced, the company's stock was around $41. A year later, it rose to $56.

Totaling the Two Major Components of Synergistic Value

As has already been noted, while it is difficult to foresee the true savings that can be realized through cost-cutting early in the process, this component of synergistic value is much more easily estimated than the value contributed by cross-selling opportunities. Many more variables come into play when predicting revenue increases. Because of this uncertainty, value increases due to cross-selling opportunities should be discounted, or even, as some analysts suggest, not taken into account at all when calculating the total expected synergistic value.

Whether and to what degree both of these components are used in calculating the synergistic value is left to the judgment of those performing the analysis. It is wise, however, to err on the conservative side so as to avoid as much as possible overestimating synergistic value and thus overpaying for an acquisition.

CALCULATING INTRINSIC VALUES: ASSUMPTIONS, ASSUMPTIONS EVERYWHERE

Along with determining the appropriate synergistic value, the intrinsic values of the two stand-alone entities must be calculated so that their sum can be factored into a final valuation of the combined entity. To accomplish this, an intrinsic value for each entity must be calculated without consideration of any elements of synergistic value. The intrinsic value of the acquiring company should already have been determined in the Corporate Self-Valuation Assessment section of *Step 2: Assessing Structural Capacity*.

Unlike synergistic values, which are based on many significant assumptions about the future that are outside of managements' control, intrinsic values are usually derived by the following more formulaic methods. This is not to say, however, that there are no significant assumptions that must be made when calculating intrinsic values. Indeed, in the case of a discounted cash flow (DCF) analysis, future cash flows must be forecasted and discount rates must be decided upon somewhat subjectively.

Two Common Valuation Methods

Two of the most common valuation methods are *discounted cash flow analysis* and the *market multiple method.* Although these methods differ significantly in approach, theoretically, they should result in at least similar valuations of the target company. The DCF analysis is more rigorous and thorough, but the assumption made by those who favor the market multiple approach is that the efficiency of the market incorporates all relevant factors into the multiples used in this method of valuation.

With either approach, it is extremely important to have operating managers involved in the validation of all key operating assumptions. The most common flaw in valuations, particularly those based on the discounted cash flow approach, is that the implicit and explicit assumptions of the analysis do not take into account how realistic certain key operating ratios are (see Figure 8-3 for likelihood of benefits in a deal). This problem can largely be avoided by reality checking key assumptions with relevant operating managers.

Both valuation methodologies are described in more detail in the following paragraphs.

Discounted Cash Flow Analysis

In this method (see Figure 8-4 for an example), cash flows are projected into the future and then discounted back to a present value using a chosen discount rate. Usually, exact cash flows are estimated for a period of between 5 and 10 years, depending on the predictability of the particular industry in question. A "terminal value" is then calculated based on an assumption of constant or steadily growing cash flow for all years after the projection period. There are three key areas that must be assessed for accuracy and relevance when using the DCF method: (1) cash flow projections during the chosen projection period; (2) terminal value at the end of the projection period; and (3) discount rate. Each area is explained in more detail below.

1. **Cash flow projections:** Future cash flows are a function of several key factors including sales, cost of sales, SG&A expenses, and balance sheet changes.

    a. **Sales:** Projections should be done on a product line basis. The key question is how realistic are the sales projections? Without reasonable sales projections, it is impossible to arrive at meaningful cash flow projections. The less reliable the sales forecasting model, the less useful the results of the discounted cash flow analysis.

    b. **Cost of sales:** This is typically the company's largest expenditure. Depending on the industry, the cost of sales could be well in excess of 50 percent of the selling price of the good or service, so this is an area where forecast accuracy is particularly important. Forecasts should be based on historical results and on industry benchmarks and trends. Any significant deviations from either should be well justified. The more granular (i.e., broken down into materials, labor, overhead, etc.) this analysis is, the better.

    c. **SG&A expenses:** All selling, general, and administrative expenses should likewise be projected on the basis of history

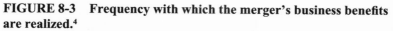

FIGURE 8-3   Frequency with which the merger's business benefits are realized.[4]

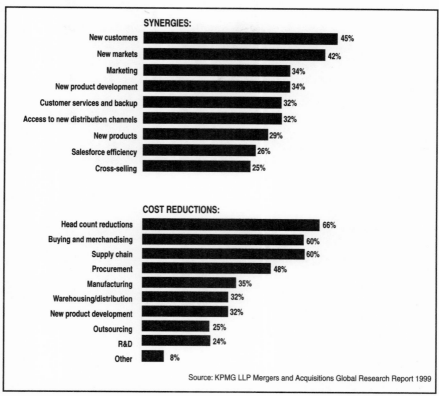

and industry norms. Again, significant deviations should be explained.

    d.   **Balance sheet:** Changes in any of the components of the balance sheet have an impact on cash flow. Some of the more important balance sheet issues to be focused on include: working capital changes, capital expenditures, depreciation methods, and any changes in capital structure expected during the projection period.

2.   **Terminal value:** It is important that by the end of the projection period it be expected that the company's operations will be at a sustainable level. In other words, by the end of the projection period cash flows should be expected to remain steady or to be growing at

[4]Unlocking Shareholder Value: the Keys to Success—Mergers and Acquisitions, a Global Research Report, 1999. Reprinted with permission from KPMG.

FIGURE 8-4   Basic DCF valuation example.[4]

($ millions)	% (Sales)	Year 1	Year 2	Year 3	Year 4	Year 5	Terminal	Equity
Revenues	100	10.00	11.00	12.10	13.31	14.64	Value	Value
Cost of Sales	60	6.00	6.60	7.26	7.99	8.78		
Gross Profit	40	4.00	4.40	4.84	5.32	5.86		
Operating Expenses	15	1.50	1.65	1.82	2.00	2.20		
EBIT	25	2.50	2.75	3.03	3.33	3.66		
Income Tax (40%)		1.00	1.10	1.21	1.33	1.46		
After-Tax Income								
(Before Interest and Taxes on Interest)		1.50	1.65	1.82	2.00	2.20		
Add: Non-cash Items		0.45	0.50	0.54	0.60	0.66		
Less: Capital Expenditures & Increase in Working Capital		0.39	0.43	0.47	0.52	0.57		
Cash Flows		1.56	1.72	1.89	2.08	2.28	16.31	
Present Value Factor*		0.877	0.769	0.675	0.592	0.519	0.519	
Present Value (PV)		1.368	1.320	1.274	1.229	1.186	8.473	
Total PV of Cash Flows								6.379
PV of Terminal Value								8.473
Total Capital Value								14.852
Less: Outstanding Interest-Bearing Debt								3.250
Total Equity Value								11.602

*Note: Discount rate is assumed to be 14 percent.

a steady rate. Given that the cash flows after the projection period are expected to remain steady or grow slowly in perpetuity, the terminal value can have a major impact on the calculated present value of the target company. The value of the cash flows after the projection period is typically estimated by dividing the final projection year cash flow by the discount rate (same method used to value a perpetuity) or by applying a market multiple to the same final projection year cash flow. With either method, the terminal value is then discounted back to the present using the discount rate.

3.   **Discount rate:** This is an area of discounted cash flow analysis where art is clearly as responsible for the outcome as is science. The Capital Asset Pricing Model typically is used for arriving at the discount rate. The principle of the model is that the required cost of equity (k_e) is equal to the risk-free (Rf) return (usually on government bonds) plus an additional risk premium. The calculation of the risk premium is based upon the historical expected return of the stock (equity) market (Rm) in excess of the risk-free return. Finally the riskiness (expressed as "beta"—β_i) of the return on a particular stock relative to the overall

market (where beta for the overall market equals 1) is factored into the calculation of the cost of equity. The equation for the cost of equity then is:

$$k_e = Rf + \beta_i(Rm - Rf)$$

The required rate of return on the debt is calculated as the interest rate on the debt multiplied by 1 minus the tax rate, to take into account the tax benefit of the interest on the debt.

The required rates of return on debt and equity are then weighted based on the capital structure of the company in order to arrive at a weighted average cost of capital (WACC). The weighted average cost of capital is the discount rate that is used to discount the pre-interest operating cash flows.

Market Multiple Method

This valuation method is based simply on applying a multiple to a target company's earnings (usually earnings before interest and taxes, or "EBIT"). The method is based on the premise that the market is very efficient in reflecting all information available to investors. The assumption is that the market is constantly valuing companies and therefore using the valuation implied by current stock prices makes sense. The accuracy of this assumption is predicated on the rational behavior of investors in the market, which, given recent radical fluctuations of valuation levels, may be called into question. The reliability of using this method is further complicated by the fact that it can be exceedingly difficult to find truly comparable companies for any particular target. Without good "comparables" it does not make much sense to rely on applying a multiple to the earnings of the target company to arrive at a valuation. Despite all the challenges with this method, it is important to understand this technique, if for no other reason than to "sanity check" the results from the discounted cash flow analysis. Also, it is important to be familiar with the multiple method since given its simplicity, it is often used by many merger and acquisition professionals as a valuation starting point (even for privately held companies).

It should be noted that the market multiple method does not directly address potentially important balance sheet–related issues, such as required investment in working capital. So when it is stated that a privately held company, with a certain sales and earnings level should sell for five to seven times EBIT, it is implicitly assumed that such a multiple takes into account all relevant valuation factors, even though the market multiple calculation is based on just one line item of the income statement. For obvious reasons, using various valuation techniques and cross-checking them for reasonableness is the approach used by most M&A professionals.

COMMENTS ON VALUING PUBLIC AND PRIVATE COMPANIES

The methods just outlined are used to value both publicly held and privately held companies. However, privately held companies are usually more difficult to value than publicly held companies. The shares of publicly held companies are traded on national securities exchanges where the market is determining their value on a daily basis. These values are in part determined by material information that is required to be disclosed on a periodic basis by federal securities laws and regulations. On the other hand, there is no market for the shares of privately held companies nor is there any requirement for the disclosure of material information about the company. Accordingly privately held companies are much more difficult to value due to the lack of market pricing and lack of disclosed information.

When comparing the value of a privately held company to a publicly held company, discounts are typically applied due to the illiquidity of the shares of the privately held company. This illiquidity stems from the fact that there is typically no market for these shares and, to the extent that a market does exist, the transactions costs in transferring the shares may be high. The discounts that may be applied to a privately held company off of a similar publicly held company will vary, based on the industry and prevailing market conditions.

CONCLUSION

Step 5: Valuing the Acquisition Target, provides a framework for thinking about determining the values of the acquiring company, the target, and the combined entity. As has been discussed, the target company may realistically be valued at more than its stand-alone intrinsic value due to its contribution to synergistic value when in combination with the acquiring company. However, the factors that drive the valuation are the assumptions made about the synergistic value of the combined entity. Since many acquisitions fail because this valuation overestimates synergistic benefits, corporate experience over the past 30 years suggests that executives should err on the side of conservatism in assigning such values.

9

STEP 6: SELECTING THE APPROPRIATE LEGAL AND TAX STRUCTURES FOR THE TRANSACTION

BACKGROUND

This step provides an overview of the legal, tax, and regulatory issues that arise most often in merger and acquisition transactions. Due to the complexity of these issues, attorneys and accountants with expertise in corporate, securities, tax, and other regulatory issues must be recruited as part of the acquisition team in order to understand each of the relevant issues and their interplay with the strategic objectives in pursuing the acquisition. As a result, this step surveys the landscape of the legal issues without suggesting the appropriateness of any legal or tax structure for any particular type of transaction.

The sixth step in the *Guide* is *Selecting the Appropriate Legal and Tax Structures for the Transaction.* Structuring merger and acquisition transactions is one of the most challenging aspects of implementing a corporate acquisition strategy. The selection of an appropriate structure for an acquisition is a complex task requiring a thorough understanding of the company being acquired, the objectives of the acquiring company and the target, and the legal, tax, and accounting treatment of each acquisition structure.

THE NUTS AND BOLTS OF STEP 6

Although there are many ways of structuring an acquisition, there are only three basic forms an acquisition can take: (1) an *asset acquisition,* (2) a *stock acquisition,* and (3) a *merger.* What follows is a brief discussion of the basic forms of mergers and acquisitions and the principal issues that should be considered in each acquisition structure. This discussion assumes a negotiated merger or acquisition of a privately held company in which legal, tax, and accounting issues will largely dictate how the transaction will be structured.

Asset Purchase Transaction

In an asset purchase transaction (see Figure 9-1), the buyer purchases all or substantially all of the seller's assets in exchange for cash, notes, or other property. The principal advantage in structuring a transaction as an asset purchase (and the reason why buyers typically prefer asset transactions over stock transactions) is that the buyer can specify those assets that it will acquire and those liabilities that it will assume. The buyer may choose to avoid certain

FIGURE 9-1   Taxable asset purchase.

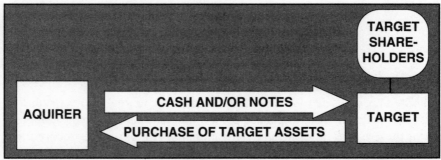

known liabilities such as known environmental liabilities, tax liabilities, pending or threatened litigation, and unfavorable contractual obligations.

The ability of the buyer to avoid certain liabilities of the seller may be limited in certain circumstances. First, under a series of legal theories grouped under the heading of *successor liability,* courts have determined that in certain circumstances a buyer will assume certain liabilities of the seller notwithstanding the fact that the transaction was structured as an asset purchase. Under one of these theories, known as the *de facto merger* doctrine, a court may determine, for policy reasons, that a buyer has acquired and is responsible for certain unassumed liabilities of the seller even though the transaction was structured as an asset purchase. In making a determination whether a *de facto* merger has taken place, a court will look to factors such as whether there is a continuity of management, personnel, physical location, assets, and general business operations; whether there is a continuity of shareholders which results from the buyer paying for the acquired assets with shares of its own stock; whether the seller ceases its business operations, liquidates, and dissolves soon after the transaction; and whether the buyer assumes those obligations of the seller ordinarily necessary for the uninterrupted continuation of normal business operations of the seller.

A second advantage of this structure from the buyer's perspective is that the buyer can acquire the seller without negotiating with the seller's shareholders individually. The ability to negotiate directly with the seller itself instead of the seller's shareholders can greatly simplify the transaction.

There are, however, a number of disadvantages to structuring a transaction as an asset purchase. One disadvantage is that the buyer must identify each of the assets being acquired and prepare the documentation necessary to transfer title to those assets. If there are a number of assets, the process of transferring title can be an expensive and time-consuming task.

A second disadvantage is that the seller may hold certain valuable contracts, licenses, and permits that cannot be assigned to the buyer without third-party consent or governmental approvals. In some cases, third parties may be unwilling to consent because they are seeking to terminate the contractual relationship, while in other cases, the third parties may be willing to consent but only after exacting a price for such consent. A sample asset purchase agreement is included as Appendix E.

Stock Purchase Transaction

In a stock purchase transaction (see Figure 9-2), the buyer purchases all, or at least a majority, of the outstanding stock of the seller from its shareholders in exchange for cash, promissory notes, or other property. The principal advantage of a stock purchase transaction is its relative simplicity. A stock purchase

FIGURE 9-2   Taxable stock purchase.

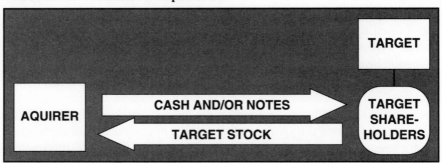

typically involves a single transaction in which the selling shareholders transfer their shares to the buyer. Unlike an asset purchase transaction, a stock purchase transaction does not involve the transfer of specific assets or the assumption of specific liabilities. The seller and its assets and liabilities remain intact since the seller, as an entity, is unaffected by its shareholders' sale of their stock.

A second advantage in structuring an acquisition as a stock purchase (and the reason why sellers typically prefer stock transactions over asset transactions), is that the liabilities of the seller remain with the target company after its stock is purchased by the buyer. However in most cases buyers will seek contractual indemnification from sellers for any breaches of representations or warranties made in the stock purchase agreement, including the existence of any undisclosed liabilities.

There are a number of significant disadvantages to stock purchase transactions. The principal disadvantage is that by acquiring the stock of the seller, the buyer is acquiring all of the seller's liabilities. However, since these liabilities remain with the seller, which is separate and distinct from the buyer, the buyer will not be directly responsible for such liabilities.

A second disadvantage is that some minority shareholders of the seller may be unwilling to sell their shares to the buyer, thereby preventing the buyer from acquiring all of the outstanding stock of the company. In certain circumstances a merger may be used to acquire control of all of the outstanding stock even though some shareholders vote against the transaction.

A third disadvantage is that stock acquisitions have less favorable tax treatment postacquisition than asset acquisitions. However, by making a Section 338 election under the Internal Revenue Code, it is possible to obtain the favorable tax treatment afforded an asset acquisition while avoiding the nontax disadvantages of asset acquisitions.

Merger

Merger is a state law process by which all of the assets and liabilities of the target company are automatically transferred to the surviving company by operation of law. The principal advantage of a merger transaction is that it is similar to a stock purchase in that it does not involve the transfer of specific assets or the assumption of specific liabilities. Instead, all of the assets and liabilities of the target company are automatically transferred to the acquiring company by operation of law.

A second advantage is that the acquiring company can obtain complete control of the target company in one step so that there is no need for a second step merger to squeeze out minority shareholders.

The principal disadvantage of a merger is that, as in a stock purchase transaction, the acquiring company assumes all of the liabilities of the target company. The liabilities include those that were disclosed by the target as well as those that were not disclosed or were not known at the time of the transaction. A merger transaction is less preferable than a stock purchase transaction in one significant respect: in a stock purchase transaction all of the liabilities of the target remain with the target after the acquisition, whereas in a merger all of the target's liabilities are directly assumed by the acquiring company. Therefore in a merger the surviving company assumes unlimited exposure for all of the liabilities of the target, whereas in a stock purchase the exposure of the acquiring company is limited to its investment in the target company's stock.

A third disadvantage of a merger is that it affords appraisal rights to shareholders of the target who vote against the merger transaction. Appraisal rights afford dissenting shareholders the right to receive cash for their stock instead of participating in the merger transaction.

A fourth disadvantage is that in certain types of mergers third-party consents may be required to transfer certain intangible rights of the target, including contracts, licenses, and permits.

Forward Merger

There are four basic forms of mergers. The first and most basic form of merger transaction is the *forward merger* (see Figure 9-3). In a forward merger, the shareholders of the target exchange their shares of target stock for shares of the acquiring company and, upon consummation of the merger, all of the assets and liabilities of the target are automatically transferred to the acquiror. A forward merger qualifies for tax-free treatment if the shareholders of the target receive at least 50 percent of their compensation in the form of stock of the acquiring company.

FIGURE 9-3   Forward merger.

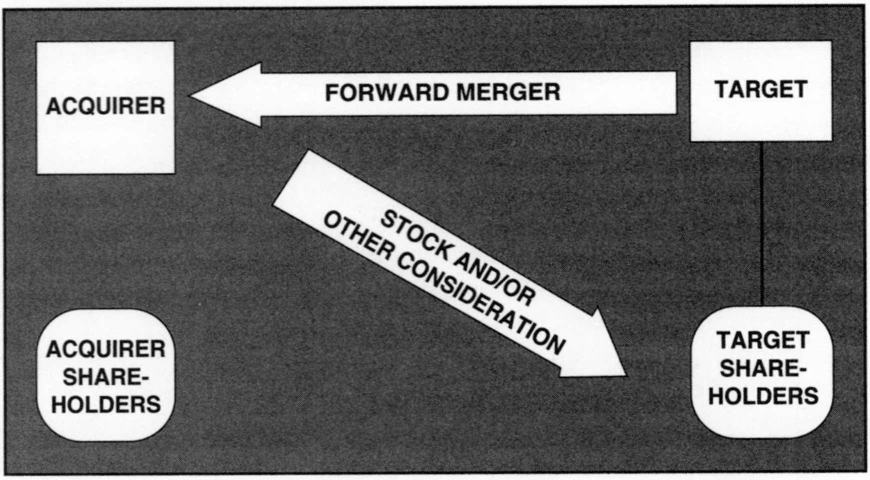

Forward mergers, however, have several important disadvantages. One disadvantage is that the acquiring company takes on all of the liabilities of the target. These liabilities include those which were disclosed by the target as well as those which were not disclosed or were not known at the time of the transaction.

A second disadvantage is that certain intangible rights may be lost upon the merger of the target into the acquiring company. These intangible rights can include contract rights, franchise rights, leases, loan agreements, government licenses, and other intangible rights held by the target. One solution to this problem is to structure the transaction as a reverse merger.

Reverse Merger

The second form of merger transaction is called a *reverse merger* (see Figure 9-4). In a reverse merger, the shareholders of the acquiring company exchange their shares of acquiring company stock for shares of the target company, and, instead of the target merging into the acquiring company, the acquiring company merges into the target. The target, not the acquiring company, is the surviving entity. All of the assets and liabilities of the acquiring company are automatically transferred to the target by operation of law.

Turner Broadcasting System: The Use of Reverse Mergers to Go Public

Owners of privately held companies have used reverse mergers to take their companies public, in the process gaining access to the equity markets. Reverse mergers can be significantly less costly than initial public offerings (IPOs)

FIGURE 9-4   Reverse merger.

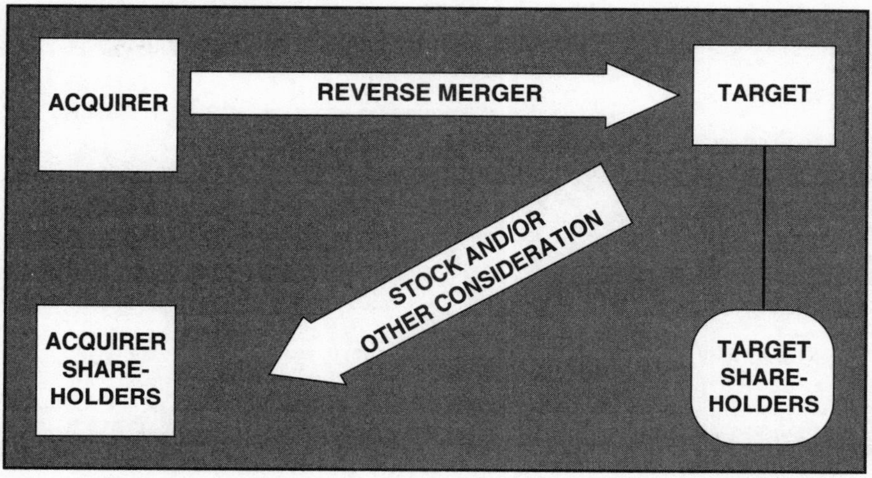

because no underwriting fees are involved. The current costs of an IPO range anywhere from $250,000 to $500,000, and underwriters make no guarantees that issuers will recoup their up-front expenses. In a reverse merger, the acquiring company simply purchases the voting stock of a publicly owned, but inactive company (a shell corporation), with no assets or liabilities, and merges its active business into the public company. The acquirer will usually change the name of the target company, appoint its own management team to corporate offices, and elect a board of directors.

In 1970 Ted Turner, then a young entrepreneur with a bold vision for the future of television, acquired Rice Broadcasting, operator of a publicly traded Atlanta television station (WJRJ-TV), with little cash investment. Merging the billboard company inherited from his father into the broadcasting company, Turner was in a position to tap the capital markets. He created Turner Broadcasting System; the first national cable super station—CNN; and the Cartoon Network. He later purchased the MGM/United Artists film library and launched Turner Film Classics. After an unsuccessful attempt to purchase the CBS-TV network, Turner eventually sold his Turner Broadcasting System to Time Warner Corp. Time Warner, the second-largest cable television operator, was acquired in 2000 by America Online, the world's largest online services company.

Forward Triangular Merger

The third form of merger transaction is a *forward triangular merger* (see Figure 9-5). In a forward triangular merger a parent company funds a subsidiary

FIGURE 9-5   Forward triangular merger.

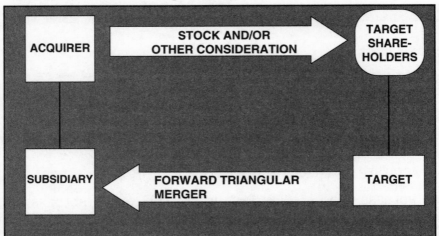

(often formed for the sole purpose of engaging in the transaction) with stock of the parent. The subsidiary then transfers the stock of the parent to the shareholders of the target in exchange for the target's assets. The target is then merged into the subsidiary and upon completion of the merger, the subsidiary is the surviving entity and the shareholders of the target are now shareholders of the parent.

A forward triangular merger limits the exposure of the parent to the liabilities of the target since the liabilities of the target are contained in the subsidiary. The subsidiary, not the parent, is subject to such liability. The forward triangular merger does not, however, resolve the issue of the potential loss of favorable intangible rights held by the target prior to the merger. The subsidiary, not the target, survives the merger, therefore the favorable intangible rights held by the target may not survive. One solution to this problem is the use of a reverse triangular merger.

Reverse Triangular Merger

The fourth form of merger transaction is a *reverse triangular merger* (see Figure 9-6). In a reverse triangular merger, the parent funds a subsidiary with stock of the parent. The shareholders of the target exchange their stock for the stock of the parent, which is held by the subsidiary. The subsidiary then merges into the target and the target survives as the subsidiary of the parent. Since the target is the surviving entity, its favorable intangible rights are preserved.

FIGURE 9-6 Reverse triangular merger.

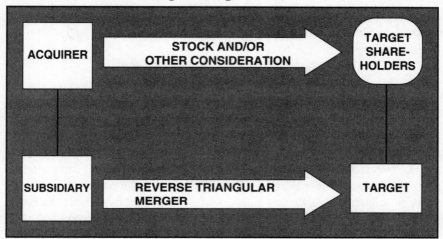

DaimlerChrysler: An Example of a Reverse Triangular Merger

Reverse triangular mergers (also called *reverse subsidiary mergers*) are frequently used in the United States. They are especially useful in situations in which there is a need to maintain the target company as a going concern. This type of acquisition is often desirable for regulatory or contractual reasons when it is important that no direct transfer of target company assets takes place.

This form of merger can also be used for combining a U.S. company and a foreign company. Daimler Benz AG used a reverse triangular merger to acquire Chrysler Corporation, the third-largest U.S. car manufacturer, in 1998. To comply with German law regarding capital increases against in-kind contributions, it was necessary for the subsidiary to be formed by a U.S. exchange agent, rather than the acquiring company, namely the DaimlerChrysler AG. The U.S. agent performed the reverse triangular merger and became the sole shareholder of the target company, Chrysler Corporation.

The shares held by the former Chrysler shareholders were converted into a right to receive shares of the German acquiring company, DaimlerChrysler. The U.S. exchange agent was then obligated to transfer the shares in the target company to the German company in the form of a capital increase against contributions in kind and to assign the shares received in return to the former shareholders of the target company, Chrysler Corporation.

FEDERAL INCOME TAX TREATMENT OF MERGERS
AND ACQUISITIONS

Corporate acquisitions may be treated as either taxable or tax-free transactions for federal income tax purposes.[1]

Taxable Asset Purchases

The tax treatment of an asset purchase transaction is fairly straightforward. The buyer will generally tender cash and/or promissory notes in exchange for the assets of the seller. The seller will recognize the gain or loss on each of its assets as either capital gain or ordinary income. The gain is the difference between the portion of the purchase price allocated to each particular asset less that asset's tax basis. From the buyer's perspective, the portion of the purchase price allocated to an asset will become the asset's tax basis. The buyer will therefore receive a "stepped-up" basis in the acquired asset equal to the portion of the purchase price allocated to that asset. There is generally double taxation for a corporate seller when it sells its assets and distributes the proceeds of the sale to its shareholders in liquidation, either as dividends or as capital gain or loss.

Taxable Stock Purchases

The tax treatment of a stock sale is also fairly straightforward. In a stock purchase transaction, the buyer will generally tender cash and/or promissory notes to selling shareholders in exchange for their stock in the seller. Each selling shareholder will recognize gain or loss on the sale in an amount equal to the difference between the amount realized from the sale of such shareholder's stock and the shareholder's tax basis in such stock. The buyer's basis in the target company's stock will be the fair market value of the consideration given in exchange for the stock.

Tax-Free Transactions

To qualify for tax-free treatment as a tax-free reorganization, a merger or acquisition must meet certain requirements set forth in the Internal Revenue Code. The transaction must also meet certain requirements developed by the courts and set forth in federal regulations. These nonstatutory requirements are: (a) *continuity of interest,* (b) *business purpose,* and (c) *continuity of business enterprise.* The continuity of interest requirement means that the share-

---

[1]State tax law considerations should also be reviewed in connection with structuring corporate acquisitions, including income tax, sales tax, property and transfer taxes, and other value-added taxes.

holders of the target must continue to own a substantial equity interest in the acquiring company after the reorganization. The business purpose require- ment means that the reorganization must be motivated by business reasons and not mere tax avoidance. The continuity of business enterprise requirement means that the business activities of the parties to the transaction must con- tinue to be operated after the reorganization.

In a tax-free merger or acquisition the acquiring company exchanges its own stock or that of a parent company for the stock or assets of the target company. In order for the transaction to be tax-free it must qualify as a tax- free reorganization under Section 368 of the Internal Revenue Code. There are three types of acquisitive reorganizations that are accorded tax-free treatment by the Internal Revenue Code:

1.   A statutory merger or consolidation, which is known for federal income tax purposes as a *Type A reorganization.*

2.   An acquisition of stock of a target company in exchange for voting stock of the acquiring company, or a *Type B reorganization.*

3.   An acquisition of substantially all of the assets of a target company in exchange for voting stock of the acquiring company, which is known as a *Type C reorganization.*

Type A and Type C reorganizations combine the assets of two companies into one, while Type B reorganizations result in the target becoming a sub- sidiary of the acquiring company. If the requirements of Section 368 are met, no gain or loss will be recognized by the target company or the target com- pany's shareholders except to the extent of any boot (cash or other property) received in the transaction.

Section 368(a)(1)(A): Statutory Merger—"A" Reorganization

A Type A reorganization (see Figure 9-7) is defined as a statutory merger or consolidation effected pursuant to state corporation laws (or the laws of the District of Columbia). In a Type A reorganization no gain or loss is recog- nized to the extent that stock of the acquiring company (or its parent) is given to the shareholders of the target company in exchange for their shares of stock in that target company. There is no limit on the type of consideration which can be used in effecting the transaction, although any consideration other than stock of the acquiring company (or its parent) must be limited to less than 50 percent of the fair market value of the total consideration given in the transaction, and any consideration other than stock of the acquiring company (or its parent) will be treated as boot and will be taxable to the tar- get shareholder.

FIGURE 9-7   Type A reorganization.

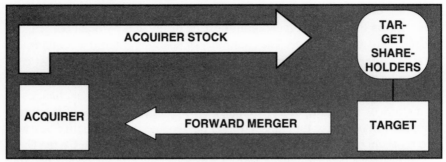

Unlike a Type B reorganization or a Type C reorganization, a Type A reorganization does not need to be effected solely with voting stock of the acquiring company (or its parent). If a transaction qualifies as a statutory merger or consolidation, it will qualify for tax-free treatment as a Type A reorganization even if nonvoting stock is issued to the shareholders of the target company.

A Type A reorganization may take the form of a forward triangular merger or a reverse triangular merger under certain circumstances. A forward triangular merger can qualify for tax-free treatment as a Type A reorganization if the following requirements are met:

1.   The acquiring company must own 80 percent of the voting stock of the subsidiary into which the target is merged, and 80 percent of the nonvoting stock of the subsidiary.

2.   The acquiring company must acquire substantially all of the assets of the target in the merger.

3.   The merger must have qualified as a Type A reorganization if the target were merged into the acquiring company rather than its subsidiary.

4.   No stock of the subsidiary is used in the transaction.

A Type A reorganization may take the form of a reverse triangular merger if the following requirements are met:

1.   The acquiring company must own 80 percent of the voting stock and 80 percent of the nonvoting stock of the subsidiary.

2.   The target company, which will be the surviving entity, must end up with substantially all of its own assets and substantially all of the assets of the subsidiary that is merged into it.

3.   The shareholders of the target must transfer control of the target in the merger.

4.   The shareholders of the target must receive voting stock of the acquiring company in the transaction.

The acquiring company generally obtains a basis equal to the target company's basis in the assets acquired, while the basis of the target company's shareholders in the stock of the acquiring company (or its parent) is equal to their basis in the target company's stock.

Section 368(a)(1)(B): Acquisition of Stock in Exchange Solely for Stock—"B" Reorganization

A Type B reorganization (Figure 9-8) is a stock-for-stock exchange, which results in the acquisition of the stock of a target company with the stock of the acquiring company. To qualify as a Type B reorganization the acquiring company must acquire the stock of the target *solely* in exchange for all or a part of its voting stock (or the voting stock of its parent) and, immediately after the transaction, the acquiring company must have control of the target.

No consideration other than stock of the acquiring company (or its parent) may be used in a Type B reorganization. "Control" is defined as the ownership of stock possessing at least 80 percent of the total combined voting power of all classes of stock entitled to vote and at least 80 percent of the total number of shares of all other classes of stock of the target company.

The result of a Type B reorganization is that the target becomes a subsidiary of the acquiring company. In a Type B reorganization, the target's shareholders will not recognize any gain or loss from the transaction. The buyer's basis in the target company's stock will be equal to the target shareholders' basis in such stock prior to the exchange.

Section 368(1)(C): Acquisition of Assets for Stock—"C" Reorganization

A Type C reorganization (Figure 9-9) is a stock-for-assets exchange. To qualify as a Type C reorganization, the target company must transfer substantially

FIGURE 9-8   Type B reorganization.

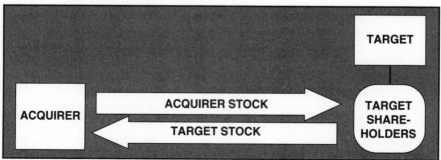

FIGURE 9-9   Type C reorganization.

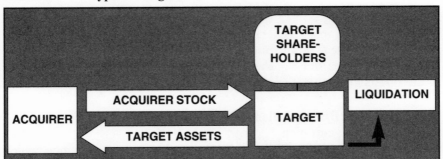

all of its assets solely in exchange for the voting stock of the acquiring company (or its parent). Substantially all of the assets of the target must be acquired in the transaction. The IRS currently interprets the "substantially all" requirement as being at least 90 percent of the fair market value of the net assets and 70 percent of the fair market value of the gross assets of the target company immediately prior to the transaction. This requirement is consistent with the purpose of the Type C reorganization provisions, which is to provide tax-free treatment to transactions that are equivalent to mergers but are not effected under state merger laws.

In addition, in a Type C reorganization the target must, as part of the transaction, liquidate and distribute its remaining assets and the shares of the acquiring company received in the transaction to its shareholders. A Type C reorganization has the same effect as the merger of the target into the acquiring company, however, there is no need to comply with state corporation law in a Type C reorganization and the acquiring company does not automatically assume all of the liabilities of the target as it would if the target were merged into the acquiring company.

A Type C reorganization may also be accomplished as a triangular transaction involving a subsidiary of the acquiring company, since the use of stock of a parent of the acquiring company may be used as consideration in this type of reorganization.

SECURITIES, ANTITRUST, TRADE AND COMMERCE LAWS

In addition to a basic understanding of the appropriate legal and tax structures for the transaction, corporate executives must have a basic understanding of the regulatory environment in which mergers and acquisitions are conducted. U.S. companies and their subsidiaries are subject to a broad range of securities, antitrust, and trade and commerce laws that may impact the structure of the merger or acquisition. As an example, Figure 9-10 describes the intense regulatory scrutiny that the AOL Time Warner deal was subjected to.

Securities Law Disclosure Requirements

The U.S. securities laws mandate disclosure of certain types of acquisitions of publicly held companies. In particular, Section 13(d) of the Securities Exchange Act of 1934 (the "Exchange Act") requires that any person or group of persons that acquires 5 percent or more of any class of specific registered securities of any corporation whose shares are registered under the Exchange Act must file a Schedule 13(d) with the issuer of the securities and with the Securities and Exchange Commission within 10 days after the acquisition.

Schedule 13(d) requires disclosure of information relating to the background of the person or group of persons conducting the acquisition, the source of the funds used and the purpose of the acquisition, the number of shares owned by such person or group of persons, and any other relevant contracts, arrangements, or understandings.

Additionally, the Securities and Exchange Commission Act of 1933 requires the submission of Form S-3, the Registration Statement for Securities Offered Pursuant to a Transaction, when securities are issued as part of a merger or acquisition. An example of a Form S-3 filing is in Appendix J, "Cisco Systems' S-3 Filing for the Komodo Technology Deal." In this deal, shares of Komodo were converted into newly issued common stock shares of Cisco.

Antitrust Law

The relevant U.S. antitrust laws which impact mergers and acquisitions include (a) The Hart-Scott-Rodino Premerger Notification Act of 1976 (HSR), (b) the Clayton Act of 1914 (the "Clayton Act"), (c) the Sherman Antitrust Act of 1890 (the "Sherman Act"), and (d) the Federal Trade Commission Act of 1914 (the "FTCA").

The Hart-Scott-Rodino Premerger Notification Act (HSR)

HSR applies to parties intending to pursue mergers or acquisitions involving voting securities or assets in the United States. The Act requires parties to certain transactions to file a notice of a pending transaction with the Federal Trade Commission (the "FTC") and the Department of Justice (the "DOJ"). The purpose of HSR is to provide the government with the opportunity to take action needed to protect competition under Section 7 of the Clayton Act, as discussed in the following paragraphs, prior to the consummation of the transaction.

The filing is required to be made by all parties to a transaction who, when taken together with their respective affiliates, meet certain gross revenue or gross assets tests. The tests include, (a) the *commerce* test, (b) the *size of the parties* test, and (c) the *size of the transaction* test. Generally speaking, these tests are met whenever a party with $100 million or more in sales or assets acquires voting securities or assets of another party with $10 million or more in sales or assets for a purchase price of more than $15 million. An acquisition of another party's voting shares of less than $15 million also requires reporting if, as a result of the transaction, the acquiring party will hold 50 percent or more of the voting securities of an issuing party that has $25 million or more in sales or assets.

After the HSR filings, the parties cannot consummate the transaction for a period of 30 days, during which time a clearance process is used to allocate the filings between various administrative agencies with expertise in the particular product or service and industry. Either the FTC or the DOJ will review the filings to determine whether the proposed transaction will have an anticompetitive impact.

The review of the proposed transaction is typically conducted in accordance with a framework set forth in the Horizontal Merger Guidelines jointly issued by the DOJ and the FTC (the "Guidelines"). The Guidelines establish the following analytical framework for evaluating proposed transactions:

- Defining the relevant product and geographic markets and identifying firms that compete in these markets.

- Measuring concentration in the relevant markets using the Herfindahl-Hirschmann Index.

- Assessing the ease of entry by new firms into the markets.

- Assessing the likely competitive impact of the transaction based on the characteristics of the markets.

- Evaluating any significant efficiencies resulting from the transaction that could not be achieved by other means.

The Clayton Act

Section 7 of the Clayton Act as amended provides that:

> No corporation engaged in commerce shall acquire, directly or indirectly, the whole or any part of the stock or other share capital . . . where in any line of commerce in any section of the country, the effect of such acquisition may be substantially to lessen competition, or to tend to create a monopoly.

Mergers and acquisitions have the effect of eliminating competition between the parties to the transaction and limiting the ability of smaller companies to compete in the marketplace.

Horizontal mergers, or mergers of competing firms in the same market, are likely to have an anticompetitive impact and are therefore carefully scrutinized by the FTC and the DOJ. The determinants of illegality in horizontal mergers are the market shares of the merging firms and the concentration of the market in which they compete.

A market's concentration is measured by the Herfindahl-Hirschmann Index (HHI), which is calculated by summing the squares of the market share percentages of each firm in the market. Based on the HHI posttransaction, a market is classified as *unconcentrated, moderately concentrated,* or *highly concentrated.* In cases of moderately or highly concentrated markets certain specified increases in the HHI raise a presumption of anticompetitive impact which can be rebutted by evidence demonstrating that the transaction is not likely to create opportunities for competition to raise prices.

Vertical mergers include mergers between suppliers and their customers. These mergers can also have an anticompetitive impact in that they may limit competing suppliers from markets for their products and services, and may limit competing customers from certain suppliers. However, these types of mergers are typically subject to less intense scrutiny than horizontal mergers.

The Sherman Antitrust Act and the Federal Trade Commission Act

Section 2 of the Sherman Antitrust Act provides:

> Every person who shall monopolize, or attempt to monopolize, or combine or conspire with any other person or persons, to monopolize any part of the trade or commerce among the several States, or with foreign nations, shall be deemed guilty of a felony.

Section 5(a)(1) of the Federal Trade Commission Act provides:

> Unfair methods of competition in commerce, and unfair or deceptive acts or practices in commerce, are hereby declared unlawful.

These sections of the Sherman Antitrust Act and the FTCA define a broad range of anticompetitive practices that restrain trade or are considered unfair and may impact the structure of a transaction.

The Failed WorldCom-Sprint Deal

Perhaps the most poignant example of the impact that antitrust laws can have on a proposed acquisition strategy is the failed WorldCom-Sprint merger. On July 13, 2000, WorldCom and Sprint called off their ambitious $120 billion merger. At the time of its announcement, the merger of the number 2 and number 3 long-distance carriers would have resulted in the largest proposed merger ever. However, on June 27, 2000, federal antitrust authorities filed a lawsuit seeking a permanent injunction to block the proposed merger on the grounds that it would pose an unacceptable threat to competition in the long-distance and Internet businesses. European officials came close to filing a suit before WorldCom and Sprint withdrew their request for overseas approval.

The Justice Department argued that "the proposed merger of WorldCom and Sprint will cause significant harm to competition in many of the nation's most important telecommunications markets. . . . By combining two of the largest telecommunications firms in these markets, the proposed acquisition would substantially lessen competition in violation of Section 7 of the Clayton Act. . . . For millions of residential and business customers throughout the nation, the merger will lead to higher prices, lower service quality, and less innovation than would be the case absent its consummation."

Justice Department officials went on to identify a number of areas in particular where the merger would violate antitrust laws, including:

- The U.S. long-distance market where, together with AT&T, the combined entity would control approximately 80 percent of the market.

- The Internet backbone market, in which WorldCom controls approximately 37 percent of the market and Sprint controls approximately 16 percent of the market.

- Long-distance services between the United States and foreign countries, where the combined entity would have approximately 30 percent of the market.

- International private telecommunications line services, where the two companies would control approximately 37 percent of the market and a monopoly on private line communications between the United States and a number of other countries.

- Custom corporate network services for large U.S. companies which, the DOJ argued, was dominated by the "Big Three."

The failure of the merger was not unexpected. Since the inception of the transaction, antitrust experts (and most likely corporate insiders at both companies) were skeptical of the ability of the transaction to pass muster under the antitrust laws. See Figure 9-10 for a timeline review of the AOL Time Warner deal that made it through similar regulatory review.

FIGURE 9-10   Intense Regulatory Scrutiny of AOL Time Warner Deal.[2]

Following are highlights in the saga of America Online Inc.'s
acquisition of Time Warner Inc., as an example of the various
steps in regulatory scrutiny.

2000

Jan. 10 — AOL, the world's largest Internet services provider,
and media giant Time Warner, parent of CNN and CNNfn, agree
to merge in an all-stock deal to create the world's biggest media
company. AOL shares are worth $72.875, valuing Time Warner
at almost $164 billion.

Feb. 29 — Companies pledge to Senate Judiciary Committee to
give competing Internet service providers access to Time
Warner's high-speed digital cable network. Chairman Sen. Orrin
Hatch, R-Utah, says committee unconvinced of value of pledge.

May 1 — Time Warner pulls ABC's signal from 3.5 million cable
subscribers during "sweeps week" celebrity version of hit show
"Who Wants to Be a Millionaire," after contract dispute with ABC
parent, Walt Disney Co., over fees.

June 23 — AOL shareholders approve merger in special
shareholder meeting. Time Warner shareholders, in separate
meeting, also signal approval.

Aug. 7 — America Online–Latin America debuts on NASDAQ
amid criticism that AOL has been less successful abroad than in
the United States.

(continued)

[2]AOL Time Warner Timeline: Mega-deal surprised Wall Street, then faced intense regulatory scrutiny, Reuters, January 11, 2001. Copyright Reuters Limited 2001. Reprinted with permission from Reuters Limited.

FIGURE 9-10   (*Continued*)

Oct. 5 — Time Warner/EMI merger falls apart due to European Union regulatory concerns.

Oct. 11 — European Union clears deal after Time Warner agrees to sever links with Germany's Bertelsmann AG. The Federal Communications Commission halts consideration of transfer of Time Warner's broadcast licenses until FTC acts.

Oct. 18 — Despite solid earnings, AOL shares hit a new low of $37.25, dragging merger value below $84 billion and leading analysts to question deal. Meanwhile, Time Warner reports solid earnings.

Nov. 20 — Time Warner agrees to let Earthlink Network, Inc., offer high-speed access over its cable pipelines in hopes of allaying regulators' concerns. AOL and Time Warner also push back their time line to close their merger into as late as early 2001. They had previously insisted it would close no later than Dec. 21.

Nov. 28 — Federal Trade Commission delays plans to sue to block AOL's purchase of Time Warner.

Dec. 5 — AOL Chief Executive Steve Case expresses confidence that the new combined company "will be running before the president is inaugurated." Inauguration Day is January 20.

Dec. 12 — FTC Chairman Robert Pitofsky meets with rival Internet service providers and concerned consumer groups. Qwest Communications International, Inc., tells FTC that concessions on access are "grossly inadequate" and cites "significant risks to competition" in high-speed Internet market.

FIGURE 9-10   (*Continued*)

> **Dec. 14** — FTC unanimously approves merger after companies
> pledge to give rivals greater access to their cable lines and
> content.
>
> **2001**
>
> **Jan. 11** — The companies complete their merger after the FCC
> gives its approval, though the agency attaches conditions meant
> to ensure open Internet access and competition in instant
> messaging, which AOL dominates.

CONCLUSION

The structuring of a transaction is impacted not only by complex business and economic considerations such as those outlined in the previous steps in *The M&A Strategy Guide,* but also by a host of legal, tax, and regulatory issues, including those outlined in this step. The merger team must include experts in each of these fields to help shape the structure of the transaction early enough in the acquisition process so that there is the maximum opportunity to address these issues in a timely manner and to minimize any adverse impact caused by these issues.

10

STEP 7: MANAGING THE INTEGRATION

BACKGROUND
The Politics of Change

Although many agree that poor strategic fit and overpayment are often responsible for unsuccessful M&A deals, poor integration planning and execution surely round out the top three causes of failure. Up until now, much of *The M&A Strategy Guide* has focused on the technical side of the transaction, which includes financial, legal, and operational issues. Too often though, executives focus on these technical aspects of doing the deal at the expense of the "soft" or "human" issues. In *Step 7: Managing the Integration,* the *Guide* addresses what might be called the political side of the transaction. Political issues include the intangibles of culture, communications, and leadership. Unfortunately, many executives ignore these political aspects as if they were a waste of time. Most likely, however, there is a nagging suspicion in the back of their minds that such issues are very important but are too difficult to manage. A common response by executives is to concentrate on factors they can control at the expense of those that they cannot. Financial or operational problems can be diagnosed and technical solutions for them can be found in a relatively straightforward manner. With people, however, there are too many variables to deal with that are beyond one's control.

But where there are people, there are political issues that must be addressed. And people are key to the backbone of any organization. To put it in perspective, one must remember that the greatest cost to a typical organization is the expense of paying its employees. U.S. companies have seen this expense increase significantly as they have had to evolve from a capital-intensive manufacturing economy to a labor-intensive service economy over the past few decades. More people, more politics.

To complicate matters further, changing demographics and globalization have made today's workforce more diverse than ever. Diversity is generally thought to be good. The belief is that diversity creates new perspectives that may lead to innovative, "out-of-the-box" thinking. Diversity, however, may lead to insurmountable disagreements among employees. Often, people from diverse corporate cultures who must work together during M&A integrations are unable to come to agreements. Egos clash; people are shuffled around into new positions; and key employees may quit. Many companies have been hurt due to talented individuals leaving in the wake of M&A deals.

Regardless of what the efficiency expert Frederick Taylor may have taught us, individuals are not interchangeable assets, but rather highly complex beings driven more by emotion than logic. Many executives, however, move individuals around on their organization charts without considering their thoughts and feelings. During the integration phase of a typical merger or acquisition, many positions will be reshuffled and lives disrupted. Such disruption cannot be avoided, yet those who lead the changes must be sensitive to these crucial human issues. One does not manage people—one leads them. And leadership is in the realm of the political.

THE NUTS AND BOLTS OF STEP 7

This step in the *Guide* provides guidance on managing the change that ensues from the integration of two companies, with special emphasis on the political issues that must be addressed. The analysis is divided into two sections. The first section presents a framework developed by Harvard Business School professor John Kotter in his book, *Leading Change*. The concepts in Kotter's book are intended to address organizational change generally; however, they are clearly applicable to the M&A integration process.

The second section identifies and discusses the four key determinants of successful integration: (1) *effective communication;* (2) *human resource issues;* (3) *legacy relationship issues* and (4) *optimization of cross-selling to the customer base.*

Nortel Networks: Taking Advantage of M&A to Help Foster Positive Change

Nortel's 1998 purchase of Bay Networks was more than an acquisition; it was a cultural "right-angle turn," according to Nortel's CEO John Roth. The merger gave Nortel access to the fast-moving world of Internet telephony (telecommunications over the Internet, as opposed to conventional long-distance phone networks). While negotiating with Bay Networks, Nortel put itself through a self-analysis that changed the company in some fundamental ways. For one, the company changed its name (from Northern Telecom). More to the point, Nortel adopted some of the management traits of the company it acquired, Bay Networks.

While Bay Networks delivered some important capabilities in Internet technology, perhaps its greatest contribution was in helping orchestrate some subtle but no less important changes in Nortel management. Roth appointed Bay's CEO, Dave House, president of the entire company, and Bay's chief technology officer was promoted to the same position for the combined company.

Together, Roth and House instituted some large-scale changes in product planning and development. They maintained the focus on product innovation and preached the value of outsourcing production to contract manufacturers. They institutionalized Silicon Valley business principles such as quick decision making. Nortel now outsources 50 percent of its circuit board production. Research and development was streamlined to get quicker decisions on key projects. Nortel R&D projects are now reviewed once a week by a portfolio management team, which makes decisions about projects it wants to tackle that week. Previously, projects in development were reviewed about once every eight months.

In another significant change, Nortel began offering employee stock options to all employees, copying a Bay Networks practice. Nortel's Roth says that Nortel has a long tradition of trying to get the best out of all employees, as opposed to getting the best employees. The company's "right-turn" strategy following the Bay Networks merger is an attempt to maintain that tradition.

Kotter on Leading Change

Unfortunately, today's executives are trained in the technical aspects of management rather than the political dimensions of leadership, which are the real keys to massive change initiatives such as mergers and acquisitions. Our business schools aim to create good managers and hope they somehow become great leaders. It is ingrained in our educational culture. Focused as we are on measuring progress through testing, we gravitate toward teaching subjects that can easily be tested. It is much easier to attach a grade to one's knowledge of financial mathematics than to that person's actionable understanding of leadership. It is relatively easy to teach technical skills such as how to launch a new product or do an initial public offering. But political leadership skills are far more elusive. How do you teach someone to conjure the magic ingredients of charisma, passion, and vision?

John Kotter, in his book *Leading Change*,[1] comments that today's business professors, for the most part, came of age before massive change was the norm. Consequently, they understand management better than leadership. For them, change occurred relatively incrementally and infrequently. They did not grow up in an environment of rapid technological shifts and globalization such as the one that surrounds us today. Kotter believes that this entrenched management mindset that pervades business education is reinforced in the corporate world.

He offers his own eight-step framework for change leadership, distilled from his research at over 100 organizations that are struggling to transform themselves into visionary companies. In order to effect successful change, Kotter suggests that leaders follow these eight steps:

1. **Establish a sense of urgency.** Too many leaders do not generate a sufficient sense of urgency in their companies to gain the momentum that massive change demands. Effective leaders dramatically paint a picture of an imminent crisis that motivates their followers into affecting change. Many executives who have gone through M&A integrations comment that if they were to do it over again, they would speed the process up. They understand that the slower the change process, the more people get complacent and resist change. Also, executives often get too bogged down in details. They attack problems without prioritizing. Consequently, they may end up spending significant amounts of time on activities that produce limited results.

   Cisco Systems, one of the paragons of successful acquisition strategy, understands the need for speed. It has carefully refined its acquisition process so that it conducts negotiations and executes transactions in as little as three weeks. It also has reduced the process of integration to a science and uses its vast experience to move newly acquired companies swiftly through the integration process. A more detailed discussion of Cisco's acquisition and integration tactics is included in the Cisco case review that is included in the final step of the *Guide*.

2. **Create a guiding coalition.** Despite all the talk of large-scale consensus-building, most successful change processes really rely on relatively small groups of smart, aggressive executives with the pas-

[1] *Leading Change*, John P. Lotter, Harvard Business School Press, January, 1996.

sion and talent to drive change. This cadre of executives must be carefully selected as part of the M&A team. Some executives may not believe that they have a vested interest in creating a combined company. They may believe that their jobs will be eliminated in cost-cutting once the dust settles. If reductions in force are required they should be well thought out and should all be completed at once if at all possible. The remaining workforce should be assured that no further cuts will be made.

3. **Develop a vision and strategy.** Executives from both of the entities entering into a transaction must come to consensus quickly with regard to a joint corporate vision and strategy. In the chaos that often accompanies the integration process, executives are often still working toward goals set before the merger or acquisition took place. It is difficult to affect organizational inertia, but both companies must focus their energies in the same direction and create new momentum.

4. **Communicate the vision.** Once the new leaders come to an agreement regarding the combined company's goals, they then must communicate their vision and strategy to the rest of the newly formed organization.

   One major key is to communicate the sense of urgency and the vision simply, vividly, and repeatedly. As with advertising, it is best to blanket the intended audience constantly with consistent messages that reinforce the general themes laid out in the vision and strategy. It is best to use various media. The word should be spread through meetings, memos, company newsletters, and all other formal and informal interactions. More suggestions on communication tactics are covered later in this step.

5. **Empower broad-based action.** This step is especially relevant in the M&A context. Executives trying to lead the newly combined entity must ensure that they have buy-in from key players from both organizations. If the perception is that executives from only one of the combining entities are calling all the shots, those from the second entity may not take action as readily. Emphasizing the perception that there is broad-based decision making is often necessary. Meetings that include a mix of participants from both of the combining entities will help solidify the belief that the new management is working as a harmonious team.

6. **Generate short-term wins.** Integration milestones should be set at very short intervals. Breaking long, complex processes into digestible pieces will drive the organization to reach goals more quickly and

effectively. These short-term goals should be clearly communicated to the organization as a whole. To keep the momentum going, the leadership should acknowledge every success (even the small ones) and celebrate them publicly across the organization. This will demonstrate to all divisions that progress is being made throughout the organization and spur them to achieve their own specific goals.

7. **Consolidate gains and produce more change.** Kotter strongly emphasizes the need to overcome any resistance to change. During complex M&A integrations, this is accomplished by breaking the process into discrete steps and ensuring that each step is addressed thoroughly before moving on to the next. Although many experienced executives put an emphasis on speed, they do not suggest doing so at the expense of thoroughness. The step-by-step format of *The M&A Strategy Guide* was designed to help executives speed the process along while attending to all of the necessary details.

8. **Anchor new approaches in the culture.** Cultural change comes at the end of the process, not at the beginning. To make positive cultural changes endure, the leadership must clearly articulate how previous changes have produced success. Step 9 of *The M&A Strategy Guide, Implementing an Acquisition Feedback Loop,* will assist in this process.

   With the crises that often accompany M&A come unique opportunities. New cultures must be formed as distinct corporate entities combine. Executives should embrace this opportunity to begin anew and rectify unproductive aspects of the former organizations. Although it may sound a bit idealistic, it is the ideal opportunity to create cultural synergies by incorporating the best cultural aspects of the two combining companies in the newly forming entity.

The M&A integration process is an extreme case of massive organizational change that must be spearheaded by aggressive leaders. The process outlined in the preceding list should help guide corporate executives to maintain momentum during the sometimes slow-going process of integration.

KEY DETERMINANTS OF SUCCESSFUL INTEGRATION
Managing integration of combining companies is a complicated task, requiring close attention to a number of variables. Key among the many determinants of successful integration are the following: (1) *effective communication;* (2) *human resource issues;* (3) *legacy relationship issues;* and (4) *optimization of cross-selling to the customer base.*

Effective, structured communication programs are essential to any successful postacquisition integration process. The news is not always "good," but it is critical that it is delivered in a manner that does not alienate key constituencies in the combined entity. Likewise, it is important that policy changes that have a psychological or financial impact on employees of the combined entity are handled with care. Issues such as compensation, titles, and norms (for example, the company picnic) must be addressed in what is perceived to be a timely and fair manner; otherwise, covert subversion of the integration process may become widespread. Legacy relationships between the two firms (potentially arch-rivals in the past) also must be acknowledged and managed from the outset. Finally, the often key issue of cross-selling to a customer base must be planned for from the outset and compensation and incentive programs must be devised to increase the likelihood of success in this area. Each of these major integration issues is covered in greater depth in the text that follows.

Effective Communication

Effective communication is important throughout the acquisition process, but it is particularly critical once the entities have combined. Just as it is important for a company to manage the media in a crisis situation, it is important for an acquiring company to manage the "rumor mill" during an acquisition. Any critical information not communicated is effectively left open for interpretation by important constituencies, often to the detriment of the integration process. Though there are different perspectives on this issue, some feel strongly that it is better to disclose negative information as early in the process as possible, in order to paint a clear picture of the future and to give employees a chance to digest and deal with the news.

There are four criteria for effective communication in a postacquisition situation. It must be (a) *simple;* (b) *structured;* (c) *consistent;* and (d) *balanced.* Each of these criteria is described in more detail in the following paragraphs.

Simple The communication should be written very clearly and simply worded to minimize the potential for misinterpretation. Wherever practical, specificity also helps to leave little room for interpretation. There will be circumstances where ambiguity is necessary, but the acquiring company should attempt to keep such instances to a minimum.

Structured It is best if the communication is perceived to be part of a program intended to keep all employees informed. A periodic newsletter (the more frequent, the better) should be developed and distributed to the entire employee base. This serves the dual purpose of helping to minimize misinformation and rumors and to make it clear to employees the intention to keep them apprised of all key developments.

Consistent   While frequent, structured, and simple communication is beneficial, it is important that it not be rushed. Information should not be communicated until it is relatively certain that it is accurate and will be implemented. Lack of consistency between what is communicated and what is implemented breeds suspicion that can be easily used by anyone whose goal is to undermine the integration process.

Balanced   Although it is generally clear which of the organizations is dominant in a transaction, it is important that the employees of the nondominant entity do not feel powerless and manipulated. It is critical that even when new policies are communicated that are significantly different from those that may have existed in the past, such communication is done in a nonauthoritarian manner. Even if new policies are not liked, as long as the process and the communication is perceived as fair and balanced, the probability of a positive outcome is greatly enhanced.

There are other issues that must be considered beyond the human aspects of communication, however.

Human Resource Issues
In any merger or acquisition scenario egos are an important factor. While there are a host of issues that can be impacted by egos in a postacquisition integration, there are three that stand out as worthy of close attention: (a) *compensation;* (b) *titles;* and (c) *norms.* Each is discussed in more detail in the following paragraphs.

Compensation   It is unusual for the compensation structure of combining entities to be precisely the same. In fact in many cases the compensation structures might be dramatically different. Given the sensitivity to compensation, this issue can cause animosity and behavior that undermines the successful integration or at least peaceful, cooperative coexistence of the employees of the two companies. Internal experts, sometimes with the aid of outside compensation consultants, must devise a plan that addresses the key points of dissension, and even if the plan does not introduce parity, it must be justified to the concerned parties. It is clear that parity sometimes does not make the most sense, but perceived fairness will be the litmus test by which employees will judge managerial actions in the postacquisition integration. A somewhat obvious rule of thumb is that mediocrity should not be introduced in the name of fairness. Likewise, top performers should not be alienated in the name of accommodating the needs of the majority. These issues mainly arise with senior management and top salesforce performers. As with any other potentially major adjustments that will be made, effective communication in the area of compensation is critical.

Titles   Though employee titles seem like a petty matter in the scheme of a multimillion- or multibillion-dollar merger, they are a factor that must be carefully considered. Again, this issue mainly impacts those in management and other high profile (such as sales) positions, but it has some effect at every level of the organization. For many individuals, a large part of their sense of self-worth is tied to their job and to some extent in their title. Careful planning for rapid postacquisition title adjustment can help stem the potential exodus of key performers.

There are two tendencies in this process that must be avoided. The first tendency is to only be concerned with the most senior levels of management. While this clearly is an area that must receive attention, the reality is that much of the productivity of the organization, particularly as it relates to direct customer interaction, takes place at least a level or two down from the top. It is important not to neglect these lower levels in the early stage of the title adjustment process. The second temptation is to develop shared titles to avoid conflict and damaged egos. While this may work in some circumstances, it is generally better to have one person clearly responsible for a particular function within the organization. Rather than shared titles, an approach that can work is to further divide the job into clearly defined, discrete functions and put individuals in charge of the more focused areas. The appropriateness of such decisions is, of course, context-sensitive.

Norms   Cultural norms in companies play an important role in developing a sense of camaraderie, teamwork, and shared mission. When companies combine, particularly companies with significantly different norms, the disruption that ensues can have a deleterious effect on productivity and employee morale. It is therefore critical to undertake a process that clearly defines existing norms in the two organizations. Those norms should then be categorized into those that have a high level of importance to employees and those that have a low level of importance to employees. The list should then be compared for overlap and complementarity. This is another area of the integration process where following the four rules for effective postacquisition communication is critical. Getting buy-in up front to any adjustments to key norms can save numerous problems down the road. The problems to be avoided include some of the most difficult to manage—those of disgruntled employees covertly undermining the integration process. To use a trite example, traditions such as the company picnic can have important emotional meaning to employees, and any adjustments perceived to be unfair or insensitive in this area have been known to have a profound effect on employee morale. While it will not be possible to keep everyone happy, the perception of a fair, open, well-communicated process is the ultimate goal in matters such as these. It is critical not to underestimate the importance of these "soft side" issues.

Soft side issues are critical to address during integration in order to realize the value of a deal. However, as discussed in *Step 4: Performing Due Diligence,* they are also important factors to address during the due diligence process. Value in a deal is often unrealized because the soft side issues are not factored into the deal from the beginning; they are only addressed during the integration. For further discussion regarding soft side issues, see Appendix H, "Corporate Cultures Play Big Role in M&A Integration."

Legacy Issues

In the postacquisition integration process, there are several issues related to the culture and history of the individual organizations that can interfere with their successful combination. Three issues that require especially close attention and management are: (a) *legacy interaction;* (b) *operating style;* and (c) *existing relationships.* Each of these issues is reviewed in detail below in the following paragraphs:

Legacy Interaction   Prior to the transaction, the combining companies may have been fierce competitors, or negotiators on the opposite sides of the table for many years or even decades. In such situations, each company may have been painted by the other in negative terms, effectively as an arch-villain to be defeated. It is very difficult to overcome such a legacy of interaction. Human resource specialists from each of the companies and perhaps consultants with outside expertise, will need to construct a strategy to minimize the detrimental effects of such a historical relationship. One approach to mitigating the effects of entrenched opinions is to form task forces and functional teams comprised of members from each of the organizations as early after the transaction as possible. Working together to overcome obstacles and to achieve goals often works wonders in erasing historical, usually highly inaccurate, perceptions of employees at the other company.

Operating Style Often combining entities have different operating styles. One company may be run in a highly regimented, almost militaristic manner, whereas the other company may be run in a laid-back manner. Such differing operating styles often arise when older companies acquire younger companies in an effort to modernize or gain access to cutting-edge technology. In such circumstances, trying to force employees of either firm entirely into the working style of the other company is highly unlikely to be successful. Instead, it makes sense to try to fuse the styles at the margins and only where absolutely necessary mandate one or the other style. The areas of operational and financial controls are where there is typically little room for compromise, but otherwise, flexibility should be the watchword. Given that operating style is a subset of cultural norms, this is another area where observing the four key rules of effective postacquisition communication is key. Any major adjustments must be communicated in a simple, structured, consistent, and balanced manner.

GM-EDS: An Example in Culture Clash General Motors (GM) bought computer service giant Electronic Data Systems (EDS) in a $2.5 billion all-stock transaction in 1984. The automaker hoped the acquisition would enable it to cut production costs and regain market share. Although buying EDS made GM the world's number one data processing company, the high-tech dream never materialized for a variety of reasons.

For one thing, differences in corporate culture and management style— GM's bureaucratic, centralized style of management compared to the more entrepreneurial, customer-driven approach at EDS—and the data processing subsidiary's unique status as an independent company within GM, doomed the merger almost from the start. EDS' founder Ross Perot, given a seat on the GM board of directors, clashed publicly with GM chairman Roger Smith, the man who engineered the GM-EDS merger, over his role in the combined company. GM silenced its most vocal critic in 1986 by buying back his stake in GM, and 12 years later, in 1996, spun off EDS as an independent, publicly traded company.

Existing Relationships The reality of company operation dictates that much of business be conducted on the basis of personal relationships. In the case of a merger of two firms there will be some relationships that overlap, but many that do not. There must be a process that guides the combined entity in reconciling which suppliers, distributors, customers, and other relevant entities will remain engaged. Given the subjective and emotional basis on which personal relationships with these entities exist, it is best if the process for determining continued interaction is objective. Use of an objective process is the only approach that will be perceived as fair. Perception of fairness is likely to be further enhanced if the criteria for assessment are "bought-into" in advance. The proliferation of customer, supplier, and distributor scorecards should facilitate the process of evaluating these relationships objectively and determining which will exist and on what terms, into the future. Again, effective communication of the rationale for these decisions is key, as is the perception of fairness and objectivity. Many employees thrive on the basis of relationships they develop during the course of their careers, so sensitivity should be employed in making changes to existing relationships in any of these areas.

Realities of Cross-Selling to Customers

Many combinations are rationalized on the basis of the anticipated ability of the combined entity to cross-sell products and services to customers. In practice, such cross-selling often proves difficult. There are three issues that must be considered and managed to increase the probability that cross-selling becomes a significant benefit of the combination: (a) *adequate analysis;* (b) *customer mindset;* and (c) *salesforce resistance.* Each of these issues is discussed in more detail in the following paragraphs.

Adequate Analysis   In order to determine whether there is likely to be significant opportunity for cross-selling, significant analysis must be performed. This analysis, which should be performed to as great an extent as possible before the combination, includes many of the elements of strategic due diligence previously detailed. Specifically, it is important to understand where the demographic characteristics and buying profiles of the customers of the individual companies indicate a strong probability of cross-selling opportunities. Given the time constraints of a transaction, it is often the case that very little such analysis is done up front. Still, corporate executives are often shocked when the anticipated volume of cross-selling does not come to fruition. So, the lesson here is to conduct such an analysis as early in the game as possible. While the proforma analysis of cross-selling potential will certainly not be perfect, it will at least provide some guidance for appropriate expectation setting, forecasting, and strategy.

Customer Mindset   The combination may be a source of cognitive dissonance for persons responsible for purchasing decisions at customer sites. In the case of a horizontal merger, for many years, they may have put the individual firms into mutually exclusive "buckets" in their mind. In the case of vertical mergers, they may not be familiar with one of the firms comprising the combined entity. While none of these issues is necessarily a "deal-stopper," it may be an impediment to effective cross-selling. Lack of information is the main potential culprit here, so the indicated remedy is education. Just as effective communication is important with employees, a similarly informative program must be implemented with customers. The key is not just to provide new marketing materials, but also to provide education as to why the combination of the firms makes sense, particularly how it will benefit customers. Those involved in the purchasing decision will appreciate the caring implied by the provision of context and information, particularly if the rationale for the combination includes genuine potential for improved customer value.

SalesForce Resistance   Educating customers will of course not be of much use if the salesforce is not educated and incentivized in parallel. This is one of the areas of cross-selling that is most often not given adequate attention. Salespersons often are simply told that they will now be able to sell new products to their customers, but they are not given adequate training on how to do it, or why it will benefit them in a meaningful way. It is critical that adequate attention is paid to properly train and incentivize the salesforce as early as possible in the postacquisition integration process. In fact, this analysis and planning should be done in advance of the finalization of the combination, otherwise, it is likely that the anticipated level of cross-selling will not be attained.

CONCLUSION
Political issues must be dealt with on a grand scale during M&A integrations. Mergers and acquisitions mean more people working together. And where there are more people, there are more political issues that must be dealt with. It is bad enough if the political aspects of an organization are ignored during stable times, but serious damage can be caused if not enough attention is paid to them during major change initiatives such as M&A integrations. When executives are too busy handling technical issues to attend to political issues, the process usually falls apart. It is exactly at such times of massive change when employees are looking for leadership.

11

STEP 8:
MONITORING
PROGRESS
THROUGH
ACQUISITION
SCORECARDING

BACKGROUND
Monitoring the Integration Process

The M&A Strategy Guide is designed as a tool that can assist corporate executives in navigating the merger and acquisition process. The first few steps of the *Guide* are designed to gather, organize, and analyze information relevant to this process. These steps include: *Thinking Through Strategic Objectives, Assessing Structural Capacity, Identifying and Screening Potential*

Acquisition Targets, and *Performing Due Diligence.* The information and analysis drawn from these steps is then used to formulate assumptions, which underlie decisions that are made in subsequent steps. The analysis and planning in steps such as *Valuing the Acquisition Target* and *Managing the Integration* are based on information-driven assumptions that then are used to guide further action.

It is important to remember that significant aspects of the M&A planning and integration process are based on assumptions rather than facts. For example, some of the key assumptions are made in the step defined as *Valuing the Acquisition Target.* If the forecasted synergies do not materialize, the transaction may result in a loss in shareholder value. As was discussed in that section, overpayment for the target company is often cited as a major cause of failed transactions. Accordingly, executives should not be mesmerized by their own projections about the synergies that may be achieved by the combined entity. Cost-cutting and cross-selling forecasts made during the valuation stage are merely estimates of future benefits that may or may not be realized.

The seminal decision in the merger and acquisition process is whether to proceed with the transaction. Once a decision to proceed has been made, the transaction has been consummated, and the integration process begins, executives must monitor how actual performance compares on an ongoing basis to the assumptions of performance that supported the decision to proceed. If a mechanism is established to monitor these differences during the integration process, there is a better chance that the integration will be a success. Through such a mechanism, executives will be able to identify problems and decide how resources should be deployed to rectify underperformance. Also, a close monitoring of progress will enable executives to modify earlier assumptions as the integration proceeds. As this process moves forward, ongoing planning can be based on more facts and less assumptions and thus enable executives to make decisions with more certainty. This is where the Acquisition Scorecard comes in.

THE NUTS AND BOLTS OF STEP 8
Step 8: Monitoring Progress Through Acquisition Scorecarding discusses how to use the performance measurement concept of "scorecarding" to monitor the M&A integration progress.

A wave of "scorecard" thinking began in 1992 with the publication of Robert S. Kaplan and David P. Norton's article, "The Balanced Scorecard—Measures that Drive Performance," in the *Harvard Business Review.* In this article and in subsequent books on the subject, the authors developed a performance measurement system that went beyond simple financial measures of performance. They created a framework that is "balanced" in that it attempts to measure and manage companies' progress toward the more elusive aspects of success such as achieving mission, vision, and customer and employee satisfaction.

In many companies, however, implementing a successful enterprise-wide "balanced scorecard" has proven elusive. There are many reasons for the challenges that companies have encountered in this effort, including lack of management understanding of scorecarding, entrenched political interests, and lack of sufficient available data.

Because so many factors beyond financial performance must be measured and managed during the M&A integration process, implementing an Acquisition Scorecard may prove to be very useful. Furthermore, an acquisition represents an excellent opportunity to make necessary changes throughout the combined entity including, for example, changes to company information systems and employee mindsets. One of the major impediments to effective postacquisition integration is the lack of objective systems of implementation and results measurement, often leading to a perception of favoritism in decision making. Such a perception can have a negative impact on the retention of key employees and therefore on the health of the combined enterprise. It is critically important to develop objective integration and results measurement systems. Development of an Acquisition Scorecard is one important piece of this puzzle.

Kaplan and Norton's "Balanced Scorecard" provides four key categories that must be monitored for managers to have a broad understanding of the health of the enterprise. Those categories (or "perspectives") include *financial; customer; internal;* and *innovation/learning.* These four categories are of course still relevant in an acquisition situation, but a fifth category must be added to effectively monitor the performance of the combined company: *HR/company culture.* Technically, this perspective could be included under the "internal" category, but its effective monitoring and management is so fundamental to the success of any acquisition that it is worthy of a distinct category in the Acquisition Scorecard.

The Acquisition Scorecard

In the Acquisition Scorecard, the HR/company culture perspective is seen at the center of the action, as decisions and outcomes in this area can quickly make or break the success of the acquisition. The next step in developing the Acquisition Scorecard it to identify key measures in each of the perspective areas.

Identifying Key Measures in Each of the Five Scorecard Areas

In each of the Scorecard areas, key measures must be selected that represent the health and effectiveness of the combined enterprise. (Some common measures in each perspective area follow.) It is important to remember that these measures will only be useful to the extent that they: (a) represent relevant issues for decision making; (b) can be measured based on available data (or data that will be tracked in the future); (c) are monitored on a regular basis; and (d) are used as the basis for decision making or for further "drill down" into key decision areas.

The accompanying chart (Figure 11-1) gives a small sample of the potential measures that might be included for each Scorecard perspective. The relevant measures will depend on the industry and operating approach of the companies, as well as the breadth and depth of the key decisions to be made. In the ideal situation, there will be overlap among the measures that have been tracked in the past by the acquirer and the target. In reality, it is typically the case that neither company will have tracked very many measures, other than financial. It is therefore important to decide quickly which Scorecard measures are most important and develop a plan for tracking them as soon as possible at the beginning of the integration process. The sooner they are tracked, the sooner there will be a baseline (or "benchmark") for under-

FIGURE 11-1   Sample measures for an acquisition scorecard.

HR / Company Culture	Financial	Innovation and Learning	Customer	Internal
• Employee Satisfaction Rating	• Net Income %	• Revenue from New Products	• Customer Complaints	• Product Defects
• Key Employee Retention %	• ROE	• Product Development Cycle Time	• On-time Delivery	• Revenue/ Employee
• OSHA / Safety Record	• Sales Growth $ / Units	• Patents Issued	• % New Sales to Existing Customers	• Inventory Turnover
• Absenteeism	• EVA	• # New Products in Pipeline	• Customer Retention/Attrition	• Asset Turnover
• Cross-Company Teams	• Cash Flow	• # R&D Employees	• Market Share Growth	• Utilization Rate (employee, machine, etc.)

standing performance improvement or degradation and for developing a suitable plan of action to improve problem areas.

Finding and Measuring Relevant Data

It is important to realize that finding and measuring the relevant data for effective scorecarding will not be easy. In many cases, this will entail developing a data warehouse to gather all the relevant data and transform it into useful information for decision making. Although this process will not be simple, if done correctly it should yield dividends in the form of improved postacquisition management and tracking of performance gains.

Executives should start with those measures for which the data are available. Typically these include financial measures initially and market measures soon thereafter. It is absolutely critical to begin tracking HR/company culture measures as soon as possible. It is widely argued today that effective management of these issues can greatly enhance the probability of a successful postacquisition integration. In the end, company performance, and most all of the relevant Scorecard measures, are dependent on the productivity of the organization's greatest intangible assets: the intellectual property and performance of its employees.

Scorecarding can be a very complex undertaking. However, an Acquisition Scorecard could prove vital in saving an M&A transaction that was based on flawed assumptions. If the management of the newly combined company can quickly identify areas of lagging performance relative to the assumptions made early in the process, it will be in a position to take appropriate action to enhance performance in these areas. Also, executives who have implemented and are closely monitoring an Acquisition Scorecard will be able to modify assumptions going forward that may otherwise have compounded the problem by incorrectly informing future planning and execution. The following checklist from John Reed, former co-CEO of Citigroup along with co-CEO Sandy Weill, provides an example of documentation that can be used to track and communicate the integration process.

FIGURE 11-2 A Progress Checklist for Citigroup.

A progress checklist for Citigroup

In 1999, John S. Reed, the then co-CEO of Citigroup (along with

co-CEO Sandy Weill), shared the following simple checklist,

 which gives a sense of how the leaders of the huge financial

services firm were keeping track of the integration of operations

in the wake of the 1998 merger between Citigroup and

Travelers.* A typical Acquisition Scorecard obviously is much

more detailed than this example; however, this shows how the

leadership of a massive company was tracking and

communicating the integration process from a business unit

perspective. As can be seen from the checklist, the only area

that Reed believed had been well integrated at that point was

the organization's asset management business.

DONE TO DO

   x   **ASSET MANAGEMENT**
                              It's full speed ahead at the smallest of
                              Citigroup's three main business lines.
                              "I'm quite comfortable that we have a

---

*"Businessweek Online," June 7, 1999 Issue. Reprinted with permission from *Business Week.*

FIGURE 11-2   *(Continued)*

decent vision," Reed says. "I'm not
spending any time worrying about that."

x   CORPORATE BANK

Reed is asking his executives questions:
Who are your customers? What are you doing
for them? What kind of capital does it
require? What kind of earnings volatility
are you going to experience? "This is a
business-building activity," Reed says.
"I would say we are in the very early
stages."

x   CONSUMER BANK

Reed and Weill discussed strategy before
doing the deal. And integration is further
along than on the corporate side. "But
still, it's got to take on real form,"
Reed says.

x   RISK MANAGEMENT

The most important process at the company,
Reed says. To combine "very disparate
risk systems," Citi has brought in an
outsider, Petros K. Sabatacakis, most
recently of American International Group.

(continued)

FIGURE 11-2 *(Continued)*

x **HUMAN RESOURCES**

Developing talent won't have much impact
on the merger's short-term success. But
it will in two to three years, says Reed.
"I don't think we want to rely on just
going out in the job market and hiring
people.... I put tremendous value—more
than most people—on the HR function."

x **TECHNOLOGY**

"The Internet is going to shape our
business," says Reed. "I think we need
a technology overlay, to take a look at
the whole company from some core architectural and technology look-see. I'm
looking to create a process that allows
the company to be moving purposefully
toward an appropriate technology archi-
tecture, capability, and capacity."

x **FINANCE**

Reed says it's not enough to seize
opportunity in the 100 countries where
Citigroup does business. You also have
to be able to gauge your need for
capital, monitor exposures, and devise
funding strategies. "Risk, HR, technology, and finance—we don't have them
fully integrated yet."

12

STEP 9:
IMPLEMENTING
AN ACQUISITION
FEEDBACK LOOP

BACKGROUND
Developing a Learning Organization

At the beginning of *Step 8: The M&A Strategy Guide* was described as a tool for gathering and analyzing information, which is used in turn to formulate assumptions and plans relevant to the M&A process. The usefulness of the *Guide* in any particular circumstance is dependant upon the timeliness and accuracy of the information that is fed into it.

The M&A process is typically fast-paced and complex. In order to ensure proper information flow, appropriate channels of communication must be kept open among a multitude of decision makers at various levels in both of the combining companies. As was mentioned earlier, the M&A experience is not only a challenge, but an opportunity for the leadership of the newly combined company to establish more effective processes. Some of the most important processes that should be put into place are those that ensure ongoing information sharing throughout the organization. Such processes are key to companies as they strive to become what are known as *learning organizations.*

Learning organizations constantly evolve toward greater effectiveness by systematically learning from their mistakes and sharing those lessons throughout their organizations. Organizing employees into teams (both cross-functional and within functions) is one of many strategies used by learning organizations. Such interaction helps employees learn more about other functions and thus how their own responsibilities fit into the overall operations of the organization. (The importance of an effective multidisciplinary acquisition team was reviewed in *Step 2: Assessing Structural Capacity.*) Armed with such knowledge (and with the proper level of empowerment), employees can begin improving processes that upper-level management might not even be aware of. This is especially important in the rush of a typical M&A transaction during which the leadership must focus on the big issues. Such widespread understanding of overall goals and the empowerment to help the organization move in the right direction will not only speed the integration process but will also help solidify relationships among employees who must quickly work effectively together.

Learning organizations are keenly aware of their own issues and problems, but they are not solely inward-focused. Each business unit at GE may be considered its own separate company. Nonetheless, these "companies" interact and learn from one another. Furthermore, GE employees track innovations at companies outside the GE family, looking for ways to apply any good ideas within their own organization.

With these lessons in mind, the ninth and final step in *The M&A Strategy Guide* discusses *Implementing an Acquisition Feedback Loop.* The objective is for the acquiring company to take the lessons learned from prior acquisitions so that they may inform future acquisitions. In the GE tradition, M&A lessons learned should not only be derived from one's own experience but also from the experiences of others. For this reason, the step ends with a discussion of the acquisition planning and integration process at Cisco Systems, which is broadly acknowledged as one of the most successful M&A-driven companies ever.

GE: PROMOTING CONSTANT AND NEVER-ENDING IMPROVEMENT
Sharing Best Practices among Business Units
Throughout the 1980s, GE, under the guidance of CEO Jack Welch, instituted one of the earliest and most extensive downsizing programs corporate America had ever seen. When Welch took over as CEO in 1981, GE had nearly

420,000 employees. Even with the 150,000 employees added due to acquisitions over the next dozen years, in 1993 total employees numbered only 230,000. The net reduction was achieved through layoffs, attrition, and transfers to other companies through sell-offs. Welch had successfully slashed the levels of bureaucracy that he believed would choke GE as it strove to compete with its new, sleeker competitors. Afterward, however, he had to find a way to get the remaining employees back on board. Not only did he need them not to resist, he needed them to help fight the impending battles with these new competitors.

Welch began his revolution and kept it going with several innovative methods of unleashing the ideas of the employees in the trenches. The most interesting and innovative of these methods is the now-famous GE "Work-Out." Work-Outs take the form of New England town meetings. Employees and managers are invited so that there is an even cross section of GE personnel. Dress is casual. Normally, a Work-Out takes three days. In the first two days of the meeting, the employees (with the help of a facilitator) brainstorm proposals that might improve processes in their different divisions. This is done in preparation for the third day, when they confront their bosses. They then fire the proposals at their bosses, who must stand at the front of the room and either agree to each proposal on the spot, reject it with reasons why, or postpone the decision in order to study it for a limited period of time. The object of the exercise is to come up with specific, actionable items that will improve GE's processes.[6]

Also, and perhaps more important, it gives the lower-level employees the opportunity to express their thoughts and feel like part of the leadership process and not just simply like followers. Everyone is included in the program. Work-Outs were initiated in 1989, and by 1996 practically all GE employees had participated in one. In the words of Jack Welch, "People who had never been asked for anything other than their time and their hands now saw their minds, their views sought after. And in listening to their ideas, it became even more clear to everyone that the people who are closest to the work really do know it better."[7]

Not Invented Here? That's Okay

GE not only fosters the sharing of best practices among its different business units; it also looks outside its organization to infuse new ideas that could

[6]Tichy, Noel, M., and Stratford, Sherman. *Control Your Destiny or Someone Else Will.* New York: Harper Business, 1993, p. 278.

[7]Slater, Robert. *Get Better or Get Beaten! 31 Leadership Secrets from GE's Jack Welch.* New York: McGraw-Hill, 1994, p. 134.

improve its processes. Jack Welch calls this "legitimate plagiarism." Robert Slater in his book, *Jack Welch and the GE Way,* recounts an interview with Welch about such a learning strategy. According to Slater, GE's CEO is unapologetic about adopting ideas created by other companies. Indeed, of the famous Six Sigma quality program, Welch exclaims: "I'm very proud of the fact that we didn't invent it. Motorola invented it. Allied followed up with it. And we've taken it. That's a badge of honor. That's not something bad. That's a great thing to do." Welch admits that there is probably always someone somewhere who is doing something smarter than the way they are doing it at GE.

According to several accounts, employees are not rewarded for simply coming up with or pinching great ideas, though. Rather, they get promotions for spreading good ideas as far and wide as possible. To facilitate this process, Welch kicks off every year with a meeting of his top 500 executives, during which managers from different divisions mingle and brainstorm. Diversity is the key. Managers who make light bulbs or locomotives swap ideas with those who finance cars or work in reinsurance.

NUTS AND BOLTS OF STEP 9
Define Key Drivers of Acquisition Success or Failure
Whereas the Acquisition Scorecard helps keep executives abreast of progress on any given acquisition, the acquisition feedback loop helps organize ongoing learning, which can be applied to future acquisitions. This feedback loop should be thought of as an *ex post facto* due diligence on a given acquisition process, the findings from which are then fed into a repository of best practices information that can be used for planning and integration of subsequent acquisitions.

The first step in developing and implementing such a feedback loop is to define the relevant drivers or measures of performance that will improve future acquisition decision making. This fundamental step is often overlooked as acquiring companies attempt to measure the success of an acquisition on an *ad hoc* basis, often shifting from one set of measures to another. It is critical to develop an "anchor set" of key drivers and measures of performance that are unlikely to change in the foreseeable future for a particular company or industry. The key drivers or performance measures should include, at a minimum, relevant *strategic, financial, operational,* and *human resource* components.

Figure 12-1 illustrates an approach to using the acquisition feedback loop to leverage knowledge creation and management in future acquisitions.

FIGURE 12-1   Acquisition feedback loop.

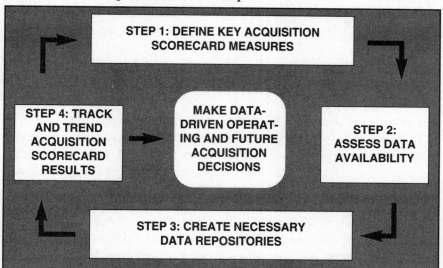

Strategic Component   The strategic performance measure must begin with a restatement of the original strategic objective(s) that motivated the acquiring company to pursue an acquisition strategy. As outlined earlier in this book, some of the common reasons why companies pursue acquisition strategies include increasing geographic reach, expanding product and service offerings, providing liquidity for company founders, and acquiring promising new technologies. The fundamental question is whether the underlying strategic goals have been achieved, and if they have not, what caused the acquisition to fail from a strategic perspective.

Financial Component   The financial component must begin with a comparison of actual financial results of the combined entity with the financial projections, which were the basis of the decision to proceed with the acquisition. Key questions include: Have the financial targets been achieved? If not, were there any flawed assumptions in the projections? If so, why were the assumptions flawed? What approach would have led to the correct set of assumptions? How should the answers to these questions inform the methodology for identifying and evaluating future acquisition candidates? How should assumptions that help value acquisition candidates be formulated in the future? Did cost-cutting and cross-selling projections prove realistic?

Operational Component   The operational component must begin with a definition of the relevant operational process measures. Such measures might include the level of technology integration, customer retention, or other strategic operational performance measures. Key questions then might include: What were the best practices that were uncovered from the various technology integration projects? What types of customer complaints resulted from the integration process? Were any operations negatively affected because of the integration process? How can such problems be avoided in the future?

Human Resource Component   The human resource component assesses the effect of the acquisition integration process on the combined entity's management team and employee relations. Key questions include: Was the management team sufficiently experienced to run the combined entity? Did all of the key players remain a part of the management team? If there were key players who left, how might we have persuaded them otherwise? Were employees properly incentivized? Were the integration teams effective? Are all the divisions of the newly formed company now working together effectively? If not, why not? How have any such problems been rectified? Are there any lessons learned that could be applied to other areas of the organization to ensure that such problems do not arise there?

Assess Data Availability

Once the relevant drivers and measures of performance have been defined, the company must determine which of the relevant data are currently tracked and available. For any data that are not currently tracked, a plan must be implemented to initiate tracking, if it is determined that the cost/benefit of monitoring the relevant measure makes sense. There will be a differing level of readiness for data necessary for each relevant driver or measure of performance. Typically, financial data will be the most readily available, with customer and internal data available in bits and pieces.

Create Necessary Data Repositories

Often it will be the case that there will be "islands" of data tracked by different functional (and often divisional) areas of each company. In order for these data to become informative, it will usually be necessary to build data warehouses or repositories. This is no small task, but it is a necessary one, if management is to make data-driven decisions during future acquisitions. Design and construction of repositories should be performed on a priority basis, according to which measures will be supported and the impact of the availability of better information anticipated.

Track and Trend Key Drivers and Measures of Performance

Once the key drivers and measures of acquisition performance are determined and the data are in place, the company can track and trend the results. The key here is to understand how the acquiring company performed on certain key metrics (measures) and if possible, understand how performance during the most recent acquisition compares to the company's performance during past acquisitions. Analysis to understand the differences, positive and negative, yields a road map to making decisions to further improve performance of the combined entity as well as future acquisition processes.

Some of the information gathered will be very objective, such as the financial information, while some will be more subjective, such as feedback on employee relations. Executives should strive to be just as disciplined in recording these subjective pieces of advice as they are with gathering the "hard" facts. It also is important to note that achieving 100 percent data availability to support some new measures could take significant time, so it is necessary to get started as soon as possible instead of waiting until all data are available. Information can be incorporated over time, as it becomes available.

It is important to make data-driven future acquisition decisions, rather than simply relying on intuition to be successful. Intuition has been used very effectively in many companies that have made many successful acquisitions. The acquisition feedback loop is not intended to replace intuition; rather it is meant to enhance the quality of management decisions by anchoring them to a set of measures that illustrate the key drivers of the acquisition process.

M&A LESSONS LEARNED FROM CISCO SYSTEMS

Cisco Systems, the world's leading supplier of computer networking systems, has refined the process of growth through acquisitions into something of an art form, acquiring 51 companies in a six-and-a-half-year period from 1993 to 2000.

In 1993 the company launched a strategic acquisition program aimed at rapidly acquiring and assimilating small companies with market-proven technologies that would complement Cisco's own broadening product line. The genesis of this acquisition strategy was a realization on the part of company management that a number of its customers were selecting products such as Crescendo Communications, Inc.'s new fast Ethernet LAN technology over Cisco routers. At that time, Cisco's management was contemplating a move into low-end LAN equipment by acquiring companies such as Cabletron or Synoptics who were leading manufacturers of hubs. John Chambers, John Morgridge and Ed Kozel, Cisco's chief technology officer, decided at that point to pursue a strategy based on the purchase of smaller leading-edge technology companies rather than larger competitors such as Cabletron or Synoptics. Cisco's first acquisition was Crescendo Communications, Inc., a privately held networking company that provided high-performance workgroup solutions. As a result of the decision to pursue this strategy, Cisco was on the road to transforming itself from a manufacturer of routers to a provider of an end-to-end networking solution. Today Crescendo switches, along with products from later acquisitions, account for nearly $7 billion in annual sales.

Cisco targets companies with industry-leading technology that will extend the Cisco product line. Such a strategy allows Cisco to be a leader in the networking space without having to develop all of its technology internally. After the acquisition, Cisco will continue to develop the technology of the acquired company and will distribute the resulting products through its extensive and sophisticated marketing and support network.

Cisco's Acquisition Criteria

John Chambers, the President and CEO of Cisco Systems, in an interview with *Business 2.0,* articulated the series of rules of thumb he uses to guide his acquisition strategy:

1. **Shared vision.** First, the management at Cisco and the acquisition target must have a shared vision of where the industry is going and the role that each company wants to play in the industry going forward. If the vision or the roles are not complementary, Chambers will not consider the acquisition.

2. **Short-term wins for employees.** Second, Chambers insists on providing what he calls "short terms wins" for the employees of the acquired company. To ensure that the employees of the acquired company will remain with Cisco, they must see a future for Cisco; they must be comfortable with the company's culture; and they must be provided with an opportunity to continue the work they were doing prior to the acquisition. Chambers realizes that in a technology company, what you are acquiring are the employees.

3. **Compatibility of long-term strategies.** Third, Chambers looks at an acquisition target's long-term strategy and how it fits into Cisco's long-term strategy. For the acquisition to work Chambers insists that there must be long-term wins for all four of a company's constituencies—its shareholders, employees, customers, and business partners.

4. **Cultural similarities.** Fourth, Chambers examines the similarities in the culture and chemistry of the two companies and has indicated

that the culture and the chemistry may be the most important factor. One culture or chemistry is not right, but cultures and chemistries that are too different will never merge successfully.

5. **Geographic proximity for large acquisitions.** Fifth, to the extent Cisco is targeting a large acquisition, there must be geographic proximity to Cisco's current operations. Chambers argues that lack of geographic proximity will eliminate many of the efficiencies of a combined entity.

Chambers' ideal acquisition target is a small start-up that has an industry leading technology in development that will be ready for market in 6 to 12 months. In acquiring the company Cisco will be buying the engineering talent and the developing product. Once a company has been acquired, Cisco will use its manufacturing capability and financial clout behind the new product to quickly bring it to market through its extensive distribution channels.

Chambers comments that if a target company does not meet all five tests he is very cautious about making the acquisition, and that if the target only meets three of the five he will not move forward.

Cisco as the Master Integrator

Not only is Cisco adept at acquiring companies, it is just as adept at quickly and effectively integrating them. In anticipation of each acquisition, Cisco will assemble a customized packet of information that includes descriptions of Cisco's structure and employee benefits, a contact sheet, and an explanation of the strategic importance of the acquired company. On the day the acquisition is announced Cisco will send teams of human resource and business development personnel to the headquarters of the acquired company where they will meet with employees of the acquired company to answer questions and set expectations.

The integration team at Cisco will work closely with management of the acquiring company to determine where each of the new employees would fit within the combined entity. Typically the acquired company's product development and marketing divisions will remain independent business units while sales and manufacturing divisions will be folded into their Cisco counterparts.

Immediately after the closing of the transaction, Cisco's integration team offers an orientation program for new employees, educating managers about Cisco's hiring and employment practices, training new salespeople in Cisco's products, and advising engineers about its product development activities.

When asked how he measures success, Chambers is quick to respond: retention of employees and revenue that you generate two to three years down the line.

The Cerent Example

For example, Cisco's 1999 purchase of Cerent Corp. for $7.2 billion in stock was one of its most successful acquisitions and set the stage for subsequent mergers. The Cerent acquisition signaled Cisco's intention of becoming a player in the fast-growing broadband communications market. By acquiring Cerent, a manufacturer of fiber-optic switching equipment, Cisco gained access to a network switching technology it did not possess internally.

While many commentators argued that Cisco grossly overpaid for Cerent, the combination of Cerent's unique expertise in optical switching gear with Cisco's worldwide distribution system effectively added $1.5 billion to Cisco's bottom-line performance.

This merger was successful in other respects. Unlike many big company/small company mergers, Cisco retained nearly all of Cerent's 400 employees, including most of the smaller company's sales staff. This was again due to Cisco's mastery of the art of integration. Even before the deal was signed the Cisco integration team began planning every detail of the integration. Two months later, when Cisco formally took control, every Cerent employee had a title, a boss, a bonus plan, a health plan, and a direct link to Cisco's corporate intranet.

As a result of these successes, Cisco has become a model of successful acquisition planning and integration. In a 1999 survey by Best Practices, a Chapel Hill, N.C., consulting firm, Cisco was ranked number one in a survey of successful merger and acquisition strategies. Firms in other industries, such as Yahoo! and U.S. West, have studied Cisco's techniques, and rivals such as Lucent Technologies and Nortel Networks are imitating Cisco's strategy.

FINAL THOUGHTS ON M&A PLANNING AND INTEGRATION

THE NEED FOR A SYSTEMATIC APPROACH TO M&A

The corporate growth strategy of mergers and acquisitions has the potential for achieving rapid increases in revenues and if the process is well-conceived and executed, for rapid increases in earnings as well. However, the pursuit of growth through acquisition also carries with it some drawbacks. It is an extremely complex undertaking and typically involves significant risks. For even a single acquisition to succeed, a large number of variables must be skillfully managed. When a company is planning to do many, rather than "one-off" or opportunistic, acquisitions, it must put into place a corporate acquisition program that takes these variables into account in a structured fashion. This book's *M&A Strategy Guide* provides such a methodological approach by outlining the steps that should be followed when pursuing corporate growth through acquisition.

Develop an Effective Corporate Strategy

Mergers and acquisitions (and corporate growth efforts in general) have recently tended to emphasize "core" business activities. The definition of "core" varies somewhat from company to company, of course, but clearly the trend is away from conglomeration and toward strategic focus. On the whole it seems prudent to stay in businesses that the management team already knows well.

This rationale takes on particular importance in the merger and acquisition arena, where situations are typically so complex and fast-moving that the acquiring company's management team has little time to advance along the learning curve.

That said, it might still be appropriate for companies to diversify into new industries. Under these circumstances, *Step 1: Thinking Through Strategic Objectives,* is in many ways the most important of the steps in *the M&A Strategy Guide.* The success of the entire M&A process relies on sound strategic thinking. Too often, busy executives focus on efficiency rather than on effectiveness. Instead of taking sufficient time to figure out what to do, they dive right in and try to figure out how to do it. Such executives first must understand the difference between efficiency and effectiveness. A metaphor might help clarify this distinction: efficiency is about climbing the tree fast whereas effectiveness is about knowing which tree to climb up in the first place.

Strategy is about effectiveness. Executives may choose to buy a certain company and then integrate it in a very efficient manner. However, they may have bought a company in an industry that they really should not be competing in. In such a case, they would be—to extend the metaphor—barking up the wrong tree. When they get to the top, they probably will realize that they will have to come down and start anew. Sometimes, this fall can be a hard one.

Conduct an Honest Self-Evaluation

The famous Greek admonition—Know thyself—is extremely important to companies considering growth through acquisition. Many acquiring companies spend significant amounts of time (as they should) conducting due diligence on potential acquisition targets. In the rush to grow through acquisition, though, they often forget to take into account their capacity to do so.

Many companies acquire others at points when they are not financially or operationally prepared to do so. The results can be disastrous. Many acquisitions are thought to be overvalued. In some respects, this is another way of saying that the acquiring company does not have the financial capacity to enter into the deal at the agreed-upon price.

Acquisition-minded companies also must review their operational capacity to pursue M&A deals. They may not have the management expertise to run the newly combined company. They may not have the technologies necessary to quickly integrate information systems. As in any business venture (but perhaps more so during an acquisition), access to good information is necessary to guide appropriate actions as the process unfolds. The acquiring company also might not have the operational processes in place to realize the synergies, that are crucial to the success of the deal. The metaphor to keep in mind here is: Don't bite off more than you can chew.

Perform Thorough Due Diligence

Although there is a step in *The M&A Strategy Guide* dedicated to performing due diligence on potential acquisition targets, one should realize that the disciplined step-by-step thinking imposed by this tool will enable executives to go beyond the relatively narrow aspects of the typical due diligence phase. Before considering an acquisition, executives must achieve a thorough understanding of a multitude of factors by means of an environmental assessment and a self-assessment as well as the typical target company due diligence. The *Guide* thoroughly outlines all of these assessment processes. It bears repeating: Do your homework.

Address the Human Side of Integration

There are so many technical issues (such as those concerning finance and operations) to attend to during M&A planning and integration that executives often do not stop to think through the implications that such massive change will have on the employees of the two merging companies. Insensitivity with regard to human relationships is at the root of many problems in typical day-to-day business affairs. Because of the sheer magnitude of changes necessitated by an M&A integration, however, the implications on employee relations are magnified manyfold.

True leaders understand that the incessant complaining about having to deal with "politics" is misplaced. Massive change, such as that brought about during M&A restructurings, demands leadership. Leading means inspiring people to take action. And where people are involved, there are politics. Managing the politics of change is what executives are paid to do.

Admittedly, it is difficult to predict how employees will react to the stress that will undoubtedly accompany the M&A integration process. Nonetheless, those leading the integration effort must monitor the crucial human aspects of the process, because, as much research has shown, how such issues are handled often make or break the deal. People should not be viewed as the problem, but rather, as part of the solution.

Monitor Progress and Keep Track of Lessons Learned

Executives must manage multiple activities that are occurring quickly and simultaneously during the integration process. In order to do this, they need more than just a plan. The common expression is that one can only manage what one measures. To this end, management must set measurable objectives and then tie these goals to realistic timelines.

In order to monitor progress, corporate executives need to decide which activities should be measured and then ensure that the information necessary to monitor these activities is readily available to management and others who are accountable to meet those goals. As has been done in *The M&A Strategy Guide,* it is best to divide goals into many discrete steps. Setting milestones at short intervals will show employees that they are making quick progress. This, in turn, will create the momentum necessary to drive people through the change process.

Companies that plan to grow through a series of acquisitions should create a formal feedback loop. Through such a mechanism, executives can keep track of lessons learned, which they then can use to improve the M&A planning and integration process for their next acquisition. Even if an acquisition is a "one-off" occurrence, establishing a feedback loop can help the management team of the newly formed company learn how to work together better and in a shorter timeframe.

Those Who Fail to Plan, Plan to Fail

The M&A planning and integration process is so complex and time-pressured that executives who try to learn as they go will surely drown in the process. Preparing in advance is a necessity. Currently, we are in the midst of another wave of significant merger activity, which will affect many corporate executives. The odds are that most corporate executives will in some way be involved in a merger or acquisition at some point in their careers. All executives would do well to prepare during the calm before they are thrust into the storm.

A P P E N D I X E S

ACKNOWLEDGMENT

The material in Appendixes A through F was provided by Andrew J. Sherman, Esq., and is an excerpt from his work, *Maneuvering Your Way Through M&A,* a reference guidebook created exclusively for the Association for Financial Professionals (AFP).

Sherman is an internationally recognized authority on the legal and strategic aspects of entrepreneurship and business growth. He is a senior partner with McDermott, Will & Emery, an international law firm with more than 925 lawyers worldwide, where he manages a multimillion-dollar corporate and transactional practice representing Fortune 1000 corporations as well as hundreds of technology-driven, net-centric, and rapidly growing businesses. He chairs the firm's regional Emerging Business and Technology practice group, as well as the firm's international Franchising, Licensing, and Distribution group. His current and previous clients include Intel, Apple Computer, America Online (AOL), Texaco, Panasonic, Revlon, Beatrice Foods, Sanyo, GAF, Owens-Corning, Shell Oil, Sears, Metrocall, Bankers Trust, Household Finance Corporation, Pritzker Organization (Hyatt Hotels), MarchFirst (Whittman-Hart and CKS/USWeb), the Western Professional Hockey League, and the Great Lakes Baseball League.

He is the author of 11 books on business growth, capital formation, and the leveraging of intellectual property, including the best-selling and critically acclaimed *Raising Capital* (Kiplingers, 2000), *The Complete Guide to Running and Growing Your Business* (Random House, 1997), *Franchising and Licensing: Two Ways to Build Your Business,* 2d edition (AMACOM Books, 1999), and *M&A from A to Z* (AMACOM Books, 1998).

141

SAMPLE CONFIDENTIALITY AGREEMENT

THIS CONFIDENTIALITY AGREEMENT ("Agreement") is made as of this＿＿day of＿＿＿＿＿＿＿＿, 20＿＿by and among Company1, Inc., a＿＿＿＿＿＿＿＿corporation ("Company1") and Company2, Inc., a＿＿＿＿＿＿＿＿corporation ("Company2") and each of the undersigned representatives of each of Company1 and Company2, respectively (the "Representatives"). Company1 and Company2 are collectively referred to hereinafter as the "Parties."

WHEREAS, the Representatives executing this Agreement shall include, but are not limited to, the following individuals: On behalf of Company1, ＿＿＿＿＿＿＿＿, and on behalf of Company2,＿＿＿＿＿＿＿; provided, however, that any additional Representatives also shall execute a copy of this Agreement;

WHEREAS, Representatives of the Parties intend to meet on ＿＿＿＿＿＿＿, 20＿＿to discuss certain transactions related to the businesses of the Parties, including a potential purchase and sale transaction between the Parties or other possible combinations of Company1 and Company2 (all of which shall be referred to hereinafter as the "Transaction");

WHEREAS, each of the Representatives, in the course of meetings and discussions relating to the Transaction, may disclose certain confidential and proprietary information regarding each Party's business plans, financial and operational data, services, products, and product development plans;

WHEREAS, each of the Parties desires to protect its proprietary rights and further desires to prevent unauthorized disclosure of any information regarding its individual business plans, financial and operational data, products and services;

WHEREAS, the Representatives collectively desire to prevent unauthorized disclosure by any one of them of any information regarding the Transaction and the business plans, financial and operational data, products and services associated therewith;

WHEREAS, the Parties intend to have the "confidential information" as defined below treated as being confidential and/or proprietary.

NOW, THEREFORE, in consideration of the premises and the mutual covenants contained herein, the parties agree as follows:

1. <u>Definition of Confidential Information</u>. In connection with the Transaction being discussed among the Representatives, each of the Parties and their Representatives may disclose certain information intended to remain as proprietary and confidential, including information regarding business plans, financial data, operational data, product development plans, products and services. The information furnished by either of the Parties or any Representative is hereinafter referred to as "Confidential Information" and such Confidential Information shall belong to the Party furnishing the same (through one or more of its Representatives) and shall be treated as Confidential Information as provided herein. Confidential Information shall also include all discussions in connection with, and all information in any medium in any way related to, the Transaction.

The term "Confidential Information" shall not include information which was or becomes generally available to the public other than as a result of a disclosure by a Representative or his affiliates, agents or advisors including, without limitation, attorneys, accountants, consultants, bankers and financial advisors (collectively "Affiliates").

2. <u>Use of Confidential Information</u>. The Representatives of a Party shall not use any Confidential Information disclosed by the Representatives of the other Party or pertaining to the Transaction for its own use or for any purpose other than to carry out the discussions between the Parties and to further the evaluation of the Transaction and the business relationship between the Parties.

3. <u>Permitted Disclosure</u>. A Party or its Representatives may disclose Confidential Information if required by a governmental agency or court of

competent jurisdiction, or the rules thereof; provided, however, each Party agrees to give to the other prompt notice of the receipt of the subpoena or other process requiring or requesting disclosure of Confidential Information.

4. Proprietary Rights. All Confidential Information furnished by a Party or its Representatives to the other Party or its Representatives shall remain the property of the Party furnishing the same and shall be promptly returned or destroyed at the request of the Party furnishing the Confidential Information.

5. No License or Right to Reproduce. Nothing contained in this Confidentiality Agreement shall be construed as granting or conferring on any Party or its Representatives, any rights, by license or otherwise, to reproduce or use in any other manner any Confidential Information disclosed hereunder by the other Party or its Representatives or pertaining to the Transaction, except to further the Transaction and the business relationship between the Parties.

6. Non-Competition. For a period of one (1) year from the date of this Confidentiality Agreement, no Party nor any of its respective Representatives shall, directly or indirectly, on behalf of itself or himself or herself or any other person, use any Confidential Information disclosed by the other Party or its Representatives or pertaining to the Transaction, except in connection with the furtherance of the Transaction and the business relationship between the Parties.

7. No Further Obligation. Neither the disclosure or receipt of Confidential Information shall obligate a Party to undertake any business relationship with the other Party in connection with the Transaction. The Parties and the Representatives understand and acknowledge that neither Party is making any representation or warranty, express or implied, as to the accuracy or completeness of the Confidential Information, and that only those representations or warranties that are made in a definitive purchase and sale or merger agreement when, as, and if executed, and subject to such limitations and restrictions as may be specified in such definitive agreement, will have any legal effect.

8. No Waiver. Failure to enforce any provision of this Agreement shall not constitute a waiver of any other term herein and any waiver of any breach shall not be construed as a waiver of any subsequent breach. If any provision of this Agreement is held to be invalid, void or unenforceable, the remaining provisions shall continue in full force and effect without being impaired or invalidated. This Agreement shall be construed and governed in accordance with the laws of the State of_____.

9. Termination. This Agreement shall terminate on the earlier of the execution of definitive agreement by the Parties, the unanimous agreement of the under-signed parties, or one year from the date hereof.

10. Entire Agreement. This Confidentiality Agreement embodies the entire understanding among the Parties and their respective Representatives

with regard to the Transaction, the Confidential Information and all other subject matter described or contained herein. This Agreement may not be amended, changed, altered or modified in any way, except by a writing signed by the Parties. This Agreement may be executed in a number of counterparts which, when taken together, shall constitute one and the same instrument.

IN WITNESS WHEREOF, the parties hereto have executed this Confidentiality Agreement as of the day and year first above written.

COMPANY 1, INC.   COMPANY 2, INC.

BY:_____   BY:_____

Individually:_____   Individually:_____

B

SAMPLE LETTER OF INTENT

Ms. Prospective Seller
SellCo, Inc.

Re: Letter of Intent Between BuyCo, Inc. and SellCo, Inc.

Dear Ms. Prospective Seller:

This letter ("Letter Agreement") sets forth the terms by which BuyCo, Inc. ("BCI") agrees to purchase shares of a newly authorized class of convertible preferred stock of SellCo, Inc. (the "Company") in accordance with the terms set forth below. BCI and the Company are hereinafter collectively referred to as the "Parties."

Section I of this Letter Agreement summarizes the principal terms proposed in our earlier discussions and is not an agreement binding upon either of the Parties. These principal terms are subject to the execution and delivery by the Parties of a definitive Stock Purchase Agreement, Employment Agreement and other documents related to these transactions.

Section II of this Letter Agreement contains a number of covenants by the Parties, including BCI's funding commitment and the execution and delivery of a Promissory Note in consideration therefor, which shall be legally binding upon the execution of this Letter Agreement by the Parties.

The binding terms in <u>Section II</u> below are enforceable against the Parties, regardless of whether or not the aforementioned agreements are executed or the reasons for non-execution.

SECTION I—PROPOSED TERMS

1. <u>Stock Purchase</u>. The Parties will execute a Stock Purchase Agreement, pursuant to which, BCI will purchase shares of a newly authorized class of convertible preferred stock of the Company (the "Shares"), for a total purchase price of $_____. The Company's Board will amend its articles of incorporation (and bylaws if necessary) and take any formal corporate action necessary to create and authorize this new class of stock. The Shares will constitute_____percent of the total capitalization of the Company on a fully-diluted, post-transactional basis. The Shares will have no dividend or liquidation preferences to the Company's common stock ("Common Stock") and will be identical in every other way to the Common Stock except that each of the Shares will have votes compared to each share of Common Stock (which has one vote). The Shares will be automatically convertible into shares of Common Stock on a one-for-one basis upon the disposition of the Shares by BCI to any party not affiliated with BCI. Simultaneous to the issuance of the Shares to BCI, BCI will give limited revocable proxies to Prospective Seller ("Seller"), entitling her to vote 50 percent of the Shares issued to BCI, respectively, on any matters on which the shareholders of the Company are entitled to vote, except matters relating to an initial public offering by or a sale of the Company where the holders of a majority of the Common Stock have already approved such an action. The foregoing exception will not apply, however, where all of the holders of Common Stock have unanimously approved an initial public offering by or a sale of the Company, provided, however, that all the holders of any class of stock of the Company will receive the same rights under such a transaction. Additionally, the proxies will be subject at all times to automatic revocation at the time that the proxy holder is no longer employed by the Company.

2. <u>Employment Agreements</u>. Prior to closing, the Company will enter into an individual employment agreement with Seller for_____-year terms at the compensation levels set forth in the Company's business plan previously presented by the Company to BCI. The employment agreement will contain such other terms and conditions as are reasonable and customary in the type of transaction contemplated hereby.

3. <u>Board of Directors of the Company and BCI</u>. Seller will be nominated to serve on the Board of Directors of BCI. BCI will be entitled to designate members to three of the eight seats on the Company's Board of Directors.

The Company's Board (and its shareholders, if necessary) will undertake all necessary corporate action to ensure the proper size and make-up of the Company's Board. Any future borrowing by the Company will require approval by the Company's Board and any such borrowing not related to the Company's ordinary course of business will require the approval of 70 percent of the Company's Board of Directors.

4. <u>Closing and Documentation</u>. The Parties intend that a closing of the agreements shall occur on or before _____, 20____, at a time and place that is mutually acceptable to the Parties. BCI or its representatives will prepare and revise the initial and subsequent drafts of the necessary agreements.

SECTION II—BINDING TERMS

In consideration of the costs to be incurred by the Parties in undertaking actions toward the negotiation and consummation of the Stock Purchase Agreement and the related agreements, the Parties hereby agree to the following binding terms ("Binding Terms"):

5. <u>Refundable Deposit</u>. BCI will pay a refundable deposit in the amount of $_____ to the Company at the time of the execution of this Letter Agreement, and will pay an additional $_____ no later than _____ days after the execution of this Letter Agreement. All sums paid hereunder shall be deductible from the purchase price to be paid for the Shares as described in Paragraph 1. In the event that BCI does not complete the purchase of the Shares, the sums payable hereunder shall be deemed an advance and subject to repayment to BCI_____ months from the date of execution of this Letter Agreement in a lump sum with interest at the rate of 1.5 percent above the highest U.S. prime rate published in *The Wall Street Journal* from the date of execution of this Letter Agreement to the date of repayment. In the event that the closing is delayed beyond _____, 20____, BCI will advance additional funds of $_____ on _____, 20____ and $_____ on _____, 20____. Each additional advance shall be repaid within six months of the date of the advance at the rate of 1.5 percent above the highest U.S. prime rate published in *The Wall Street Journal* from the date of advance to the date of repayment. The Company shall execute and deliver a Promissory Note in consideration of the advance of funds hereunder and pursuant to the terms stated above.

6. <u>Right of First Refusal for Additional Capital Contributions</u>. The Company agrees to grant BCI a right of first refusal for any future equity financing (except in the case of an initial public offering). Holders of Common Stock shall have a pre-emptive right, however, to contribute such proportionate

share of any such equity financing in order to maintain their respective interests in the Company. In the event that a valuation cannot be agreed upon by the contributing parties hereunder, an independent appraisal of the Company shall be obtained from a qualified investment banker at the Company's expense.

7. Due Diligence. The directors, officers, shareholders, employees, agents and other representatives (collectively, the "Representatives") of the Company shall (a) grant to BCI and its Representatives full access to the Company's properties, personnel, facilities, books and records, financial and operating data, contracts and other documents; and (b) furnish all such books and records, financial and operating data, contracts and other documents or information as BCI or its Representatives may reasonably request.

8. No Material Changes. The Company agrees that, from and after the execution of this Letter Agreement until the earlier of the termination of the Binding Terms in accordance with Paragraph 14 below or the execution and delivery of the agreements described herein, the Company's business and operations will be conducted in the ordinary course and in substantially the same manner as such business and operations have been conducted in the past and the Company will notify BCI of any extraordinary transactions, financing or business involving the Company or its affiliates.

9. No-Shop Provision. The Company agrees that, from and after the execution of this Letter Agreement until the termination of the Binding Terms in accordance with Paragraph 14 below, the Company will not initiate or conclude, through its Representatives or otherwise, any negotiations with any corporation, person or other entity regarding the establishment of a line of credit, the sale of substantially all of the assets of or the management of the Company. The Company will immediately notify the other Parties regarding any such contact described above.

10. Lock-Up Provision. The Company agrees that, from and after the execution of this Letter Agreement until (a) the consummation of the transactions contemplated in Section I and the execution of definitive agreements thereby, or (b) in the event that definitive agreements are not executed, until the repayment of all amounts advanced hereunder, plus accrued interest, that without the prior written approval of BCI and subject to any anti-dilution provisions imposed hereunder, (x) no shares of any currently issued Common Stock of the Company shall be issued, sold, transferred or assigned to any party; (y) no such shares of Common Stock shall be pledged as security, hypothecated, or in any other way encumbered; and (z) the Company shall issue no additional shares of capital stock of any class, whether now or hereafter authorized.

11. <u>Confidentiality</u>. Prior to Closing, neither Party nor any of their Representatives shall make any public statement or issue any press releases regarding the agreements, the proposed transactions described herein or this Letter Agreement without the prior written consent of the other Party, except as such disclosure may be required by law. If the law requires such disclosure, the disclosing party shall notify the other Party in advance and furnish to the other Party a copy of the proposed disclosure. Notwithstanding the foregoing, the Parties acknowledge that certain disclosures regarding the agreements, the proposed transactions or this Letter Agreement may be required to be made to each Party's representatives or certain of them, and to any other party whose consent or approval may be required to complete the agreements and the transactions provided for thereunder, and that such disclosures shall not require prior written consent. BCI and its employees, affiliates and associates will (a) treat all information received from the Company confidentially, (b) not disclose such information to third parties without the prior written consent of the Company, except as such disclosure may be required by law, (c) not use such information for any purpose other than the consideration of the matters contemplated by this Letter of intent, including related due diligence, and (d) return to the Company any such information if this Letter Agreement terminates pursuant to Paragraph 14 below.

12. <u>Expenses; Finder's Fee</u>. The Parties are responsible for and will bear all of their own costs and expenses incurred at any time in connection with the transaction proposed hereunder up to $_____. Any additional or extraordinary expenses above this amount shall be borne by BCI; provided, however, the Company shall be responsible for any finder's fees payable in connection with the transactions contemplated hereby.

13. <u>Break-Up Fee</u>. The Company agrees to pay BCI a break-up fee of $_____ in the event that the sale and purchase of the shares contemplated in <u>Section I</u> is not accomplished by_____, 20____as a result of the Company's failure or refusal to close pursuant to the terms set forth above and not due to any refusal or delay on the part of BCI to close by that date.

14. <u>Effective Date</u>. The foregoing obligations of the Parties under <u>Section II</u> of this Letter Agreement shall be effective as of the date of execution by the Company, and shall terminate upon the completion of the transactions contemplated in <u>Section I</u> above or, if such transactions are not completed, then at such time as all of the obligations under this <u>Section II</u> have been satisfied, unless otherwise extended by all of the Parties or specifically extended by the terms of the foregoing provisions; provided, however, that such termination shall not relieve the Parties of liability for the breach of

any obligation occurring prior to such termination. Please indicate your agreement to the Binding Terms set forth in <u>Section II</u> above by executing and returning a copy of this letter to the undersigned no later than close of business on_____, 20____. Following receipt, we will instruct legal counsel to prepare the agreements contemplated herein. The Binding Terms shall become binding on the Company upon the advance of funds pursuant to Paragraph 5 and the execution of Promissory Note in consideration therefor.

Very truly yours,

/s/ <u>Prospective Buyer</u>

Prospective Buyer, President

BuyCo, Inc.

ACKNOWLEDGED AND ACCEPTED:

SellCo, Inc.

By: Prospective Seller, President

Dated:_____

APPENDIX C

SAMPLE WORK SCHEDULE

Sample Work Schedule

TIMETABLE	TASK	RESPONSIBLE PARTIES
Six weeks before closing	a. Letter of intent is signed; board resolutions to authorize negotiations obtained	Seller and buyer and their counsels
	b. Due diligence request delivered to seller	Buyer's counsel
Five weeks before closing	a. Due diligence materials organized and delivered	Seller's counsel
	b. Review of due diligence materials	Buyer's counsel
	c. Prepare draft of asset purchase agreement, informational schedules and exhibits to purchase agreement, employment and consulting agreements, etc.	Buyer's counsel
	d. Order lien searches on seller's assets to review encumbrances	Buyer's counsel
	e. Comprehensive review of seller's financial statements	Buyer's accounting firm
Three to four weeks before closing	a. Review, negotiation and redraft of asset purchase agreement (may continue until the night before closing)	Buyer's and seller's counsels
	b. Preparation and negotiation of opinion(s) of counsel	Buyer's and seller's counsels
	c. Complete review of all initial due diligence materials and make follow-on requests, where necessary	Buyer's counsel
	d. Ensure that all board and shareholder approvals have been obtained (as required by state law)	Buyer's and seller's counsels
	e. Prepare checklist and commence process for all third-party regulatory and contractual approvals (banks, landlords, insurance companies, key customers, etc.)	Buyer's and seller's counsels

Sample Work Schedule   *(Continued)*

TIMETABLE	TASK	RESPONSIBLE PARTIES
Two weeks before closing	a. Mutual review of press releases or other third-party communications regarding the deal (or sooner as required by the SEC)	Buyer's and seller's counsels
	b. Prepare schedule of closing documents (including opinions, results of lien searches, compliance certificates, etc.)	Buyer's counsel
One week before and up to closing	a. Finalize any last-minute negotiations to the asset purchase agreement	Buyer's and seller's counsels
	b. Obtain Closing Certificates from State Authorities (e.g., good standing certificates, taxes paid and current, charter and amendments)	Seller's counsel
	c. Checklist to ensure that all conditions to closing have been met or waived	Buyer's and seller's counsels
	d. Dry-run closing to identify open issues (highly recommended 2–3 days before closing)	Buyer and seller
	e. Closing	All parties
	f. Resolution of post-closing matters and conditions	All parties

A   P   P   E   N   D   I   X

SAMPLE DUE DILIGENCE CHECKLIST

In analyzing the seller, the following legal documents and records, where applicable, should be carefully reviewed and analyzed by the acquisition team and its legal counsel:

I. <u>Corporate Matters</u>
    A. Corporate records of the seller.
        1. Certificate of incorporation and all amendments.
        2. By-laws as amended.
        3. Minute books, including resolutions and minutes of all director and shareholder meetings.
        4. Current shareholders list (certified by the corporate secretary), annual reports to shareholders, and stock transfer books.
        5. List of all states, countries and other jurisdictions in which the seller transacts business or is qualified to do business.
        6. Locations of business offices (including overseas).
    B. Agreements among the seller's shareholders.
    C. All contracts restricting the sale or transfer of shares of the company, such as buy/sell agreements, subscription agreements,

offeree questionnaires, or contractual rights of first refusal as
well as all agreements for the right to purchase shares, such as
stock options or warrants as well as any pledge agreements by
an individual shareholder involving the seller's shares.

II. Financial Matters
A. List of and copies of management and similar reports or mem-
oranda relating to the material aspects of the business operations
or products.
B. Letters of counsel in response to auditors' requests for the preceding five (5) years.
C. Reports of independent accountants to the Board of Directors
for the preceding five (5) years.
D. Revolving credit and term loan agreements, indentures and other
debt instruments, including, without limitation, all documents
relating to shareholder loans.
E. Correspondence with principal lenders to the seller.
F. Personal guarantees of seller's indebtedness by its shareholders
or other parties.
G. Agreements by the seller where it has served as a guarantor for
the obligations of third parties.
H. Federal, state and local tax returns and correspondence with federal, state and local tax officials.
I. Federal filings regarding the Subchapter S status (where applicable) of the seller.
J. Any private placement memorandum (PPM) (assuming, of
course, that the seller is not a Securities Act of 1934 "Reporting
Company") prepared and used by the seller (as well as any document used in lieu of a PPM, such as an investment profile or a
business plan).
K. Financial statements, which should be prepared in accordance
with Generally Accepted Accounting Principles (GAAP), for
the past five (5) years of the seller, including:
1. Annual (audited) balance sheets.
2. Monthly (or other available) balance sheets.
3. Annual (audited) and monthly (or other available) earnings
statements.
4. Annual (audited) and monthly (or other available) statements of shareholders' equity and changes in financial
position.

    5. Any recently prepared projections for the seller.

    6. Notes and material assumptions for all statements described in K (1)–(5), above.

L. Any information or documentation relating to tax assessments, deficiency notices, investigations, audits or settlement proposals.

M. Informal schedule of key management compensation (listing information for at least the ten most highly compensated management employees or consultants).

N. Financial aspects of overseas operations (where applicable), including status of foreign legislations, regulatory restrictions, intellectual property protection, exchange controls, method for repatriating profits, foreign manufacturing, government controls, import/export licensing and tariffs, etc.

O. Projected budgets, accounts receivable reports (including detailed aging report, turnover, bad debt experience, and reserves) and related information.

III. Management and Employment Matters

A. All employment agreements.

B. Agreements relating to consulting, management, financial advisory services, and other professional engagements.

C. Copies of all union contracts and collective bargaining agreements.

D. Equal Employment Opportunity Commission (EEOC) (and any state equivalent) compliance files.

E. Occupational Safety and Health Administration (OSHA) files, including safety records and worker's compensation claims.

F. Employee benefit plans (and copies of literature issued to employees describing such plans), including the following:

    1. Pension and retirement plans, including union pension or retirement plans.

    2. Annual reports for pension plans, if any.

    3. Profit sharing plans.

    4. Stock option plans, including information concerning all options, stock appreciation rights, and other stock-related benefits granted by the company.

    5. Medical and dental plans.

    6. Insurance plans and policies, including the following:

        a. Errors and omissions policies.

        b. Directors' and officers' liability insurance policies.

       7.   Any employee stock ownership plan (ESOP) and trust agreement.

       8.   Severance pay plans or programs.

       9.   All other benefit or incentive plans or arrangements not covered by the foregoing, including welfare benefit plans.

   G.   All current contracts and agreements with or pertaining to the seller and to which directors, officers or shareholders of the seller are parties, and any documents relating to any other transactions between the seller and any director, officer or shareholders, including receivables from or payables to directors, officers or shareholders.

   H.   All policy and procedures manuals of the seller concerning personnel; hiring and promotional practices; compliance with the Family and Medical Leave Act, etc.; drug and alcohol abuse policies; AIDS policies; sexual harassment policies; vacation and holiday policies; expense reimbursement policies; etc.

   I.   The name, address, phone number and personnel file of any officer or key employee who has left the seller within the past three years.

IV.   <u>Tangible and Intangible Assets of the Seller</u>

   A.   List of all commitments for rented or leased real and personal property, including location and address, description, terms, options, termination and renewal rights, policies regarding ownership of improvements, and annual costs.

   B.   List of all real property owned, including location and address, description of general character, easements, rights of way, encumbrances, zoning restrictions, surveys, mineral rights, title insurance, pending and threatened condemnation, hazardous waste pollution, etc.

   C.   List of all tangible assets.

   D.   List of all liens on all real properties and material tangible assets.

   E.   Mortgages, deeds, title insurance policies, leases and other agreements relating to the properties of the seller.

   F.   Real estate tax bills for the real estate of the seller.

   G.   List of patents, patents pending, trademarks, trade names, copyrights, registered and proprietary Internet addresses, franchises, licenses and all other intangible assets, including registration numbers, expiration dates, employee invention agreements and policies, actual or threatened infringement actions, licensing agreements, and copies of all correspondence relating to this intellectual property.

H. Copies of any survey, appraisal, engineering or other reports as to the properties of the seller.

I. List of assets which may be on a consignment basis (or which may be the property of a given customer, such as machine dyes, molds, etc.).

V. Material Contracts and Obligations of the Seller

A. Material purchase, supply and sale agreements currently outstanding or projected to come to fruition within 12 months, including the following:

1. List of all contracts relating to the purchase of products, equipment, fixtures, tools, dies, supplies, industrial supplies, or other materials having a price under any such contract in excess of $5,000.

2. List of all unperformed sales contracts.

B. Documents incidental to any planned expansion of the seller's facilities.

C. Consignment agreements.

D. Research agreements.

E. Franchise, licensing, distribution and agency agreements.

F. Joint venture agreements.

G. Agreements for the payment or receipt of license fees or royalties and royalty-free licenses.

H. Documentation relating to all property, liability and casualty insurance policies owned by the seller, including for each policy a summary description of:

1. coverage;

2. policy type and number;

3. insurer/carrier and broker;

4. premium;

5. expiration date;

6. deductible;

7. any material changes in any of the foregoing since the inception of the seller; and

8. claims made under such policies.

I. Agreements restricting the seller's right to compete in any business.

J. Agreements for the seller's current purchase of services, including, without limitation, consulting and management.

K.   Contracts for the purchase, sale, or removal of electricity, gas, water, telephone, sewage, power, or any other utility service.

L.   List of waste dumps, disposal, treatment and storage sites.

M.   Agreements with any railroad, trucking or any other transportation company or courier service.

N.   Letters of credit.

O.   Copies of any special benefits under contracts or government programs which might be in jeopardy as a result of the proposed transaction (e.g., small business or minority set-asides, intra-family transactions or favored pricing, internal leases or allocations, etc.).

P.   Copies of licenses, permits and governmental approvals applied for or issued to the seller which are required in order to operate the businesses of the seller, such as zoning, energy requirements (natural gas, fuel, oil, electricity, etc.) operating permits or health and safety certificates.

NOTE: This section is critical and will be one key area of the negotiations. Therefore, it is suggested that the buyer and its advisory team request copies of *all* material contracts and obligations of the seller and then organize them as follows:

Q.   Schedule of all contracts and obligations of seller which are to be assumed by buyer after closing*

R.   Status of each contract or obligation:

1.   To what extent will third-party consents be required for the assignment or assumption of these contracts or obligations?

2.   Sample Responses:

a.   _____ current not required

b.   _____ received notice of default on _____, 20_____; cured on _____, 20_____ consent to assignment requested _____, 20_____ and obtained _____, 20_____.

c.   _____ notice of default received; default not yet cured! Consent to assumption required, but not yet requested.

*e.g., Contracts which have a remaining term in excess of six months.

VI.   Litigation and Claims—Actual and Contingent
    A.   Opinion letter from each lawyer or law firm prosecuting or defending significant litigation to which the seller is a party describing such litigation.
    B.   List of material litigation or claims for more than $5,000 against the seller asserted or threatened with respect to the quality of the products or services sold to customers, warranty claims, disgruntled employees, product liability, government actions, tort claims, breaches of contract, etc., including pending or threatened claims.
    C.   List of settlement agreements, releases, decrees, orders, or arbitration awards affecting the seller.
    D.   Description of labor relations history.
    E.   Documentation regarding correspondence or proceedings with federal, state or local regulatory agencies.

NOTE: Be sure to obtain specific representations and warranties from the seller and its advisors regarding any knowledge pertaining to potential or contingent claims or litigation!

VII.   Miscellaneous
    A.   Press releases (past two years)
    B.   Resumes of all key management team members
    C.   Press clippings (past two years)
    D.   Financial analyst reports, industry, surveys, etc.
    E.   Texts of speeches by the seller's management team, especially if reprinted and distributed to the industry or the media
    F.   Schedule of all outside advisors, consultants, etc. used by the seller over the past five years (domestic and international)
    G.   Schedule of long-term investments made by the seller
    H.   Standard forms (purchase orders, sales orders, service agreements, etc.)

Reprinted with permission from the Association for Financial Professionals (AFP).
Maneuvering Your Way Through M&A:
A Reference Guidebook for Financial Professionals
created by Andrew J. Sherman, Esq.

SAMPLE ASSET PURCHASE AGREEMENT

THIS ASSET PURCHASE AGREEMENT ("Agreement") is made and entered into this_____day of _____, 20____, by and among Growth Co. Corp., a Maryland limited liability company (the "Buyer") and Target Co., Inc., a New York corporation (the "Seller"), and Jane C. Doe and John F. Doe individually (each a "Shareholder" and collectively, the "Shareholders").

W I T N E S S E T H :

WHEREAS, the Seller is engaged in the equipment manufacturing business and activities related thereto (herein referred to as the "Business"); and

WHEREAS, Seller and the Shareholders (constituting all of the beneficial shareholders of the Seller), desire to sell, convey, transfer, assign and deliver to Buyer the Business and substantially all of the assets, properties and operations used in the Business, and Buyer desires to purchase the Business and such assets, properties and operations, on the terms and subject to conditions contained in this Agreement, and other agreements related hereto.

NOW, THEREFORE, in consideration of the mutual benefits to be derived from this Agreement, the receipt and sufficiency of which are hereby acknowledged, the parties hereto hereby agree as follows:

1. SALE AND PURCHASE OF ASSETS.

    1.1   Sale of Assets to Buyer. Upon the terms and subject to the conditions herein set forth, at the Closing referred to in Section 3, Seller shall sell, transfer, assign, convey and deliver to Buyer, and Buyer shall purchase and acquire from Seller, all of the properties, assets and goodwill that are used in the Business, of whatever kind and nature, real or personal, tangible or intangible (including all rights of the Seller arising from its operation of the Business) and excluding only those assets referred to in Section 1.2 of this Agreement (collectively, the "Assets"), as those Assets exist on the Closing Date (as defined in Section 3). The Assets include, but are not limited to, the following:

        (a)   all of Seller's machinery, equipment, equipment leases, chemicals, supplies, vehicles, furniture, fixtures, tools, computers and all other personal property, wherever located, which are used in the Business, including, but not limited to, the items listed on Schedule 1.1(a);

        (b)   all interests of Seller in real property, including leases, options, rights of way, zoning and development rights and easements, described on Schedule 1.1(b);

        (c)   all inventory of Seller used in the Business, wherever located, including, without limitation, the parts, chemicals and materials listed on Schedule 1.1(c);

        (d)   all of Seller's computer software used in the Business, and all rights, title and interest of Seller in, to and under all trademarks, trademark rights, trademark applications, patents, patent rights, patent applications, trade secrets, inventions, training and equipment manuals, technology, methods, manufacturing, engineering, technical and any other know-how, processes, projects in development, trade names, service marks, other intellectual property rights and other proprietary information of the Seller used in or relating to the Business. All material intellectual property, including all trade names and patents used or held by Seller, are listed on Schedule 1.1(d);

        (e)   all of Seller's rights under any written or oral contracts, unfilled service and/or purchase orders, agreements, leases, instruments, registrations, licenses, certificates, distribution agreements or other documents, commitments, arrangements or authorizations relating to the Business, including, but not limited to, the agreements and other instruments identified on Schedule 1.1(e) (the "Contracts"); provided, that nothing contained in this Agreement shall be construed as an attempt to agree to assign any contract which is by itself non-assignable without the consent of the other party or parties thereto, unless such consent shall be given;

(f) all rights in connection with all permits, certificates, licenses, approvals, registrations and authorizations of Seller which may be necessary or desirable in order to conduct the Business (the "Permits");

(g) all of Seller's rights under manufacturers' and vendors' warranties relating to those items included in the Assets and all of Seller's similar rights against third parties relating to items included in the Assets;

(h) all of Seller's accounts receivable, notes and other receivables, unbilled costs and fees, all prepaid items, amounts on deposit of Seller, and other current assets existing on the Closing Date, including, but not limited to, the receivables and other assets set forth on Schedule 1.1(h), but excluding cash and cash equivalents;

(i) all goodwill, customer and vendor lists, telephone numbers, and other intangible property, and all of Seller's rights to commence or maintain future and existing actions relating to the operation of the Business or the ownership of the Assets, for events occurring after the Closing Date, and the right to settle those actions and retain the proceeds therefrom;

(j) all shares of stock and partnership interests owned by Seller, if any;

(k) all of Seller's rights under the insurance or similar policies in effect on or prior to the Closing Date set forth on Schedule 1.1(k);

(l) all financial, operational, and any other files, logs, books and records and data of the Business of Seller, (collectively, "Books and Records") and including, without limitation, all correspondence, accounting records, personnel records, purchase orders and invoices, customer records, supplier records, advertising and promotional materials and files, and other business records which are owned by Seller relating to the Business.

1.2 Excluded Assets. The following assets (the "Excluded Assets") shall be retained by the Seller and shall not be sold or assigned to Buyer:

(a) all cash on hand and cash equivalents and cash-value life and other split-life insurance policies of Seller;

(b) the corporate minute books and stock books of Seller; and

(c) any lease, commitment or other agreement listed on Schedule 1.2(c) with respect to which the Buyer does not desire to acquire concurrent with its purchase of the Assets under this Agreement, including any employee advance.

1.3 Method of Conveyance. The sale, transfer, conveyance and assignment by the Seller of the Assets to the Buyer in accordance with

Section 1.1 hereof shall be effected on the Closing Date by the Seller's execution and delivery to the Buyer of a general assignment and bill of sale,
in substantially the form attached hereto as Exhibit A (the "General Assignment and Bill of Sale"). At the Closing, all of the Assets shall be transferred
by the Seller to the Buyer free and clear of any and all liens, encumbrances,
mortgages, security interests, pledges, claims, equities and other restrictions or charges of any kind or nature whatsoever (collectively, "Liens")
except for a lessor's interest in any leased assets or as otherwise listed in
Schedule 4.5(a).

2.   **PURCHASE PRICE.** The purchase price to be paid by the Buyer for
the Assets to be sold, transferred and conveyed by the Seller pursuant to this
Agreement shall be:

    (a)   _____; and
    (b)   _____.

3.   **CLOSING.**
        3.1   Date of Closing. Subject to the terms and conditions set forth
herein, the closing of the transactions contemplated hereby (the "Closing")
shall be held at 10:00 a.m. at the offices of counsel for the Seller on or before
_____, 20_____, provided that all conditions to the Closing have
been satisfied, or at such other time, date and place as shall be fixed by
agreement among the parties hereto. The date on which the Closing shall
occur is referred to herein as the "Closing Date." At the Closing, the parties
shall execute and deliver the documents referred to in Section 3.2.
        3.2   Items to be Delivered at Closing. At the Closing and subject
to the terms and conditions herein contained:
        (a)   Seller shall deliver or cause to be delivered to Buyer
    the following:
                (i)   one or more Bills of Sale and such other good and
        sufficient instruments and documents of conveyance and trans-
        fer executed by Seller, in a form reasonably satisfactory to
        Buyer and its counsel, as shall be necessary and effective to
        transfer and assign to, and vest in, Buyer all of Seller's right,
        title and interest in and to the Assets, including without limi-
        tation, (A) good and valid title in and to all of the Assets owned
        by Seller, (B) good and valid leasehold interests in and to all
        of the Assets leased by Seller as lessee, and (C) all of the
        Seller's rights under all agreements, contracts, instruments and
        other documents included in the Assets to which Seller is a
        party or by which it has rights on the Closing Date;

(ii)   all third-party consents required to be delivered as a condition to Closing as set forth in Section 8.2(d), which may be necessary or desirable in connection with the transfer of the Assets, including the Contracts and the Permits;

(iii)   all of the agreements, contracts, commitments, leases, plans, computer programs and software, data bases whether in the form of computer tapes or otherwise, manuals and guidebooks, customer lists, supplier lists, and other documents, books, records, papers, files, office supplies and data belonging to the Seller which are part of the Assets;

(iv)   one or more Assignment and Assumption Agreements executed by Seller;

(v)   executed lease for the Seller's home offices (the "Darien Property"), attached hereto as Exhibit M and assignment of lease for the Seller's Potomac warehouse and office (the "Potomac Property"), transferring the leasehold and subleasehold interests in said properties to Buyer;

(vi)   a written opinion of Joseph P. Doe, Esq., counsel for Seller, dated the Closing Date, in the form of Exhibit F hereto;

(vii)   a certificate, signed by a duly authorized officer of the Seller and dated the Closing Date, representing that the conditions contained in Section 8.2(b) of this Agreement have been satisfied;

(viii)   certified copies of resolutions of the Seller's Board of Directors and its Shareholders with respect to the approval of this Agreement and the transactions contemplated hereby (Exhibit O);

(ix)   Employment Agreements, executed by Jane C. Doe and John F. Doe, respectively (Exhibits G and H, respectively); and

(x)   any other opinions, certificates or other documents and instruments required herein to be delivered by the Seller or the Shareholders.

(b)   Buyer shall deliver to the Seller the following:

(i)   the Purchase Price pursuant to Section 2 hereof;

(ii)   a certificate, signed by a duly authorized officer of the Buyer and dated the Closing Date, representing that the conditions contained in Section 8.1(a) of this Agreement have been satisfied;

(iii)   certified copies of resolutions of the Manager of the Buyer with respect to the approval of this Agreement and the transactions contemplated hereby;

(iv)   executed counterparts of the lease amendments with respect to the _____ and _____ Properties;

(v)   the executed Promissory Notes;

(vi)   the Operating Agreement of the Buyer;

(vii)   the Pledge Agreement and the Pledged Collateral Account Agreement executed by the Pledgor in accordance with Section 8.1(f) hereof;

(viii)   executed Employment Agreements as provided in Section 8.2(f); and

(ix)   any other certificates or other documents and instruments required herein to be delivered by Buyer.

4.   REPRESENTATIONS AND WARRANTIES OF THE SELLER. In order to induce the Buyer to enter into this Agreement and to consummate the transactions contemplated hereby, the Seller and each of the Shareholders, jointly and severally, hereby represents and warrants to the Buyer as follows:

4.1   Organization and Authority. Seller is a corporation duly organized, validly existing and in good standing under the laws of the State of Maryland. Seller has the full power and authority to enter into and perform this Agreement, to own, operate and lease its properties and assets, to carry on its business as it is now being conducted, and to execute, deliver and perform its obligations under this Agreement and consummate the transactions contemplated hereby. Each Shareholder has the full power and authority to enter into and perform this Agreement. Seller has delivered to the Buyer complete and correct copies of its Articles of Incorporation and Bylaws, each as amended to date. Seller is duly qualified to do business as a foreign corporation and in good standing in _____ .

4.2   Authorization of Agreement. The execution, delivery and performance by the Seller of this Agreement and of each and every document and instrument contemplated hereby and the consummation of the transactions contemplated hereby and thereby have been duly and validly authorized and approved by all necessary corporate action of the Seller. This Agreement has been duly executed and delivered by the Seller and each of the Shareholders and constitutes (and, when executed and delivered, each such other document and instrument will constitute) a valid and binding obligation of the Seller and each of the Shareholders, enforceable against the Seller and each of the Shareholders in accordance with its terms.

4.3   Capitalization and Share Ownership of Seller. The Seller's authorized capital stock consists of 1,000 shares of common stock, no par value. There are 1,000 shares of the Seller's common stock presently outstanding, all of which shares are owned by the Shareholders, free and clear of all Liens. All of the Shareholders' shares have been duly authorized and validly issued, are fully paid and non-assessable. No equity securities (or debt securities convertible into equity securities) of the Seller, other than the Shareholders' shares, are issued and outstanding. There are no existing contracts, subscriptions, options, warrants, calls, commitments or other rights of any character to purchase or otherwise acquire any common stock or other securities of the Seller.

4.4   Non-Contravention; Consents and Approvals.

(a)   Neither the execution and delivery by the Seller of this Agreement nor the consummation by the Seller or the Shareholders of the transactions contemplated hereby, nor compliance by the Seller or the Shareholders with any of the provisions hereof, will

(i)   conflict with or result in a breach of any provision of the Articles of Incorporation or Bylaws of the Seller;

(ii)   result in the breach of, or conflict with, any of the terms and conditions of, or constitute a default (with or without the giving of notice or the lapse of time or both) with respect to, or result in the cancellation or termination of, or the acceleration of the performance of any obligations or of any indebtedness under, any contract, agreement, lease, commitment, indenture, mortgage, note, bond, license or other instrument or obligation to which the Seller or any Shareholder is a party or by which the Seller, the Shareholders or any of the Assets may be bound or affected, (other than such breaches, conflicts and defaults set forth in Schedule 4.4(a) hereto, which shall have been waived at or prior to the Closing);

(iii)   result in the creation of any Lien upon any of the Assets; or

(iv)   violate any law or any rule or regulation of any administrative agency or governmental body, or any order, writ, injunction or decree of any court, administrative agency or governmental body to which the Seller, the Shareholders or any of the Assets may be subject.

(b)   Except as set forth in Schedule 4.4(b) hereto, no approval, authorization, consent or other order or action of, or filing with or notice to any court, administrative agency or other governmental authority or any other person is required for the execution and delivery by Seller or the Shareholders of this Agreement or the consummation by the Seller and the Shareholders of the transactions contemplated hereby.

(c) A description of all Permits held by Seller and necessary or desirable for the operation of the Business are set forth in Schedule 4.4(c) hereto. All Permits listed in Schedule 4.4(c) are valid, and neither Seller nor any Shareholder has received any notice that any government authority intends to modify, cancel, terminate, or deny renewal of any Permit. No current or former stockholder, officer, director or employee of Seller or any affiliate of Seller owns or has any proprietary, financial or other interest in any Permit which Seller owns or uses. Seller has conducted the Business in compliance with the requirements, standards, criteria and conditions set forth in the Permits and other applicable orders, approvals, variances, rules and regulations and is not in violation of any of the foregoing. The transactions contemplated by this Agreement will not result in a default under or a breach of or violation of or adversely affect the rights and benefits afforded to the Seller by any Permits. Except as set forth in Schedule 4.4(c) hereto, no approval by a governmental authority is required for transfer to Buyer of such Permits.

4.5 Ownership of Assets.

(a) The Seller has and will have at the Closing good, valid and marketable title to each and every item of the tangible and intangible personal property and assets included in the Assets, and valid leasehold interests in all leases of tangible personal and real property included in the Assets, free and clear of any Liens except as set forth in Schedule 4.5(a). At the Closing, the Seller will transfer to Buyer good, valid and marketable title to the Assets, free and clear of any and all Liens, except as set forth in Schedule 4.5(a).

(b) No affiliate of the Seller has, or has indirectly acquired, any right, title or interest in or to any of the Assets.

(c) The Seller has not sold, transferred, assigned or conveyed any of its right, title and interest, or granted or entered into any option to purchase or acquire any of its right, title or interest, in and to any of the Assets or the Business. No third party has any option or right to acquire the Business or any of the Assets.

4.6 Balance Sheet; Existing Condition; Ordinary Course. Attached hereto as Schedule 4.6 are (i) the Seller's unaudited balance sheet (the "1996 Balance Sheet") as of December 31, 1996 (the "Balance Sheet Date"), together with the related unaudited statements of income, shareholders equity and cash flows for the year then ended; and (ii) the Seller's unaudited balance sheets as of December 1995 and 1994, together with the related unaudited statements of income, shareholders equity and cash flows for the years ended December 31, 1995 and 1994 (such unaudited financial statements for 1994, 1995 and 1996 being referred to herein collectively as the "Financial Statements"). The Financial Statements (i) are true, complete and correct; (ii) are in accordance with the books and records of the Seller; (iii) fairly, completely and accurately present the financial position of the Seller as of the respective dates thereof and the results of its operations for the periods presented; and (iv) were prepared in conformity with generally accepted accounting principles consistently applied throughout the periods covered thereby. Since the Balance Sheet Date, except as set forth in Schedule 4.6 hereto, there has not been with respect to the Seller:

(a) any material adverse change in the Assets or the Business of the Seller from their condition as set forth on the 1996 Balance Sheet;

(b) any damage, destruction or loss, whether covered by insurance or not, materially and adversely affecting the Business or Assets of the Seller or any sale, transfer or other disposition of the Assets other than in the ordinary course of business;

(c) any declaration, setting aside or payment of any dividend, or any distribution with respect to the capital stock of the Seller or any direct or indirect redemption, purchase or other acquisition by the Seller of shares of its capital stock, or any payment to any affiliate of any inter-company payable or any transfer of Assets to any affiliate; or

(d) except as set forth on Schedule 4.6(d), any increase in the compensation payable by the Seller to any Shareholder or any of the Seller's officers, employees or agents, or in the payment of any bonus, or in any insurance, payment or arrangement made to, for or with any such officers, employees or agents. Since the Balance Sheet Date, Seller has conducted its Business in the ordinary course and has made no material change to its marketing, purchasing, collections or accounting procedures.

4.7 Litigation. There is no litigation, suit, proceeding, action, claim or investigation, at law or in equity, pending or, to the best knowledge of the Seller or any Shareholder, threatened against, or affecting in any way the Assets, the Seller or any Shareholder's ability to own or operate the Business, or which questions the validity of this Agreement or challenges any of the transactions contemplated hereby or the use of the Assets after the Closing by the Buyer. Neither the Seller, nor any of the Shareholders, nor any of the Assets is subject to any judgment, order, writ, injunction or decree of any court or any federal, state, municipal or other governmental authority, department, commission, board, bureau, agency or other instrumentality.

4.8   Compliance with Laws. Except as set forth in Schedule 4.8, the Seller's Business has at all times been conducted in compliance with all applicable laws, regulations, ordinances and other requirements of governmental authorities (including applicable federal, state and local laws, rules and regulations respecting occupational safety and health standards). Except as set forth in Schedule 4.8, neither the Seller nor any Shareholder has received any notice, advice, claim or complaint from any employee or governmental authority that the Seller has not conducted, or is not presently conducting, its business and operations in accordance with all applicable laws and other requirements of governmental authorities.

4.9   Permits and Licenses. The Seller has all permits, certificates, licenses, approvals, registrations and authorizations required in connection with the conduct of the Business. The Seller is not in violation of, and has not violated, any applicable provisions of any such permits, certificates, licenses, approvals, registrations or authorizations. Except as set forth on Schedule 4.9, all permits, certificates, licenses, approvals, registrations and authorizations of the Seller which are necessary for the operation of the Seller's Business are freely transferable.

4.10   Contracts.

(a)   Schedule 4.10(a) contains a true and complete list of all material contracts and agreements related to or involving the Business or the Assets or by which any of the Assets is subject or bound in any material respect, including, without limiting the generality of the foregoing, any and all: contracts and agreements for the purchase, sale or lease of inventory, goods, materials, equipment, hardware, supplies or other personal property; contracts for the purchase, sale or lease of real property; contracts and agreements for the performance or furnishing of services; joint venture, partnership or other contracts, agreements or arrangements involving the sharing of profits; employment agreements; and agreements containing any covenant or covenants which purport to limit the ability or right of the Seller or any other person or entity to engage in any aspects of the business related to the Assets or compete in any aspect of such business with any person or entity (collectively, the "Scheduled Contracts"). As used herein, the terms "contract" and "agreement" mean and include every material contract, agreement, commitment, arrangement, understanding and promise whether written or oral. A complete and accurate copy of each written

Scheduled Contract has been delivered or made available to the Buyer or, if oral, a complete and accurate summary thereof has been delivered to the Buyer. Except as set forth on Schedule 4.10(a), the Scheduled Contracts are valid, binding and enforceable in accordance with their respective terms, are in full force and effect and were entered into in the ordinary course of business on an "arms-length" basis and consistent with past practices. The Seller is not in breach or default of any of the Scheduled Contracts and, except as set forth on Schedule 4.10(a), no occurrence or circumstance exists which constitutes (with or without the giving of notice or the lapse of time or both) a breach or default by the other party thereto. Neither the Seller nor any Shareholder has been notified or advised by any party to a Scheduled Contract of such party's intention or desire to terminate or modify any such contract or agreement. Neither the Seller nor any Shareholder has granted any Lien on any Scheduled Contract included in the Assets.

(b)   Except as set forth on Schedule 4.10(b) and this Agreement, neither the Seller nor any Shareholder is a party to, and neither the Seller nor any Shareholder nor any of the Assets is subject or bound in any respect by, any written or oral contract and agreement related to or involving the Business which will affect in any manner the Buyer's ownership, use or operation of the Assets, including, without limitation any contracts or agreements (i) for the purchase, sale or lease of inventory, goods, equipment or for the performance or furnishing of services; (ii) for the furnishing of services for which the Seller has received payment in advance of furnishing such services and has not yet furnished such services; and (iii) containing any covenant or covenants which purport to limit the ability or right of the Seller or any other person or entity to engage in any aspects of the business related to the Assets or compete in any aspect of such business with any person or entity.

(c)   Except as set forth on Schedule 4.10(c), all Scheduled Contracts included in the Assets will be fully and validly assigned to the Buyer as of the Closing.

(d)   Except as set forth in Schedule 4.10(d), there is no Scheduled Contract or any other Contract included in the Assets which cannot be terminated without any further obligation, payment or penalty upon thirty-days' notice or more to the other party or parties to such Contract.

4.11   Condition of Purchased Assets. Each and every one of the tangible Assets to be purchased by Buyer pursuant to this Agreement is in good operating condition and repair, ordinary wear and tear excepted, and is fit and suitable for the purposes for which they are currently used by Seller. The Assets include all of the properties and assets of Seller required, necessary or desirable to enable Buyer to conduct the operation of the Business in the same manner in which the Business has been conducted prior to the date hereof by Seller.

4.12   Customers. Seller has delivered to Buyer a complete and accurate list of all customers which has been included in Schedule 4.12. Except as set forth in Schedule 4.12, no current customer (i) has cancelled, suspended or otherwise terminated its relationship with the Seller; or (ii) has advised the Seller or either Shareholder of its intent to cancel, suspend or otherwise terminate such relationship, or to materially decrease its usage of the services provided by Seller.

4.13   Employee Benefit Plans. Except as set forth in Schedule 4.13, there are not currently, nor have there ever been, any Benefit Plans (defined below) in place or established by Seller. "Benefit Plan" means any bonus, incentive compensation, deferred compensation, pension, profit sharing, retirement, stock purchase, stock option, stock ownership, stock appreciation rights, phantom stock, leave of absence, layoff, vacation, day or dependent care, legal services, cafeteria, life, health, accident, disability, workers' compensation or other insurance, severance, separation or other employee benefit plan, practice, policy or arrangement of any kind, whether written or oral, including, but not limited to, any "employee benefit plan" within the meaning of Section 3(3) of ERISA. All group health plans of the Seller have been operated in compliance with all applicable federal and state laws and regulations.

4.14   Warranties. Schedule 4.14 sets forth a complete and correct copy of all of the Seller's standard warranties (collectively, the "Warranties" or individually a "Warranty") currently extended by the Seller to the customers of the Seller. There are no warranty claims outstanding against the Seller.

4.15   Trademarks, Patents, Etc. Except as set forth in Schedule 4.15, the Seller has clear title to its patents, trademarks, trade names, brand names, service marks, service names, copyrights, inventions or licenses and rights and applications with respect to the foregoing (collectively, the "Marks and Patents"). All the Marks and Patents are valid and have not been abandoned, and there are no prior claims, controversies, lawsuits or judgments which affect the validity of the Seller's rights to the Marks and Patents nor are there any legal proceedings, claims or controversies instituted, pending or, to the best knowledge of the Seller or the Shareholders, threatened with respect to any of the Marks and Patents, or which challenge the Seller's rights, title or interest in respect thereto. Except as set forth on Schedule 4.15, none of the Marks and Patents are the subject of any outstanding assignments, grants, licenses, Liens, obligations or agreements, whether written, oral or implied. All required renewal fees, maintenance fees, amendments and/or other filings or payments which are necessary to preserve and maintain the Marks and Patents have been filed and/or made. The Seller owns or has the right to use all Marks and Patents and the like necessary to conduct its Business as presently conducted and without conflict with any patent, trade name, trademark or the like of any other person or entity.

     4.16   Insurance. Set forth in Schedule 4.16 is a complete and accurate list of all insurance policies which the Seller maintains with respect to its Business or the Assets. Such policies are in full force and effect. Such policies, with respect to their amounts and types of coverage, are adequate to insure fully against risks to which the Seller, the Business or the Assets are normally exposed in the operation of the Business. There has not been any material adverse change in the Seller's relationship with its insurers or in the premiums payable pursuant to such policies. The insurance coverage provided by the Seller's insurance policies shall not be affected by, and shall not lapse or otherwise be terminated by reason of, the execution of this Agreement. Neither the Seller or either Shareholder has received any notice respecting the cancellation of such insurance policies.

     4.17   Environmental Matters.

     (a)   Except as set forth on Schedule 4.17(a) attached hereto, Seller has obtained all permits, licenses, and other authorizations (collectively, the "Licenses") which are required in connection with the conduct of the Business under all applicable Environmental Laws (as defined below) and regulations relating to pollution or protection of the environment, including Environmental Laws and regulations relating to emissions, discharges, releases or threatened releases of pollutants, contaminants, chemicals, or industrial, toxic or hazardous substances or wastes into the environment (including without limitation, ambient air, surface water, groundwater, or land) or otherwise relating to the manufacture, processing, distribution, use, treatment, storage, disposal, transport, or handling of pollutants, contaminants, chemicals, or industrial, toxic or hazardous substances or wastes.

     (b)   Except as set forth in Schedule 4.17(b), Seller is in substantial compliance in the conduct of the Business with all terms and conditions of the Licenses and is in substantial compliance with all other limitations, restrictions, conditions, standards, prohibitions, requirements, obligations, schedules and timetables contained in the Environmental Laws or contained in any regulation, code, plan, order, decree, judgment, injunction, notice (written or verbal) or demand letter issued, entered, promulgated or approved thereunder.

(c)   Except as set forth on Schedule 4.17(c), neither Seller nor any Shareholder is aware of, nor has Seller received any written or verbal notice of, any past, present or future events, conditions, circumstances, activities, practices, incidents, actions or plans which may interfere with or prevent compliance or continued compliance with any Environmental Laws or any regulations, code, order, decree, judgment, injunction, notice (written or verbal) or demand letter issued, entered, promulgated or approved thereunder, or which may give rise to any common law or legal liability, or otherwise form the basis of any claim, action, demand, suit, proceeding, hearing, study or investigation, based on or related to the Seller's, processing, storage, distribution, use, treatment, disposal, transport, or handling, or the emission, discharge, release or threatened release into the environment, of any pollutant, contaminant, chemical, or industrial, toxic or hazardous substance or waste.

(d)   There is no civil, criminal or administrative action, suit, demand, claim, hearing, notice or demand letter, notice of violation, investigation, or proceeding pending or threatened against Seller or the Shareholders in connection with the conduct of the Business relating in any way to any Environmental Laws or regulation, injunction, notice or demand letter issued, entered, promulgated or approved thereunder.

(e)   For purposes of this Agreement, "Environmental Laws" means collectively, all federal, state and local environmental laws, common law, statutes, rules and regulations including, without limitation, the Comprehensive Environmental Response, Compensation and Liability Act (42 U.S.C. Sec. 9061 et seq.), as amended, the Hazardous Materials Transportation Act (49 U.S.C. Sec. 1801 et seq.), as amended, the Resource Conservation and Recovery Act (42 U.S.C. Sec. 6901 et seq.), as amended, the Federal Water Pollution Control Act (33 U.S.C. Sec. 1251 et seq.), as amended, the Safe Drinking Water Act (42 U.S.C. Sec. 300f et seq.), as amended, the Clean Air Act (42 U.S.C. Sec. 7401 et seq.), as amended, the Toxic Substances Control Act (15 U.S.C. Sec. 2601 et seq.), as amended, the Federal Emergency Planning and Community Right-to-Know Act (42 U.S.C. Sec. 11001 et seq.), as amended, any so-called "superfund" or "super-lien" law and such statutes and ordinances as may be enacted by state and local governments with jurisdiction over any real property now owned or leased by the Seller or any real property upon which the Seller now conducts its Business and any permits, licenses, authorizations, variances, consents, approvals, directives or requirements of, and any agreements with, any governments, departments, commissions, boards, courts, authorities, agencies, officials and officers applicable to such real property or the use thereof and regulating, relating to, or imposing liability or standards of conduct concerning any pollutant, contaminant, chemical, or industrial, toxic or hazardous substance or waste.

4.18   Notes, Accounts or Other Receivables. Set forth on Schedule 1.1(h) is a complete list of Seller's notes, accounts or other receivables included in the Assets as existing on the Closing Date. All of the Seller's notes, accounts or other receivables included on Schedule 1.1(h) are properly reflected on the books and records of the Seller, and are in their entirety valid accounts receivable arising from bona fide transactions in the ordinary course of business.

4.19   Real Estate.

(a)   The Seller does not own any real property.

(b)   The Seller has valid leasehold interests in all of the real property which it leases or purports to lease, free and clear of any Liens, other than the interests of the lessors, including the Darien Property and the Anytown Property.

(c)   The Seller enjoys peaceful and undisturbed possession under all of the leases pursuant to which Seller leases real property (the "Real Property Leases"). All of the Real Property Leases are valid, subsisting and in full force and effect and there are no existing defaults, or events which with the passage of time or the giving of notice, or both, would constitute defaults by the Seller or, by any other party thereto.

(d)   Neither Seller nor any Shareholder has received notice of any pending condemnation, expropriation, eminent domain or similar proceedings affecting all or any portion of any real property leased by the Seller and no such proceedings are contemplated.

4.20   No Guarantees. The Seller has not guaranteed or pledged any Assets with respect to any obligation or indebtedness of any person or entity and no person or entity has guaranteed any obligation or indebtedness of the Seller.

4.21   Taxes.

(a)   The Seller has timely filed or will timely file all requisite federal, state and other Tax (defined below) returns, reports and forms

("Returns") for all periods ended on or before the Closing Date, and all such Tax Returns are true, correct and complete in all respects. Neither the Seller nor any Shareholder has any knowledge of any basis for the assertion of any claim relating or attributable to Taxes which, if adversely determined, would result in any Lien on the assets of such Seller or any Shareholder or otherwise have an adverse effect on the Seller, the Assets or the Business.

(b)   For purposes of this Agreement, the term "Tax" shall include any tax or similar governmental charge, impost, or levy (including, without limitation, income taxes, franchise taxes, transfer taxes or fees, sales taxes, use taxes, gross receipts taxes, value added taxes, employment taxes, excise taxes, ad valorem taxes, property taxes, withholding taxes, payroll taxes, minimum taxes or windfall profits taxes) together with any related penalties, fines, additions to tax or interest imposed by the United States or any state, county, local or foreign government or subdivision or agency thereof.

4.22   Labor Matters. Schedule 4.22 sets forth a true and complete list of all employees of Seller together with a brief summary of their titles, duties, terms of employment and compensation arrangements, including the salary and any bonus, commission or other compensation paid to each employee during the twelve (12)-month period prior to the date hereof and the current employment and compensation arrangements with respect to each such employee. Further, with respect to employees of and service provided to Seller:

(a)   Seller is not a party to any collective bargaining or similar labor agreements, no such agreement determines the terms and conditions of employment of any employee of Seller, no collective bargaining or other labor agent has been certified as a representative of any of the employees of the Seller, and no representation campaign or election is now in progress with respect to any of the employees of the Seller;

(b)   Seller is and has been in compliance in all material respects with all applicable laws respecting employment and employment practices, terms and conditions of employment and wages and hours, including without limitation, any such laws respecting employment discrimination and harassment, workers' compensation, family and medical leave, the Immigration Reform and Control Act, and occupational safety and heath requirements, and has not and is not engaged in any unfair labor practice;

(c)   There is not now, nor within the past three years, has there been, any unfair labor practice complaint against Seller, pending or to

Seller's best knowledge, threatened before the National Labor Relations Board or any other comparable authority; nor any labor strike, slow-down or stoppage actually ending or, to Seller's best knowledge, threatened against or directly affecting Seller; there exist no other labor disputes with regard to Seller's employees or relative to Seller's Employee Manual ("Manual"), including, without limitation, any reports of harassment, substance abuse, disciplinary, safety or punctuality problems in contravention of Seller's Manual, or other acts or omissions filed or recorded by or against any employee of Seller. Seller's cessation of operations will not violate any laws, rules, regulations or employment policies applicable to its employees.

(d)   As of the Closing Date, each employee of the Seller has received any pay owed him or her with respect to vacation, compensatory or sick time and any other employee benefits due employee, except as otherwise set forth in Schedule 4.22(d).

4.23   Absence of Undisclosed Liabilities. Neither the Seller nor any Shareholder has any material liabilities or obligations with respect to the Business, either direct or indirect, matured or unmatured or absolute, contingent or otherwise, other than (a) those reflected in the 1996 Balance Sheet and (b) those liabilities or obligations incurred, consistently with past business practice, in or as a result of the normal and ordinary course of business since the Balance Sheet Date.

4.24   Liabilities. The liabilities to be assumed by Buyer pursuant to this Agreement consist solely of liabilities of Seller under Contracts included in the Assets which relate solely to the operation of the Business and the Assumed Liabilities in Schedule 1.2.

4.25   Accuracy of Documents and Information. The information provided to the Buyer by the Seller and the Shareholders with respect to the Seller, the Assets and the Business, including the representations and warranties made in this Agreement and in the Schedules attached hereto, and all other information provided to the Buyer in connection with their investigation of the Seller, does not (and will not at the Closing Date) contain any untrue statement of a material fact and does not omit (and will not omit at the Closing Date) to state any material fact necessary to make the statements or facts contained herein or therein not misleading.

4.26   Brokers and Agents. Neither Seller nor any Shareholder has employed or dealt with any business broker, agent or finder in respect of the transactions contemplated hereby.

5.   NON-COMPETITION. Each of the Shareholders agrees that for a period of six (6) years from the date of this Agreement, he or she shall not, directly or indirectly: (a) engage in competition with the Buyer in any manner or capacity (e.g., as an advisor, consultant, independent contractor, principal, agent, partner, officer, director, stockholder, employee, member of any association, or otherwise) or in any phase of the business conducted by the Buyer during the term of this Agreement in any area where the Buyer is conducting or initiating operations during the period described above; provided, however, that ownership by a Shareholder as a passive investment, of less than one percent (1 percent) of the outstanding shares of capital stock of any corporation listed on a national securities exchange or publicly traded in the over-the-counter market shall not constitute a breach of this provision; (b) hire or engage or attempt to hire or employ any individual who shall have been an employee of the Buyer at any time during within one (1) year prior to such action taken by a Shareholder, whether for or on behalf of such Shareholder or for any entity in which such Shareholder shall have a direct or indirect interest (or any subsidiary or affiliate of any such entity), whether as a proprietor, partner, co-venturer, financier, investor or stockholder, director, officer, employer, employee, agent, representative or otherwise; or (c) assist or encourage any other person in carrying out, directly or indirectly, any activity that would be prohibited by the above provisions of this Section if such activity were carried out by Shareholder, either directly or indirectly; and in particular each Shareholder agrees that he or she will not, directly or indirectly, induce any employee of the Buyer to carry out, directly or indirectly, any such activity. In the event of any conflict between this provision and the terms of an Employment Agreement in full force and effect, the Employment Agreement will govern.

6.   REPRESENTATIONS AND WARRANTIES OF THE BUYER. In order to induce the Seller to enter into this Agreement and to consummate the transactions contemplated hereby, each of the Buyers, jointly and severally, hereby represents and warrants to the Seller as follows:

6.1   Buyer's Organization. The Buyer is a limited liability company duly organized, validly existing and in good standing under the laws of the State of Maryland. The Buyer has all requisite power and authority to own and operate and lease its properties and assets, to carry on its business as it is now being conducted and to execute, deliver and perform its obligations under this Agreement and consummate the transactions contemplated hereby.

6.2   Authorization of Agreement. The execution, delivery and performance by the Buyer of this Agreement and of each and every agreement and document contemplated hereby and the consummation of the transactions contemplated hereby and thereby have been duly authorized by all necessary corporate action of the Buyer. This Agreement has been duly and validly executed and delivered by Buyer and constitutes (and, when executed and delivered, each such other agreement and document will constitute) a valid and binding obligation of the Buyer, enforceable against the Buyer in accordance with its terms.

      6.3   Non-Contravention; Consents. Neither the execution and delivery by the Buyer of this Agreement nor the consummation by the Buyer of the transactions contemplated hereby, nor compliance by the Buyer with any of the provisions hereof, will (i) conflict with or result in a breach of any provision of the Articles of Organization or Operating Agreement of the Buyer; (ii) result in the breach of, or conflict with, any of the terms and conditions of, or constitute a default (with or without the giving of notice or the lapse of time or both) with respect to, or result in the cancellation or termination of, or the acceleration of the performance of any obligations or of any indebtedness under any contract, agreement, commitment, indenture, mortgage, note, bond, license or other instrument or obligation to which the Buyer is now a party or by which the Buyer or its respective properties or assets may be bound or affected (other than such breaches, conflicts and defaults as shall have been waived at or prior to the Closing); or (iii) violate any law or any rule or regulation of any administrative agency or governmental body, or any order, writ, injunction or decree of any court, administrative agency or governmental body to which the Buyer may be subject. No approval, authorization, consent or other order or action of, or filing with or notice to any court, administrative agency or other governmental authority or any other person is required for the execution and delivery by the Buyer of this Agreement or consummation by the Buyer of the transactions contemplated hereby (other than such consents as shall have been obtained at or prior to the Closing).

      6.4   Litigation. There is no litigation, suit, proceeding, action, claim or investigation, at law or in equity, pending, or to the best knowledge of the Buyer, threatened against, or affecting in any way, the Buyer's ability to perform its obligations as contemplated by this Agreement.

      6.5   The Equity Interest. The Equity Interest has been duly authorized and issued in accordance with the terms hereof and the Operating Agreement.

7.   FURTHER AGREEMENTS OF THE PARTIES.

      7.1   Operation of the Business. From and after the Balance Sheet Date until the Closing Date, except to the extent contemplated by this Agreement or otherwise consented to in writing by the Buyer, the Seller shall have continued to operate its Business in substantially the same manner as presently conducted and only in the ordinary and usual course and substantially consistent with past practice and in substantial compliance with (i) all laws and (ii) all leases, contracts, commitments and other agreements, and all licenses, permits, and other instruments, relating to the operation of the Business, and will use reasonable efforts to preserve intact its present business organization and to keep available the services of all employees, representatives and agents. The Seller and each of the Shareholders shall have continued to use its, his or her reasonable efforts, consistent with past practices, to promote the Business and to maintain the goodwill and reputation associated with the Business, and shall not take or omit to take any action which causes, or which is likely to cause, any material deterioration of the Business or the Seller's relationships with material suppliers or customers. Without limiting the generality of the foregoing, (a) the Seller will have maintained all of its equipment in substantially the same condition and repair as such equipment was maintained prior to the Balance Sheet Date, ordinary wear and tear excepted; (b) the Seller shall not have sold, transferred, pledged, leased or otherwise disposed of any of the Assets, other than in the ordinary course of business; (c) the Seller shall not have amended, terminated or waived any material right in respect of the Assets or the Business, or do any act, or omit to do any act, which will cause a breach of any material contract, agreement, commitment or obligation by it; (d) the Seller shall have maintained its books, accounts and records in accordance with good business practice and generally accepted accounting principles consistently applied; (e) the Seller shall not have engaged in any activities or transactions outside the ordinary course of business; (f) the Seller shall not have declared or paid any dividend or made any other distribution or payment of any kind in cash or property to the Shareholder or other affiliates; and (g) the Seller shall not have increased any existing employee benefits, established any new employee benefit plans or amended or modified any existing Employee Plans, or otherwise incurred any obligation or liability under any employee plan materially different in nature or amount from obligations or liabilities incurred in connection with the Employee Plans.

      7.2   Consents; Assignment of Agreements. Seller shall obtain, at the earliest practicable date, all consents and approvals of third parties (whether or not listed on Schedule 4.4) which are necessary or desirable for the consummation of the transactions contemplated hereby (including, without limitation, the valid and binding transfer of the Assets to Buyer) (the "Consents"). The Consents shall be written instruments whose form and substance are reasonably satisfactory to Buyer. The Consents shall not, without Buyer's express consent, impose any obligations on Buyer or create any conditions adverse to Buyer, other than the conditions or obligations specified in this Agreement.

7.3   No Discussions. The Seller shall not enter into any substantive negotiations or discussions with any third party with respect to the sale or lease of the Assets or the Business, or the sale of any capital stock of the Seller, or any other merger, acquisition, partnership, joint venture or other business combination until the earlier to occur of the (a) Closing Date or (b) the termination of this Agreement.

7.4   Employee Matters. The Seller shall permit the Buyer to contact and make arrangements with the Seller's employees for the purpose of assuring their employment by the Buyer after the Closing and for the purpose of ensuring the continuity of the Business, and the Seller agrees not to discourage any such employees from being employed by or consulting with the Buyer. Nothing herein shall obligate the Buyer to employ or otherwise be responsible for any of the Seller's employees (other than the persons with whom the Buyer has entered or will enter into an employee agreement in accordance with Section 8.2 hereof) or pay any employee any compensation or confer any benefit earned or accrued prior to the Closing Date, except as set forth in Schedule 4.22(d).

7.5   Notice Regarding Changes. The Seller shall promptly notify the Buyer in writing of any change in facts and circumstances that could render any of the representations and warranties made herein by the Seller materially inaccurate or misleading.

7.6   Furnishing of Information. The Seller will allow Buyer to make a complete examination and analysis of the Business, Assets and records, financial or otherwise, of the Seller. In connection with the foregoing review, Seller agrees that it shall furnish to the Buyer and Buyer's representatives all such information concerning the Seller's Business, Assets, operations, properties or affairs as may be reasonably requested.

7.7   Notification to Customers. At the Buyer's request and in a form approved by the Buyer, the Seller agrees to notify all customers of the Business identified by Buyer and all customers of the Business during the year preceding the Closing as identified by Buyer, either separately or jointly with the Buyer, of the Buyer's purchase of the Business and Assets hereunder and that all further communications or requests by such customers with respect to the Business and Assets shall be directed to the Buyer. Without limiting the foregoing, promptly following the Closing, the Seller shall send a letter, in a form approved by the Buyer, to each debtor with respect to the notes, accounts or other receivables included in the Assets directing that all payments on account of such receivables made after the Closing shall be made to the Buyer.

7.8   Collection of Receivables. The Seller agrees that it will reasonably cooperate with the Buyer in collecting the notes, accounts and other receivables included in the Assets from any customers and will immediately deliver to the Buyer the amount paid on any and all receivables it collects after the Closing Date in connection with the Business, less out-of-pocket expenses incurred by Seller at the request of Buyer.

7.9 Brokers and Agents. Buyer, on the one hand, and the Seller, on the other hand, agree to indemnify and hold the other harmless from and against all fees, expenses, commissions and costs due and owing to any other broker, agent or finder on account of or in any way resulting from any contract or understanding existing between the indemnifying party and such person.

8. CONDITIONS PRECEDENT TO CLOSING.

8.1 Conditions Precedent to the Obligations of Seller. Seller's and Shareholders' obligations to consummate the transactions contemplated by this Agreement shall be subject to the fulfillment, at or prior to Closing, of each of the following conditions (any or all of which may be waived in writing, in whole or in part, by the Seller and the Shareholders):

(a) The Buyer shall have performed and complied in all material respects with each obligation and covenant required by this Agreement to be performed or complied with by them prior to or at the Closing.

(b) The representations and warranties of the Buyer contained herein shall be true and correct in all material respects at and as of the Closing Date as if made at and as of such time.

(c) Buyer shall have delivered to the Seller the items set forth in Section 3.2(b) of this Agreement.

(d) No action, suit or proceeding by any person shall have been commenced and still be pending, no investigation by any governmental or regulatory authority shall have been commenced and still be pending, and no action, suit or proceeding by any person shall have been threatened against the Buyer, the Seller or the Shareholders, (i) seeking to restrain, prevent or change the transactions contemplated hereby or questioning the validity or legality of any such transactions, or (ii) which if resolved adversely to any party, would materially and adversely affect the business or condition, financial or otherwise, of the Buyer or the Seller.

(e) All proceedings to be taken by the Buyer in connection with the transactions contemplated hereby and all documents incident thereto shall be reasonably satisfactory in form and substance to the Seller and its counsel, and the Seller and said counsel shall have received all such counterpart originals or certified or other copies of such documents as it or they may reasonably request.

(f) Buyer shall have delivered to the Seller the Pledge Agreement together with the marketable securities and other collateral securing the Note.

(g) Buyer shall have delivered to the Seller all such other certificates and documents as the Seller and its counsel shall have reasonably requested.

8.2 <u>Conditions Precedent to the Obligations of the Buyer</u>. The obligation of the Buyer to consummate the transactions contemplated by this Agreement shall be subject to the fulfillment, at or prior to Closing, of each of the following conditions precedent (any or all of which may be waived in writing, in whole or in part, by the Buyer):

(a) The Seller shall have performed and complied in all material respects with each obligation and covenant required by this Agreement to be performed or to be complied with by it on or prior to the Closing Date.

(b) The representations and warranties of the Seller and the Shareholders contained herein or in any Schedule attached hereto shall be true and correct in all material respects at and as of the Closing Date as if made at and as of such time.

(c) The Seller and the Shareholders shall have delivered or caused delivery of the items set forth in <u>Section 3.2(a)</u> hereof.

(d) Except as otherwise set forth in this Agreement, the Buyer shall have received written evidence, in form and substance satisfactory to it, that all material consents, waivers, authorizations and approvals of, or filing with or notices to, governmental entities and third parties required in order that the transactions contemplated hereby be consummated have been obtained or made.

(e) There shall not have occurred since the Balance Sheet Date any material damage or loss by theft, casualty or otherwise, whether or not insured against by the Seller or the Shareholders, of all or any material portion of the Assets, or any material adverse change in or interference with the Business or the properties, assets, condition (financial or otherwise) or prospects of the Seller.

(f) Buyer shall have entered into an employment agreement with Jane C. Doe and John F. Doe, in substantially the forms attached hereto as Exhibit G and Exhibit H, respectively.

(g) No action, suit or proceeding by any person shall have been commenced and still be pending, no investigations by any governmental or regulatory authority shall have been commenced and still be pending, and no action, suit or proceeding by any person shall have been threatened against the Buyer, the Seller or the Shareholders, (i) seeking to restrain, prevent or change the transactions contemplated hereby or questioning the validity or legality of any such transactions, or (ii) which if resolved adversely to any party, would materially and adversely affect the business or condition, financial or otherwise, of the Buyer, or the Seller.

(h)   All proceedings to be taken by the Seller and the Shareholders in connection with the transactions contemplated hereby and all documents incident thereto shall be reasonably satisfactory in form and substance to the Buyer and its counsel, and the Buyer and said counsel shall have received all such counterpart originals or certified or other copies of such documents as it or they may reasonably request.

(i)   Seller shall have delivered to the Buyer all such other certificates and documents as the Buyer or its counsel shall have reasonably requested.

9.   INDEMNIFICATION; SURVIVAL OF REPRESENTATIONS AND WARRANTIES.

9.1   Indemnification by Seller and Shareholders. Each of the Sellers and the Shareholders, jointly and severally, covenants and agrees to indemnify, defend, protect and hold harmless the Buyer and any of the Buyer's officers, directors, stockholders, representatives, affiliates, assigns, successors in interest, and current and former employees, each only in their respective capacities as such (collectively, the "Buyer Indemnified Parties"), from, against and in respect of:

(a)   any and all liabilities, claims, losses, damages, punitive damages, causes of action, lawsuits, administrative proceedings, demands, judgments, settlement payments, penalties, and costs and expenses (including, without limitation, reasonable attorneys' fees, travel expenses, expert witness fees and disbursements of every kind, nature and description) (collectively, "Damages"), suffered, sustained, incurred or paid by Buyer or any other Buyer Indemnified Party in connection with, resulting from or arising out of, either directly or indirectly:

(i)   any misrepresentation or breach of any warranty of the Seller or any Shareholder set forth in this Agreement or any Schedule or certificate delivered by or on behalf of the Seller or any Shareholder in connection herewith; or

(ii)   any non-fulfillment of any covenant or agreement on the part of the Seller or any Shareholder set forth in this Agreement; or

(iii)   the Business, operations or Assets of the Seller prior to the Closing Date or the actions or omissions of the Seller's directors, officers, shareholders, employees, or agents prior to the Closing Date (except with respect to the Assumed Liabilities); or

(iv)   the Excluded Liabilities.

(b)   any and all Damages incident to any of the foregoing or to the enforcement of this Section 9.1.

9.2   Limitation and Expiration. The indemnification obligations under this Section 9.2 or in any other certificate or writing furnished in connection with the transactions contemplated hereby shall terminate on the later of (a) the date that is six (6) months after the expiration of the longest applicable federal or state statute of limitation (including extensions thereof); or (b) if there is no applicable statute of limitation, four (4) years after the Closing Date; or (c) the final resolution of a claim or demand (a "Claim") as of the relevant dates described above in this Section.

9.3   Indemnification by Buyer. The Buyer covenants and agrees to indemnify, defend, protect and hold harmless the Shareholders, the Seller and any of the Seller's officers, directors, stockholders, representatives, affiliates, assigns, successors in interest, and current and former employees, each only in their respective capacities as such (collectively, the "Seller Indemnified Parties"), from, against and in respect of:

(a)   any and all Damages sustained, incurred or paid by Seller or any other Seller Indemnified Party in connection with, resulting from or arising out of, either directly or indirectly:

(i)   any breach of any warranty of the Buyer set forth in this Agreement or any Schedule or certificate delivered by or on behalf of the Buyer in connection herewith; or

(ii)   any non-fulfillment of any covenant or agreement on the part of the Buyer set forth in this Agreement; or

(iii)   the ownership of the purchased Assets or the operation of the Business by the Buyer following the Closing Date.

(b)   any and all Damages incident to any of the foregoing or to the enforcement of this Section 9.3.

9.4   Notice Procedures; Claims. The obligations and liabilities of the parties under this Section with respect to, relating to, caused (in whole or in part) by or arising out of claims of third parties (individually, a "Third-Party Claim" and collectively, "Third-Party Claims") shall be subject to the following conditions:

(a)   The party entitled to be indemnified hereunder (the "Indemnified Party") shall give the party obligated to provide the indemnity (the "Indemnifying Party") prompt notice of any Third-Party Claim (the "Claim Notice"); provided that the failure to give such Claim Notice shall not affect the liability of the Indemnifying Party under this Agreement unless the failure materially and adversely affects the ability of the Indemnifying Party to defend the Third-Party Claim. If the Indemnifying Party promptly acknowledges in writing its obligation to indemnify in accordance with the terms and subject to the limitations of such party's obligation to indemnify contained in this Agreement with respect to that claim, the Indemnifying Party shall have a reasonable time to assume the defense of the Third-Party Claim at its expense and with counsel of its choosing, which counsel shall be reasonably satisfactory to the Indemnified Party. Any Claim Notice shall identify, to the extent known to the Indemnified Party, the basis for the Third-Party Claim, the facts giving rise to the Third-Party Claim, and the estimated amount of the Third-Party Claim (which estimate shall not be conclusive of the final amount of such claim or demand). The Indemnified Party shall make available to the Indemnifying Party copies of all relevant documents and records in its possession.

(b)   If the Indemnifying Party, within a reasonable time after receipt of such Claim Notice, fails to assume the defense of any Third-Party Claim in accordance with Section 9.4(a), the Indemnified Party shall (upon further notice to the Indemnifying Party) have the right to undertake the defense, compromise or settlement of the Third-Party Claim, at the expense and for the account and risk of the Indemnifying Party.

(c)   Anything in this Section 9.4 to the contrary notwithstanding, (i) the Indemnifying Party shall not without the written consent of the Indemnified Party, settle or compromise any Third-Party Claim or consent to the entry of judgment which does not include as an unconditional term thereof the giving by the claimant or the plaintiff to the Indemnified Party of an unconditional release from all liability in respect of the Third-Party Claim; (ii) if such Third-Party Claim involves an issue or matter which the Indemnified Party believes could have a materially adverse effect on the Indemnified Party's business, operations, assets, properties or prospects of its business, the Indemnified Party shall have the right to control the defense or settlement of any such claim or demand, at the expense of the Indemnified Party without contribution from the Indemnifying Party; and (iii) the Indemnified Party shall have the right to employ its own counsel to defend any claim at the Indemnifying Party's expense if (x) the employment of such counsel by the Indemnified Party has been authorized by the Indemnifying Party, or (y) counsel selected by the Indemnifying Party shall have reasonably concluded that there may be a conflict of interest between the Indemnifying Party and the Indemnified Party in the conduct of the defense of such action, or (z) the Indemnifying Party shall not have employed counsel to assume the defense of such claim in accordance with Section 9.4(a).

(d)   In the event that the Indemnified Party should have a claim against the Indemnifying Party hereunder which does not involve a claim or demand being asserted against or sought to be collected from it by a third party, the Indemnified Party shall promptly send a Claim Notice with respect to such claim to the Indemnifying Party. If the Indemnifying Party does not notify the Indemnified Party within thirty (30) calendar days that it disputes such claim, the amount of such claim shall be conclusively deemed a liability of the Indemnifying Party hereunder.

(e)   Nothing herein shall be deemed to prevent any Indemnified Party from making a claim hereunder for potential or contingent claims or demands, provided that (i) the Claim Notice sets forth (A) the specific basis for any such potential or contingent claim or demand and (B) the estimated amount thereof (to the extent then feasible); and (ii) the Indemnified Party has reasonable grounds to believe that such a claim or demand will be made.

9.5   Survival of Representations, Warranties and Covenants. All representations, warranties and covenants made by the Seller, the Shareholders, and the Buyer in or pursuant to this Agreement or in any document delivered pursuant hereto shall be deemed to have been made on the date of this Agreement (except as otherwise provided herein) and, if a Closing occurs, as of the Closing Date. The representations of the Seller and the Shareholders will survive the Closing and remain in effect until, and will expire upon, the termination of the relevant indemnification obligation as provided in Section 9.2. The representations of Buyer will survive and remain in effect until and will expire upon, the later of the third anniversary of the Closing Date or the satisfaction in full of any payment obligation pursuant to the Promissory Note.

9.6   Indemnification Trigger. Notwithstanding the provisions of Section 9.1 or 9.3 above, neither Seller nor Buyer shall be liable to the other for any indemnification under this Section 9.6 unless and until the aggregate amount of Damages due to an Indemnified Party exceeds Two Hundred Thousand Dollars ($200,000) (the "Trigger Amount"). Once the Trigger Amount has been exceeded, the Indemnified Party shall be entitled to indemnification for all Damages, including the amount up to the Trigger Amount and any amount in excess thereof. The foregoing trigger provision shall not apply, however, with respect to any Damages suffered, sustained, incurred or paid by an Indemnified Party related to Taxes or assessments by any governmental authority, or with respect to any claim of actual fraud or intentional misrepresentation relating to a breach of any representation or warranty in this Agreement.

9.7   Remedies Cumulative. The remedies set forth in this Section 9.7 are cumulative and shall not be construed to restrict or otherwise affect any other remedies that may be available to the Indemnified Parties under any other agreement or pursuant to statutory or common law.

10.   POST-CLOSING MATTERS.

10.1   Transition Services. The Seller agrees to provide reasonable assistance to the Buyer in connection with the transition of the Business to the Buyer. The Shareholders will provide assistance to Buyer in accordance with their respective Employment Agreements.

10.2   Further Assurances. The Seller and each of the Shareholders hereby covenants and agrees to (a) make, execute and deliver to the Buyer any and all powers of attorney and other authority which the Seller may lawfully make, execute and deliver, in addition to any such powers and authorities as are contained herein, which may reasonably be or become necessary, proper or convenient to enable the Buyer to reduce to possession, collect, enforce, own or enjoy any and all rights and benefits in, to, with respect to, or in connection with, the Assets, or any part or portion thereof; and (b) upon the Buyer's request, to take, in the Seller's name, any and all steps and to do any and all things which may be or become lawful and reasonably necessary, proper, convenient or desirable to enable the Buyer to reduce to possession, collect, enforce, own and enjoy any and all rights and benefits in, to, with respect to, or in connection with, the Assets, and each and every part and portion thereof. The Seller and each of the Shareholders also covenants and agrees with the Buyer, its successors and assigns, that the Seller and each of the Shareholders will do, execute, acknowledge and deliver, or cause to be done, executed, acknowledged and delivered, any and all such further reasonable acts, instruments, papers and documents as may be necessary to carry out and effectuate the intent and purposes of this Agreement. From and after the Closing Date, Seller will promptly refer all inquiries with respect to ownership of the Assets or the Business to Buyer.

10.3   <u>Payment of Liabilities; Discharge of Liens</u>. The Seller shall satisfy and discharge as the same shall become due, all of Seller's liabilities, obligations, debts and commitments including but not limited to Tax liabilities, in accordance with this Agreement, other than the Assumed Liabilities.

10.4   <u>Transfer of Permits; Additional Consents</u>. Subsequent to the Closing, Seller shall use its reasonable efforts to effectively transfer to Buyer all Permits which were not so transferred at or prior to the Closing and to obtain all approvals, consents and authorizations with respect to such transfers. In addition, subsequent to the Closing, to the extent requested by Buyer, Seller shall use its reasonable efforts to obtain any required consents of the other parties to the Scheduled Contracts included in the Assets to the assignment thereof to the Buyer which were not obtained at or prior to the Closing.

10.5   <u>Inspection of Documents, Books and Records; Financial Reports</u>. Subsequent to the Closing, Buyer shall make available for inspection by Seller or its authorized representatives during regular business hours and upon reasonable notice, any original documents conveyed to Buyer under this Agreement. Upon reasonable notice to the Buyer, for five years from the Closing Date forward, Seller or its representatives shall be entitled, at Seller's expense, to audit, copy, review and inspect the Buyer's books and records at the Buyer's offices during reasonable business hours. For so long as any payment obligation is outstanding under this Agreement, Buyer shall make available to Seller and its representatives, copies of Buyer's annual corporate tax returns and any quarterly financial statements or reports prepared or compiled by or for Buyer.

10.6   <u>Acceleration of Notes</u>. In the event that Buyer shall subsequently sell, convey, transfer or assign assets of the Buyer, to a non-affiliated third party (other than as collateral under a lien or security arrangement), the value of which is greater than 25 percent of the total assets of the Buyer at the time of the transfer, all amounts of principal and interest then outstanding under both Notes shall become immediately due and payable.

11.   RISK OF LOSS. Prior to the Closing, the risk of loss (including damage and/or destruction) of all of the Seller's property and assets, including without limitation the Assets, shall remain with the Seller, and the legal doctrine known as the "Doctrine of Equitable Conversion" shall not be applicable to this Agreement or to any of the transactions contemplated hereby.

12.   MISCELLANEOUS.

12.1   Entire Agreement. This Agreement, and the Exhibits and Schedules to this Agreement constitute the entire agreement between the parties hereto with respect to the subject matter hereof and supersede all prior negotiations, agreements, arrangements and understandings, whether oral or written, among the parties hereto with respect to such subject matter, (including, without limitation, the letter of intent dated _____, 20_____, as amended, between the Seller and the Buyer).

12.2   No Third-Party Beneficiary. Nothing expressed or implied in this Agreement is intended, or shall be construed, to confer upon or give any person, firm, corporation, partnership, association or other entity, other than the parties hereto and their respective successors and assigns, any rights or remedies under or by reason of this Agreement.

12.3   Amendment. This Agreement may not be amended or modified in any respect, except by the mutual written agreement of the parties hereto.

12.4   Waivers and Remedies. The waiver by any of the parties hereto of any other party's prompt and complete performance, or breach or violation, of any provision of this Agreement shall not operate nor be construed as a waiver of any subsequent breach or violation, and the failure by any of the parties hereto to exercise any right or remedy which it may possess hereunder shall not operate nor be construed as a bar to the exercise of such right or remedy by such party upon the occurrence of any subsequent breach or violation.

12.5   Severability. If any term, provision, covenant or restriction of this Agreement (or the application thereof to any specific persons or circumstances) should be held by an administrative agency or court of competent jurisdiction to be invalid, void or unenforceable, such term, provision, covenant or restriction shall be modified to the minimum extent necessary in order to render it enforceable within such jurisdiction, consistent with the expressed objectives of the parties hereto. Further, the remainder of this Agreement (and the application of such term, provision, covenant or restriction to any other persons or circumstances) shall not be affected thereby, but rather shall be enforced to the greatest extent permitted by law.

12.6   Descriptive Headings. Descriptive headings contained herein are for convenience only and shall not control or affect the meaning or construction of any provision of this Agreement.

12.7   Counterparts. This Agreement may be executed in any number of counterparts and by the separate parties hereto in separate counterparts, each of which shall be deemed to be one and the same instrument.

12.8 <u>Notices</u>. All notices, consents, requests, instructions, approvals and other communications provided for herein and all legal processes in regard hereto shall be in writing and shall be deemed to have been duly given (a) when delivered by hand; (b) when received by facsimile transmission, with printed confirmation of transmission and verbal (telephonic) confirmation of receipt; (c) one day after being sent by a nationally-recognized overnight express service; or (d) five (5) days after being deposited in the United States mail, by registered or certified mail, return receipt requested, postage prepaid, as follows:

If to the Seller: Target Co., Inc.
16602 Side Avenue
Anytown, USA 01206
Attn: President

If to the Buyer: Growth Co. Corp.
12345 Main Street
Anytown, USA 01234
Attn: Chief Executive Officer

or to such other address as any party hereto may from time to time designate in writing delivered in a like manner.

12.9 <u>Successors and Assigns</u>. This Agreement shall be binding upon and shall inure to the benefit of the parties hereto and their respective successors and assigns. None of the parties hereto shall assign any of its rights or obligations hereunder except with the express written consent of the other parties hereto.

12.10 <u>Applicable Law</u>. This Agreement shall be governed by, and shall be construed, interpreted and enforced in accordance with, the internal laws of the State of Maryland.

12.11 <u>Expenses</u>. Each of the parties hereto agrees to pay all of the respective expenses incurred by it in connection with the negotiation, preparation, execution, delivery and performance of this Agreement and the consummation of the transactions contemplated hereby.

12.12 <u>Confidentiality</u>. Except to the extent required for any party to obtain any approvals or consents required pursuant to the terms hereof, no party hereto shall divulge the existence of the terms of this Agreement or the transactions contemplated hereby without the prior written approval of all of the parties hereto, except and as to the extent (a) obligated by law or (b) necessary for such party to defend or prosecute any litigation in connection with the transactions contemplated hereby.

12.13 <u>Attorneys' Fees</u>. In the event any suit or other legal proceeding is brought for the enforcement of any of the provisions of this Agreement, the parties hereto agree that the prevailing party or parties shall be entitled to recover from the other party or parties upon final judgment on the merits reasonable attorneys' fees and expenses, including attorneys' fees and expenses for any appeal, and costs incurred in bringing such suit or proceeding.

IN WITNESS WHEREOF, the parties have executed and delivered this Agreement on the date first above written.

GROWTH CO. CORP.

By:_____, Chief Executive Officer

TARGET CO., INC.

By:_____, Chief Executive Officer

UNDERSTANDING INTELLECTUAL PROPERTY CONSIDERATIONS IN MERGERS AND ACQUISITIONS

As financial professionals doing business in the new economy, you should not be surprised that there is an increasing focus on the intangible assets of the seller's business. The amount and quality of time and attention that must be devoted to a thorough examination of the seller's brands, customer relationships, knowledge, workers, goodwill, proprietary formulae, strategic alliances, cross-licensing arrangements, and other intangibles present complex valuation challenges and demand an understanding of the intellectual property laws that protect these key assets. To understand balance sheets of companies that operate in this new environment, you must first understand the different types of intellectual property and how each type is protected.

PATENTS

A patent grants an inventor the right to exclude others from making, using, selling (or offering to sell), or importing his or her invention throughout the United States for a limited period of time. To obtain a patent, the inventor would submit an application to the U.S. Patent and Trademark Office (USPTO).

The first step in determining whether to protect a new product or invention with a patent is to understand the costs and benefits of patent protection. The patent application and registration process generally lasts three to five years and often involves costly legal and consulting fees. As a result, it is crucial that you first determine whether the benefits of being able to exclude others from manufacturing, distributing or exploiting the subject matter outweigh the high costs of prosecuting and protecting the patent. You should also consider whether there are adequate alternatives for protecting the invention. Is adequate protection available under state trade secret laws? To what extent does the business plan exploit technology before the patent is issued? For example, attorneys' fees alone in an average patent infringement civil suit could easily cost hundreds of thousands of dollars.

The statutory requirement that the application must be filed within one year of the public use or publication of the invention applies significant limitations on the level of marketing, research, or testing.

Registration is a complicated process. The actual patent application is made up of several distinct parts, including a clear description and written drawings of the invention. The review and ultimate determination of the patentability of the invention will depend on the company's ability to demonstrate to the examiner that the statutory requirements have been satisfied.

Once the patent has been issued, the seller must embark on an aggressive patent protection program. This entails (a) the use of proper notices and labeling of the registered patent for the product; (b) monitoring the developments in the industry; (c) policing the activities of licensees, employees, and others who came into contact with the patented machine or technology; (d) exploiting the marketplace that has been created by the patented product; and (e) aggressively pursuing known or suspected infringers of the patent.

Although the costs of patent litigation may be high, the rewards of stopping an infringer are also very worthwhile. Damages and equitable remedies (such as an injunction or an accounting for profits) are available, and federal patent law allows a court to triple the damages for extraordinary cases (also known as treble damages).

TRADEMARKS

A *trademark* for the purposes of this article refers to any word, name, symbol or device used to indicate the origin, quality, and ownership of products and services. To be afforded federal protection, the trademark must be either actually used in interstate commerce, or the seller must have a bona fide intention to use the mark. Not all words and symbols are eligible for trademark protection. A properly selected, registered and protected trademark can be of great utility to a growing company that is fighting to establish, maintain and expand its market share. There is perhaps no better way to maintain a strong position in the marketplace than to build goodwill and consumer recognition in the identity selected for products and services that can be protected under federal and state trademark laws.

One of the most important benefits to be gained from federal registration is that it serves as constructive notice to the rest of the country that the trademark belongs to the registrant. This becomes an important right if it is later discovered that a remote company in a different geographic market subsequently decides to sell competing products under the registrant's marks, damaging goodwill and creating confusion when the registrant enters that local market. So long as a registration predates another's use of the mark, the registrant has the right to demand that they discontinue use of the mark as well as the right to institute a civil action for damages and even lost profits. Before registering a name, a trademark search should be conducted to determine whether a competitor already has secured rights in this trade name or any similar name for the same or a related type of product. Because common law trademark rights are grounded in actual and prior use, even federal registration does not give a registrant a right to stop others who have used the same mark in their local markets *prior* to the registrant's application.

Under the current law, a company may file an application for registration of a trademark, based on actual use *or* upon a "bona fide intention" to use the mark in interstate commerce (known as an "intent-to-use" filing). This process allows the applicant to conduct some market research and further investigation, without the need to actually put the mark into the stream of commerce.

Regardless of whether the filing is made under the *actual use* or *intent to use* provisions, an application must be prepared and filed in the classification that is appropriate for the goods and services offered. A trademark examiner will then review the application to determine if it meets the statutory requirements and whether similar trademarks have already been registered in the same or similar lines of business. The seller or its attorney must respond to all (if any) of the concerns of the examiner. This process continues until the application is either finally refused or recommended by the examiner for publication in the *Official Gazette* (which serves as notice to the general public). Anyone who believes that they would be injured by registration may file a Notice of Opposition within 30 days of the publication date. If the parties fail to resolve any differences there will be a hearing before the Trademark Trial and Appeal Board (TTAB). The TTAB is also the appropriate body to appeal a final refusal of the examiner. Registration is effective for 10 years but may be renewed for additional 10-year terms thereafter so long as it is still in actual use in interstate commerce. The registration may, however, be cancelled after six years unless an affidavit of continued use is filed with the USPTO that demonstrates that the registrant has not abandoned the trademark.

Once your trademark has been registered with the USPTO, the seller will enjoy several commercial and legal benefits which include: (a) the right to protect against businesses in the future from using its marks; (b) the right to bring legal action in federal court for trademark infringement; (c) recovery of profits, damages, and costs in a federal court infringement action and the possibility of treble damages and attorneys' fees; (d) the right to deposit the registration with the U.S. Department of Customs in order to stop the importation of goods bearing an infringing mark; and (e) a basis for filing trademark applications in foreign countries.

A trademark that is an actual use in commerce but that does not qualify for registration on the Principal Register for one or more reasons (i.e., merely descriptive or a surname) may be registered with the USPTO on the Supplemental Register. Registration on the Supplemental Register does not provide the trademark the same level of protection afforded by registration on the Principal Register. Registration on the Supplemental Register does allow the owner of the trademark to put the world on notice of his or her use and rights to the mark. Further, registration of a descriptive trademark on the Supplemental Register may be advantageous for a period of time while the mark's use is increased to the point where it becomes so substantial as to cause the trademark to acquire "secondary meaning." It is at this time that the mark may qualify for registration on the Principal Register. It may be advantageous for a start-up company to take advantage of registration on the Supplemental Register, if registration is denied on the Principal Register until its products or services are sold, and the mark, through increased use, gains secondary meaning.

When the battle with the USPTO is finally over, a new battle against the rest of the world begins. Once the mark is registered, the seller must develop an active trademark protection program designed to educate company staff, consultants, distributors, suppliers and all others that may come in contact with the company's marks as to proper usage and protection of the marks. As with trade secret laws, the courts will usually help only those who have attempted to help themselves. A company that tolerates misuse of its marks by the public and/or fails to enforce quality control standards in any licensing of the mark may lose its trademark rights, and, therefore, one of its most valuable weapons in the war for market share.

A well-managed trademark protection program begins with a formal compliance manual drafted with the assistance of trademark counsel and the company's advertising agency. The compliance manual should contain detailed guidelines for proper trademark usage, grammar and quality. In addition to a compliance manual, strategies should be developed to monitor competitors and other third parties to prevent improper usage or potential infringement of the mark. If an infringing use is discovered by a clipping service, company field representative, trade association, or supplier, then the owner of the mark must be vigilant in protection of the mark. This will require working closely with trademark counsel to ensure that all potential infringers receive letters demanding that such practices be immediately discontinued and infringing materials destroyed. As much evidence as possible should be gathered on each potential infringer and accurate files kept in the event that trademark infringement litigation is necessary to settle the dispute. The registrant considering litigation should carefully weigh the costs and likely result of the suit against the potential loss of goodwill and market share. It may be wiser to allocate those funds towards advertising rather than towards legal fees, especially if the likelihood of winning is remote.

Trademark rights are often the most valuable asset of an emerging growth company in today's competitive marketplace. The goodwill and consumer recognition that trademarks and service marks represent have tremendous economic value and are, therefore, usually worth the effort and expense to properly register and protect them. This will also require a commitment by management to implement and support a strict trademark compliance program, which should include usage guidelines for all departments inside the company, as well as for suppliers, licensees, service providers and distributors. Clipping services, semiannual trademark searches, media awareness programs, designation of in-house compliance officers, warning letters to infringers and diluters, and even litigation are all part of an aggressive trademark protection program.

COPYRIGHTS

A copyright is a form of protection available to the author of original "literary, dramatic, musical, artistic, graphical, sculptural, architectural and certain other intellectual works which are fixed in any tangible medium of expression." The owner of a copyright generally has the exclusive right to do or authorize others to do the following: *reproduce* the copyrighted work; *prepare derivative* works; *distribute and transmit* copies of the work; and *perform or display* the copyrighted work, typically for the life of the author, plus 75 years.

A question may arise as to authorship of a work when it was prepared by an employee. The Copyright Act defines a "work for hire" as being either an employee preparing a work within the scope of his or her employment or a work specially ordered or commissioned if the parties expressly agree in a signed written instrument that the work shall be owned by a party other than the author as a work for hire.

Typically the author of the work is the owner of the copyright. Under the doctrine of "work made for hire," works developed by an employee are considered to be works owned by the employer, but, under a recent major Supreme Court case, this presumption does not necessarily apply to freelance workers or independent contractors *unless* there is a written agreement stating that it is the clear intent of the parties that the copyright to the work will belong to the "commissioning party" and not the "creating party."

The author of a work protectable by copyright should, whenever possible, use a notice of copyright that puts the world on notice that the author claims the work as a copyright. The prescribed notice consists of: (a) © or the word "copyright;" (b) the year of first publication of the work; and (c) the name of the copyright owner. However, the lack of copyright notices does not necessarily mean that the author does not intend to protect its rights to the work.

Pursuant to the Copyright Act of 1976, copyright protection arises *as soon as the work is created and fixed in a tangible medium* of expression. The work need not be registered prior to its publication; however, registration is necessary if the author wants to take advantage of the many benefits and protections offered under the Copyright Act, which includes the right to sue for infringement and the ability to obtain damages and to stop others from using the work. Therefore, materials are protected, *without registration,* provided they contain the required statutory notice of copyright. Prior to registration, it is advisable to examine whether registration would compromise the confidentiality of any trade secrets which may be contained in the work. For example, the contents of a new marketing brochure is a natural candidate for copyright registration; however, the contents of a confidential operations manual should not be registered due to its proprietary contents.

To be able to enforce rights in court for copyright infringement, the author must register and deposit copies of the work in the Library of Congress depository. The Copyright Office will then examine the application for accuracy and determine that the work submitted is copyrightable subject matter. The Copyright Office, unlike the Patent and Trademark Office, will not compare the works to those already registered, and does not conduct interference or opposition proceedings. The copyright laws do provide remedies for private civil actions. Remedies for copyright infringement include injunctions against unauthorized use, attorneys' fees, damages for lost profits, and certain statutory damages. These enforcement rights and remedies must be weighed, however, against the fact that once a written work is registered, it may be viewed by the public, including competitors. Thus, it may make more sense to protect proprietary materials as trade secrets, rather than expose them to the public through the Library of Congress.

The federal copyright laws make willful copyright infringement for commercial profit a crime. The court is required to order a fine of not more than $10,000, or imprisonment not exceeding one year, or both, as well as seizure, forfeiture, and destruction or other disposition of all infringing reproductions and all equipment used in their manufacture.

TRADE SECRETS

A trade secret may consist of any type of information, including a formula, pattern, compilation, program, device, method, technique or process that derives independent economic value from not being generally known to other persons who can obtain economic value from its disclosure or use. A company uses its trade secrets to provide it with an advantage over competitors, and, therefore, a trade secret must be treated by its owner as confidential and proprietary. The scope of protection available for trade secrets may be defined by a particular contract or fiduciary relationship as well as by state statutes and court decisions. Unlike other forms of intellectual property protection, there are no federal civil statutes protecting trade secrets. Trade secrets are protected by state law.

Owners of small and growing companies whose success is due in part to the competitive advantage it enjoys by virtue of some confidential formula, method, design, or other type of proprietary know-how, generally understand the importance of protecting trade secrets against unauthorized disclosure or use by a current or former employee, licensee, supplier or competitor.

Disclosure can cause severe and irreparable damage, especially to a smaller company where trade secrets may be the company's single most valuable asset.

Courts have generally set forth three requirements for information to qualify for trade secret protection: (1) the information must have some commercial value, (2) the information must not be generally known or readily ascertainable by others, and (3) the owner of the information must take all reasonable steps under the circumstances to maintain its confidentiality and secrecy. Examples of trade secrets include business and strategic plans, research and testing data, customer lists, manufacturing processes, pricing methods, and marketing and distribution techniques. In order for a company to maintain the trade secret status of an asset, it must follow a reasonable and consistent program for ensuring that the confidentiality of the information is maintained.

Misappropriation refers to the wrongful taking of the seller's trade secrets by someone who had a duty not to take this information for his or her own competitive advantage. Therefore, in order to be able to bring an action for misappropriation, the seller must establish a legal duty owed by those who come in contact with the information not to disclose or use the information. The simplest way to create this duty is by agreement. The owner of a small or growing business should have a written employment agreement with each employee who may have access to the employer's trade secrets. The employment agreement should contain provisions regarding the nondisclosure of proprietary information as well as covenants of nonexploitation and noncompetition applicable both during and after the term of employment. These covenants will be upheld and enforced by a court if reasonable, consistent with industry norms, and not overly restrictive. The agreement should only be the beginning, however, of an ongoing program to make employees mindful of their continuing duty to protect the trade secrets of the employer. In some states, the unauthorized removal or use of trade secrets may also be a felony under criminal statutes.

Employment is not the only context in which this duty of nondisclosure might arise. An entrepreneur submitting proposals or business plans to prospective investors, lenders, licensees, franchisees, joint-venturers, lawyers, accountants, or other consultants should take steps to ensure confidentiality at the commencement of any such relationship where trade secrets may be disclosed in presentations, meetings and documents.

The most important and most immediate remedies available in any trade secret misappropriation case are the temporary restraining order and preliminary injunction. This remedy immediately restrains the unauthorized user from continuing to use or practice the trade secret, pending a hearing on the owner's charge of misappropriation. Prompt action is necessary to protect the trade secret from further unauthorized disclosure. If the case ever makes it to trial, the court's decision will address the terms of the injunction and may award damages and profits resulting from the wrongful misappropriation of the trade secret. However, the seller should be aware that there are certain risks to evaluate before instituting a trade secret suit. The company may face the risk that the trade secret at issue, or collateral trade secrets, may be disclosed during the course of the litigation. This is all the more reason why preventive and protective measures are a far more attractive alternative than litigation.

TRADE DRESS

Trade dress is a combination or arrangement of elements that comprises the interior and/or exterior design of a business, usually in the context of a retail or restaurant business. For example, trade dress can be symbols, designs, product packaging, labels and wrappers, exterior building features, interior designs, greeting cards, or uniforms that build brand awareness and loyalty with consumers. Trade dress is protected by federal and state trademark laws if it distinguishes the goods or services of one company from those of its competitors. Protectable trade dress consists of three elements: (1) a *combination* of features (used in the presentation, packaging or "dress" of goods or services); (2) which is *nonfunctional;* and (3) whose *distinctiveness* reveals to consumers the source of goods or services.

The best way to avoid trade dress infringement claims is *PREVENTION.* To prevent such claims, avoid copying competitors' trade dress, investigate competitors' potential trade dress rights, and consult a skilled trademark attorney. Also, it may be advisable to use disclaimers and to be more cautious when there is a potentially aggressive opponent.

SHOW-HOW AND KNOW-HOW

Certain types of intellectual property are treated as such primarily because some third party is willing to buy or license it from a company or individual who possesses a particular expertise. In such cases, *show-how* consists of training, technical support, and related educational services, whereas *know-how* usually takes the form of information that has been reduced to written rather than spoken form. Know-how and show-how usually arise in the context of a licensing agreement where the licensee is requesting support services in addition to the tangible technology or patent, which is the central subject matter of the agreement. To the extent that the know-how or show-how is confidential and proprietary, it will generally be governed by the law of trade secrets unless otherwise covered by a patent. To the extent that the know-how or show-how is nonproprietary and constitutes common knowledge, it will be governed by the terms and conditions of the agreement between the parties.

IDEAS AND CONCEPTS

As a general rule, the law of intellectual property seeks to protect and reward the creative firm, innovator or entrepreneur for their efforts by prohibiting misappropriation or infringement by competitors. It is, therefore, crucial that the legal considerations to protect these "crown jewels" are incorporated into the strategic marketing plan of any emerging business. If proper steps are not taken to protect these new products, services and operational techniques, then it will be extremely difficult to maintain and expand the company's share of the market, because others will be free to copy these ideas as if they were their own.

The proper protection and, where possible, registration of intellectual property is essential to building and sustaining a company's growth. The procedures and expenses that are necessary to protect these valuable *intangible assets* are crucial to the continued well-being of the company and its ability to continue to survive in a competitive marketplace.

THE DUE
DILIGENCE
PROCESS IN
MERGERS AND
ACQUISITIONS:
TREASURY'S ROLE

*Summary of a Presentation Made at the Association for Financial
Professionals Annual Conference in Philadelphia,
November 14, 2000*

By Daniel M. Perkins, Presenter
Managing Partner
Arthur Andersen Financial and Commodity Risk Consulting Practice

An understanding of the treasurer's role in the due diligence process of a
merger or acquisition will help provide the best analysis of the acquisition

target with the aim of preparing for eventual integration. It will also help you to organize and focus on your responsibilities throughout the integration process, which will pay off for all parties involved.

The most important thing to remember: The treasurer must be involved in the due diligence process. This isn't always the case. In fact, to be an essential part of the process, the treasurer often has to step up and want to be involved. At many companies, the due diligence is done by an investment bank or merger and acquisition staff specialists and the treasurer isn't involved.

With that in mind, what is it the treasurer and his or her people should be doing during this process? Why is their involvement so important to a successful merger or acquisition?

These checklists or rules include my own experiences and [those of] others who have gone through this process.

The Due Diligence Process

Keeping in mind that each transaction is very different and each company handles the due diligence process very differently, let's review how the process generally works.

A target is identified and management gives the process the go-ahead. Sometimes treasury is involved at this stage, sometimes not. But once announced, it is important to have a multifaceted task force involved in the due diligence. And that task force should include treasury. When I'm involved in these projects I insist on it because, as I've said, it is critical to success.

After the announcement, you have the investigation. Sometimes it is done by treasury, sometimes by an M&A group. From a treasury career perspective, the more you learn about this process the more helpful it will be in your career. After the investigation you have the findings and recommendations to proceed. A lot of times this is done at the board level, but keep the antennae up. You may not be involved in it from the beginning, but sooner or later you will be.

Team Approach

In terms of negotiation, the team approach is important. This is when treasury and other specialists, such as the legal and benefits departments, have to stand up and make sure they represent their departments in negotiation.

In my experience, it is important to create a team at the acquiring company. It is important to get comfortable with the new staff. Usually, it is a one-way street; there is one buyer and one seller; somebody is being taken over. A merger of equals is unusual.

So, as treasurer, you have to get involved with the company being taken over and find out what the issues are that need to be solved. You should discover problems now, during the due diligence process, not after closing. Not finding them during this process is often why deals break apart.

Once the treasurer has been named part of the due diligence team, then it's fairly important for him or her to identify what topics treasury has to examine in the process. There are literally dozens of questions you need to be asking and areas you need to examine.

Some obvious ones:

- What's going to happen in the new structure with cash management and banking?

- What kind of short-term investments do they have?

- What's the policy of the old company; what's the policy of the new company?

- What type of bank debt do they have? This is extremely critical to understand.

- What does one company do about foreign exchange versus the other? There is almost always a difference.

- What liabilities do they have in terms of leases, and purchase and sale agreements? Because of the new FAS 133 requirements, finding out about leases and their embedded options is critical.

- What kind of pension and savings plan do they have? Some companies may have DB (defined benefit) pension plans; maybe the acquiring company does not. Look at insurance risk management the same way you'd look at the banking side. These are the key treasury topics to examine.

- What kind of insurance programs do they have and how sophisticated is their risk management?

Let's drill down in each one of these areas.

Cash Management

There are a number of things to consider in the cash management and banking area. The first thing you must do is a flow diagram of the cash management system to understand the company being acquired. You need to know where their lockboxes are, the disbursement structure, and what kind of payroll they have.

You also need to look at the cash concentration. Is it all in one country, or is it across many countries? A good way to do that is to get their organization chart and understand who has responsibilities, and who has seniority in terms of authorities and approval.

By doing this, you can start assessing whether these people are going to stay or leave once the acquisition is completed. Understanding their [level of] technical expertise is extremely important, because in every instance there is somebody who is strong in financing, someone else strong in cash management, and someone who is strong in international and, of course, somebody who isn't. So this is a good opportunity to assess what the treasury structure might look like and the experience of its personnel.

Key Dates
More tactically, you should be reviewing key dates and getting answers to a number of questions, such as:

- When are the interest and principal due on the loans of the target?

- What are the fees that are generated?

- Are there some critical ratio and covenant tests that maybe you've had and they don't have or vice versa?

- When do they make payments on various debts, such as lease payments?

- Are they using consultants that have milestones to reach?

Also, obtain copies of the last 12 months of bank officer visit reports to understand the depth of relationship between the target and the bank. Look at copies of recent account analyses to understand how the structure works. At one company that I was involved in acquiring, this was extremely interesting. The company never did account analyses. My company did and kept tremendous records. It was eye opening just to find out what the account analyses were at the acquired company.

Bank Accounts
Another obvious thing that is sometimes overlooked: You should understand the acquired company's bank accounts. There is an issue of control, as well as an opportunity here.

For each account, understand its purpose and type. Find out who the authorized signers are and who has limits on certain dollar amounts. You want to ask questions such as: Does the CFO sign up to a certain amount or is it all done electronically? What are the safeguards on check stock?

This can be a big issue. At one of my past treasury positions, I had an assistant controller who was leaving the company and moving to California.

We had a holding company in Switzerland where I was investing money for the company and she was keeping the books for it. Right before she left, she came to me and said, "You know there's about $10 million in that Swiss account; if I move this money to an account for us in Switzerland, nobody would find this for about six months."

I thought she was joking, but I wasn't sure. I looked at her and said, "You know, $10 million sounds pretty good but I'd hate to spend the rest of my life locked in a Swiss jail."

It was an interesting temptation, and it points out the kind of things that can happen when there is change, as there always is in a merger or acquisition. It is often an opportunity to move cash or to lose cash, and it's critical that you understand where the opportunities are.

Remember, all of this has to be done quickly. This is why I often advocate a SWAT team approach. For example, the offshore and special purpose accounts—the accounts that you think don't have much in them because nobody's reported on them for three or six months—can be fairly critical and you'll need the team to identify and review each one of them.

Don't forget to look into the company's corporate secretary and what resolutions, terms, and conditions are involved.

Also review the mapping of the bank accounts and understand the sweeping arrangements. It's also a good time to look at electronic services. If they have a treasury workstation, what kind of information is on it and how is it shared? Find out what they are actually reporting, the kind of information reported, and the security procedures for wires and who has access.

Accounting for Cash

There are a number of things on my checklist concerning accounting for cash.

- Is there matched pay?
- Do you have controlled disbursements?
- What type of ACH payroll–third party do they have?
- Is there a netting arrangement?
- Does the company have overseas units and do they have a netting arrangement? Do you understand how those overseas netting arrangements work?

All of the different modules within a treasury workstation need to be both understood and examined, particularly at this point in time. Because that's where the opportunity is, potentially, to have things go right.

You have to understand how they forecast cash. You have to look at things as basic as: What are their customer payment terms? What do their Day's Sales Outstanding (DSO) reports look like?

I'm involved in a project now where an international company clearly has tremendous issues with DSOs. They don't understand the difference between DSO targets within the U.S. versus what they are in Europe and some parts of Asia. So understanding that is fairly critical.

Also consider the target company's current and proposed initiatives implementation status. What was their treasury trying to achieve? There may be a number of things that they were trying to achieve and, due to the acquisition or merger, aren't sure if they are going to complete them. So understand where these rank in terms of importance. Reconciliation of bank statements at many levels can be critical. There are some companies that don't even reconcile their bank statements. I advise you to do it immediately. Invariably, we're called in to do that because nobody wants to do that job.

Petty cash can be an issue, depending on the kind of company it is. With a real estate or offshore drilling company, some petty cash is usually around. Another critical thing is employee loans. What are the arrangements with the company you're taking over versus your own company?

And, certainly, look at the treasury department audit reports. It's a rule for Andersen clients that they have to have the treasury audited at least once a year, sometimes in great depth through a lot of derivatives, not very much in others. What that report looks like doesn't always come up when you're doing an acquisition, so it is important to look for it. It will help you learn a lot about what's happening in the target company's treasury and certainly where the risks are.

An area where we spend a lot of time is the foreign currency accounts, because many people don't understand them. For example, if it's cash in Canada, what currency is it in? Or is it really just cash from the U.S.? Understanding that connection is fairly critical.

Get a handle on the prices for services and frequency of price changes. We had one situation where we acquired a company that had just negotiated a service fee reduction with their bank. They didn't know that that company was going to be acquired. So when the two of them got together, they looked at the total package, went back to the bank and they negotiated another 30 percent reduction. Now, some of it was due to the fact that they got larger volume but, in effect, by putting the two companies together, you got to see what the pricing was and it really helped reduce costs and get better service.

In terms of seeing what kind of compensating balances or impress balances they have, smaller acquired companies think paying by compensating balance is a good idea. We all learned that it isn't a good idea, but paying by fees is. It doesn't happen at every company. So it's important to understand what kind of services they use and if the structure is the same.

Treasury should get a list, very quickly, of the target company's top 20 customers and vendors, because it helps you really understand where the cash flow is coming from and who's paying it and the value of that. And, certainly, if there's been a lockbox study or disbursement study, get a copy of that because that's something that really is helpful in putting together the new structure.

Watch for the sweetheart deals or what we call the board relationships. For example, someone's brother-in-law or cousin runs the bank down the street, and the target company has been giving them a lot of money. Make sure you know about that. Understand the resistance around it. There may be a board relationship where you can't just say, "Hey, that relationship doesn't make economic sense." Sometimes, as outside consultants, we can say it, but you can't always do that even if you are the acquiring company.

Finally, watch for cash that might be in a different name than the acquired company. I know of an example where there was a significant amount of money in a holding company that really belonged to the target company that the acquiring company didn't know about.

Investment Portfolio

Another important area to look at is the investment portfolio. We have nine points on our checklist. Clearly, in companies that have lots of cash, such as insurance companies or Microsoft, and not much debt, this can be a fairly big issue. You have to look at the marketability of the portfolio, and get answers to questions such as:

- What is the current cost on a market-to-market basis?

- Is there any collateral held for a debt that they have?

- What supporting documentation do they have?

- What is the cash flow for this particular type of investment?

Look at maturity dates, just like you would with debt, and understand the safekeeping and custody issues. We had one client who actually had an outside investment manager handle its daily cash. So understand who does this type of work for the target company.

Look at the liquidity of the funds that they have invested and the broker agreements and the depth of the relationship. Just as you keep a scorecard on banks and their services, you should keep one on the brokers, too.

Review what type of investment policy they have. We're all conservative. We all say we don't invest in risky things, but questions abound about investment policies and the creditworthiness of certain investments, and things continue to change very rapidly in our deregulating environment.

Find out when the investments mature and what you can do about it. Maybe you're going to need cash when the actual merger completes. Look at money markets and the overall portfolio return. Understand what the benchmarks are. Insurance companies do this pretty well. Corporations with excess cash sometimes don't; they just keep it in the money market or get the best they can in the sweep.

Know who is authorized to invest and who does the confirmations. This is a big issue, particularly from a control perspective. Separation of duties in this area is really critical and it doesn't always happen. Andersen's office in Boston did a survey asking treasury departments, "Who invests and who gets the confirmation?" It turned out in 30 percent of those surveyed that the same people both invested and got the confirmation.

You would think this was an obvious rule, but it is overlooked all the time. Usually because it is a small treasury department and the CEO has said "You are responsible for this." Thus, there isn't the effort to educate the junior accountant that the treasurer is the one that ought to get the confirmations.

It is also critical to understand the acquired company's sweep arrangements to make sure they are consistent with what you want. Invariably in a merger, you find the sweep arrangements already in place at the acquired company and it's not easy to get the cash back up to the parent, particularly to fund certain debt and pay-downs.

Debt Agreements

Now, let's review things to remember about bank debt. Obtaining copies of the debt agreements and all exhibits is important. Certainly, you get copies quickly if it's a large piece of debt. But the smaller debts—the revolvers and other working capital debt—are important too.

Finding out the right contact names can be interesting. You acquire a company and all the management you've acquired leaves, and you don't even know who the bank contact is. For example, a company is in Texas, the parent is in New York, the cash manager and operations are in Chicago—who's the contact? This can be a fairly important issue too.

Schedules may include amortization fees. How do you make sure the debt is covered at the right time? Who's tracking it? What are the events of default and the change of control? New names of management could be an issue and, if not taken care of, you could lose the credit.

Your understanding of covenant calculations on debt is very important and can be a deal breaker.

Also, look at prepayment notices and penalties; this is fairly critical. I know of a company that acquired a Brazilian company. They looked at the cost of the debt in Brazil, which was 23 percent, then said, "We're going to prepay that and go borrow in dollars." But it turns out they triggered a clause that cost them 45 percent and left them with a misunderstanding of the currency risk. So prepayments have to be looked at carefully.

On the other hand, reducing the amount of the interest expense fairly quickly is important. You should see if there are any securitized assets and ask why they have been sold and who has recourse.

A list of guarantees or letters of credit could also be considered debt, which brings up a good point. What is debt? It's changing. There are a number of things that we see in terms of change of credit, and who provides a company with credit. A lot of companies use supplier credit by not making payment terms.

Foreign Currency

In my experience, the way you look at foreign currency is very important. Let's say you acquire a company, and that company has a very sophisticated centralized foreign currency management organization. They come into a different organization that has no centralization; the individual units figure out what to do and think that hedging is speculation. This can make for a real clash of cultures.

So it is key to understand how the acquired company measures currency risk, and find out if they have contracts. You need to look at the details of open contracts, look at spot and forward contracts, look at things like futures or options and other derivatives, and understand that an embedded derivative is a risk for you.

Be sure to ask the question, What kind of policy do they have? I'm not going to go into details about what kind of policy you should have. I think what's more important is, Do you understand what they're doing? A simple statement from them of "We don't speculate," is not enough.

Another one on this checklist: What are the netting agreements? Does a bank have a netting arrangement? There are sometimes bilateral or multilateral netting arrangements between subsidiaries of a company. Do they run the netting system or use a bank or some vendor you've never heard of? Netting agreements are important because lots of cash flows through a netting arrangement.

2 APPENDIX G

In terms of foreign exchange, you need to know about authorized company traders. If you've ever acquired a U.K. company, they talk about their "trading desk." It's a treasury desk, but they refer to themselves as traders, and Europeans have a very different concept of ethics trading. Yes, they're probably just hedging, but they talk about "the deals." They talk about "the transactions."

Issues that can come up here are: What's the confirmation procedure? Who gets to see foreign currency activities? Who understands it? If they don't understand confirmation and wire transfers, you can imagine the problems you might have in this area.

When I'm working with a company, I like to hear about their losses in foreign currency. If I hear someone say that "we only lost a couple hundred thousand or half a million or a million" and they seemed okay with that, then fine, I'd get a sense that they're okay. When they start bragging about the gains they made in hedging foreign currency, my antennae go up because I can relate it back to my own experience at Fiat, where we managed foreign currency risk and had a mandate to manage it aggressively.

We made $5 million trading foreign currency risk. But the U.S. operating division lost $50 million and had to close down in the United States. So understanding the losses the target [company] has and how you can live with those losses is a really key question. And be wary when they brag, "I made the greatest hedge ever."

I think the issue about the accounting impact and FAS 133 is a bit overdone. FAS 133 is the first change in accounting regulations for foreign currency in 19 years, since FAS 52. But you need to figure out how ready people are for this very important regulation. Some training might be in order.

Other Liabilities
Other liabilities include leases. You must understand the terms and conditions of leases, including what creates a default. The change of control, is that a default? Could be. So that means the lease can be broken. You should ask yourself: Is that what I want? Do I want to take advantage of that? Or do I want to live with it?

Also consider escalation clauses and adjustment clauses. Remember FAS 133, here. Because of this accounting regulation, you have to understand whether it's a purchase or sale, and, embedded in it, is there a derivative? Very simply, if it says, "If the price of energy changes 10 percent, then my price of my payment can go up 10 percent," that's an embedded derivative. It's not a simple buy and sell agreement. It means you have to both report it and understand it.

If you're going through an acquisition right now, that's something you really need to look at, because there's risk associated with it. Also look at renewal and purchase options; that is, really dig into what's in the leases.

Look at letters of credit. Many people in our business don't understand their use. Is it financing or is there more to it? You may use a standby letter of credit and somebody else may be using it for importing information or importing products. In fact, understand the jargon of it. Is there some collateral associated with it? What is its purpose? And must any change be approved by the beneficiary? Letters of credit may very well be more complicated than you first thought.

THE SIGNIFICANCE OF LETTERS OF CREDIT

by Robin Speck
Banking Operations Manager
The St. Paul Companies

You have to be very careful with letters of credit, especially if they are part of the business that your company is doing—in my case, an insurance company. We accept letters of credit as part of the policy that we're writing for a particular client. You have to make sure that when you accept these, they are on your prevent list because it's very important.

You have to understand: If they're not on your prevent list, then, what is your recourse? How do you go back to your client and say, "Unfortunately, this bank does not meet with our criteria as an approved bank." What recourse would we take from that point? Also, you need to understand what area within your lines of business is responsible for those letters of credit. You have to make sure that your mapping process works, so that the acquiring company may take care of everything within their treasury group. But, when you map it over into your current environment, it may actually go into your underwriting or business unit. So it's real important that you take care of those finer details to make sure that everything falls properly within your process of controls and understanding.

Invariably, there's a change of ownership. The new owners don't like the credit structure, so they ask for a guarantee from the parent company. Now here's what Fiat used to do. Fiat used to give no guarantees to anybody. But they would write comfort letters. Did that make the banks happy? Maybe, but the unwritten rule was, Fiat didn't believe that the comfort letters meant anything.

They never had to pay up on a comfort letter. So what does this really mean to the target company, or its parent? Is there a comfort letter? Is there a guarantee? What does it really mean? Is it really secure credit or not? As you look at other liabilities or obligations, dig for those words. See how solid they are.

Legal charges are another liability you should be aware of. This is often left up to the legal department while you focus on other things, but maybe no one from legal is on the team. So potential legal charges must be added into the liability equation.

Pension and Savings

This brings us to another area—pension and savings—that often is not considered part of treasury's concern in a merger or acquisition, but should be. Skills are important here. Maybe you have deep pension skills in the department, maybe not. Maybe the acquired company has the skills in its treasury department. Either way, it's important to look at a checklist.

Look at the plans and the characteristics of the portfolio. Ask, "When was the last liability study? Is it matched? Are there certain investment managers who select it? Do you have somebody like a Wyatt Corporation investing for you? Do you have selection of managers outsourced?"

It's a very interesting area because, again, when you talk jargon, the pension area is a lot different than the cash management area, and understanding the terminology is key to understanding what is going on. Some treasurers have responsibility for this and for some it's in human resources. Yet there is a financial aspect that really is the responsibility of treasury when it comes to pensions.

Thus, I recommend any treasurer to ask questions here too. Who are the trustees? Who are the custodians? Look at the fee schedules. Have there been audit reports? There is a lot of actuarial information and it is very report driven.

What are the defined contribution options? ESOPs and any option programs are areas to look into in some detail. Look at reports to the fiduciary committee. They put a lot of wording and jargon around pensions. Rightfully so, but certainly it's something that you need to learn more about if you don't know it. And identify who in the organization can help you.

Insurance and Risk Management

Another area that usually falls under the treasurer, but sometimes doesn't, is insurance and risk management. This is a very interesting area. Understanding is needed here, as you start looking at your insurance policies. The treasurer should be responsible for this, at least in my view, and certainly in a merger and acquisition role. So look at global policies and the details. Is it proprietary? Do they have business interruption insurance, and coverage for crime, and errors and omissions?

What are some of the employment practices? Do they have insurance for different entities or is there umbrella coverage? Another issue in terms of liability is open claims and a claims history. Find out what claims have been like and what has been going on. Companies are very different and you have to make sure you review this area thoroughly.

I can't emphasize enough that the way you score bankers and pension managers for good or bad service, high or low rates—do the same with your insurance brokers.

Also check for nonqualified plans and Rabbi trusts (so named because the form was devised to assure a rabbi of a pension even if he transfers to another congregation). A guarantee on self-insurance for worker's comp can be overlooked. Union and nonunion issues on employee benefits and pensions can be important. This is particularly important for companies that have unions and then suddenly find out the target company doesn't have a union.

Approvals

Let's discuss approvals. This is a critical point when you're in a transition. Transactions will not be completed until the internal approval paperwork is signed. You can go after this deal, but you have to make sure everything is signed. Your Audit and Finance Committee must formally approve any transaction over $X million. In other words, you've got to understand who can approve the size of the acquisition or merger transactions. And certainly, the Board would be informed of all acquisitions before they're consummated. That's pretty logical, but you've got to do your due diligence; you've got to look at the documents and what the company says is their approval structure.

Now, finally, after the closing, treasury has an expanded role. Let's say you are part of the new treasury function. There is more cash, more bank accounts, a lot more debt, and maybe more cash for investment. Certainly there are more pension dollars. But keep in mind, there is more currency risk, too.

Conclusion

You now have an extensive checklist of things that should be reviewed and researched during the due diligence process, so hold onto the list and speak up for the treasury department at the beginning of the process. Make sure you are on the team. There's no excuse for waiting until someone says "Transfer the cash!" to be heard.

TREASURY CHECKLIST DURING DUE DILIGENCE

The treasurer has a key role in the due diligence process of a merger or acquisition, and should be reviewing a number of functions within the target company or merging companies. Here is a checklist of the areas and functions that a treasurer and his or her department should review to ensure that a merger or acquisition is a success.

Cash Management and Banking

Flow diagram of cash management system:
- Lockboxes
- Disbursement
- Payroll
- Cash concentration, etc., in all countries

Organization chart and outline:
- Key responsibilities
- Seniority
- Signing authorities, approval limits, etc.
- Areas of technical expertise
- Prior experience

Calendar of key dates:
- Interest and/or principal
- Fees
- Ratio and covenant tests
- Lease payments
- Consulting milestones

Copies of reports outlining last 12 months of bank officers' visits

Copies of recent account analyses

Bank accounts:
- Purpose, type, account number
- Authorized signers, facsimiles
- Dollar signatory limits
- Safeguards on check stock
- Average account balances
- Offshore and special purpose accounts
- Copies of corporate resolutions and terms and conditions

- ZBA mapping
- Sweep arrangements

Electronic services:

- Workstation
- Balance reporting
- Security procedures for wires
- Access and passwords
- Cash accounting procedures
- Match pay
- Controlled disbursement
- ACH: taxes, payroll, third-party payments
- Netting
- Multibank balance reporting

Cash forecasting methodology

Customer payment terms; DSO reports

Current and proposed initiatives; implementation status

Reconcilement of statements—many levels of completion

Petty cash

Employee loans

Treasury department audit reports

Foreign currency accounts.

Service prices: frequency of price changes

Compensating balances/imprest balances

Top 20 customers and vendors

Latest lockbox study/disbursement study

Sweetheart deals

Short-Term Investing

Characteristics of portfolio

- Marketability
- Cost/today's price/rate
- Collateral held
- Supporting documentation
- Cash flow

- Maturity dates
- Safekeeping/custody
- Electronic account
- Liquidity

Broker agreements and depth of relationship
Investment policy
Schedule of investments
Money market fund prospectus and portfolio
Portfolio return
Who is authorized to invest?
Confirmations
Sweep arrangements

Bank Debt

Copy of debt agreement and all exhibits
Contact names at all lender institutions
Amortization schedule
Fee schedule
Covenant calculations
Events of default: "change of control"
Prepayment notice and penalty
Collateralized or securitized assets

Foreign Exchange

Measurement methodology of underlying FX risks
All details of open contracts
Spot and forward contracts
Options, futures, or other derivative products
FX policy
Netting arrangements
Authorized company traders
Confirmation procedure
Treasury reporting of FX gains and losses for last two years
Understanding accounting impact of FX gains/losses
Readiness for FAS 133

Other Liabilities

Leases
- All terms and conditions, including events of default, change of control
- Escalation and adjustment clauses
- Renewal and purchase options

Letters of credit
- Import or standby
- Purpose
- Any change must be approved by beneficiary

Guarantees/comfort letters

Pension and Savings Plans

Plan and portfolio characteristics
Latest asset-liability study
Investment managers
Trustees
Custodians
Fee schedules
Audit reports
Actuarial reports
Trust accounting reports
Employee communications
Defined contribution investment options
Reports to fiduciary committee
Minutes of fiduciary meetings
Employee option programs
ESOPs, option plans

Insurance and Risk Management

Global policies and coverage details
- Property
- Directors and officers
- Business interruption
- Fidelity and crime

- Errors and omissions
- Employment practices
- Fiduciary
- Entity coverage
- Umbrella

Open claims, claims history

Brokers: global/local coverage

SAMPLE DATA REQUIREMENTS OF USF&G/ THE ST. PAUL COMPANIES DEAL

When The St. Paul Companies announced it would merge with USF&G, the Andersen Due Diligence Group was called in. Within this group was a smaller group of specialized consultants whose duties were to review the treasury departments and help with their integration.

Here is a list of the documents Andersen required and questions they asked of the two treasury departments. This should give you an idea of what to be ready for should you ever be involved in a merger or acquisition.

Treasury organization
- Organization chart
- Description of primary roles and tasks of treasury/cash management positions
- Interviews with treasurer and direct reports

Treasury/cash management initiatives
- Listing of past treasury/cash management initiatives, implementation status, and achieved value
- Listing of proposed treasury/cash management initiatives and associated potential annual value

Banking relationship information/structure
- List of primary banking relationships
- List of bank accounts and associated purpose
- Bank statements for significant accounts
- Account analyses for each bank relationship

Receipt processing
- Are receipts processing in-house or via lockbox?
- Listing of processing locations, types of receipts processed through the sites, and associated volumes (dollars and items).
- Perform float study to understand impact of additional volumes.

Disbursements
- Annual dollar amounts of disbursements by disbursement type (e.g., A/P, claims, payroll)
- Listing of disbursement drawee banks and methods of funding
- Listing of areas/departments responsible for initiating payments

Short-term investments
- Portfolio characteristics
- Short-term investment philosophy

Foreign exchange risk management
- Policies and procedures
- Total FX exposure

MERGERS AND ACQUISITIONS: THE HUMAN FACTOR

A [conversational] case study, held at the Association for Financial Professionals Annual Conference in Philadelphia, November 14, 2000, by Daniel Perkins, Managing Partner, Arthur Andersen Financial and Commodity Risk Consulting Practice, and Robin Speck, Banking Operations Manager, The St. Paul Companies.

Daniel Perkins:

When The St. Paul Companies announced it would merge with USF&G, I was with Arthur Andersen. My small group came on as specialized consultants to help with the integration of the treasury departments. We were responsible for reviewing all treasury functions. We also had to coordinate with other parts of the Andersen Due Diligence Group, which were reviewing the accounting, accounts receivable, and processing functions, and how to integrate the whole finance function. My group's role was very specialized, but it was a monumental exercise by the Arthur Andersen group as a whole.

Let me put it in this context. Paul Liska, CFO of The St. Paul Companies, was recently written up in *CFO* magazine as one of the top CFOs because of his ability to cut costs and generate a merger that worked so well and generated some large numbers—several hundred million dollars. But the reason that The Street was favorable about the St. Paul–USF&G merger was it was done quickly and it was done successfully. And part of that process was the due diligence team effort.

I can't emphasize this enough. This is an area where, when companies are put together, everybody's looking at them to see if they're going to be successful. If you do it right, it's worth multiples in terms of capitalization for your company. If you do it wrong, The Street will take you apart. This is a sensitive issue, but the St. Paul–USF&G merger points out why there is much to be gained by going through the process well and quickly.

There is always a human element to any merger or acquisition. And we'd like to discuss how it impacted Robin and her functions. In our particular role at Arthur Andersen, we asked for certain data requirements and for things like an organization chart, description of the primary roles, and tasks of the treasury. We did interviews with the treasurer and the direct reports, including Robin. We did many of the things found on the due diligence checklist (Treasury Checklist during Due Diligence, previously listed in this Appendix).

Robin, how did you feel that went in terms of the initial organization information? Was it easy to get the information?

Robin Speck:
Parts of the due diligence that Arthur Andersen had asked for were relatively easy to put our hands on, whereas some of it was not. It all depends on how you're structured and in what areas of the organization this information is housed—whether or not you can go readily to that group and retrieve the information or you have to work a little bit harder because the area that should be keeping track of it has or has not done what they've needed to do to have the information readily available.

Daniel Perkins:
We asked for information such as the different cash management initiatives. What are they currently doing? What are they going to implement currently? What kind of value do they get out of the services that they're changing, the things that they're going to do? Now, it's interesting because you may be doing a day job and all of a sudden this merger comes along, and then you're asked, "What about the potential annual value of the cash management initiatives?" As consultants, we do that all the time. We look at benefit relative to the process or the opportunity. You don't always do that in your day job. That's the kind of thing I would imagine you didn't just have handy, that was a harder thing to get to. So that's one of the things where, as a team, you can work toward.

Something a little easier, potentially, is looking at the bank relationship structure. So a list of the primary banks, what's the bank account's associated purpose, the bank statements that were for significant accounts, and account analyses. Was this pretty easy?

Robin Speck:

Yes and no.

Yes, it was easy in terms of what we managed at the corporate head-quarters; however, because we had a lot of subsidiaries that were very autonomous, we did not have access to their banking relationship informa-tion. Trying to pull that information in from the subsidiaries was very diffi-cult because, as you've probably all encountered, in most situations as they become more and more autonomous, they want less and less involvement from the home office. So, depending upon the dynamics, it's going to be easy or hard to gather what the consultants are looking for.

Daniel Perkins:

You know, one thing that we did look at was the receipt processing. Are receipts processed in-house or via lockbox? Now, again, being an insurance company or if you are a utility, you may process things in-house. You might buy the equipment to actually process things in-house. And you probably know that that's a bit of a dynamic. If you're a manufacturing company with business-to-business payments, you're not going to be processing a lot of checks in-house; but have more of a retail kind of arrangement. So it's an interesting question. Should you be processing in-house, should it be out-sourced? That is the kind of thing where there's some turf being defended; somebody built it up and wants to hear you say, "Hey, buying that equipment was a good idea."

Getting a listing of processing locations, the type of receipts, sites, asso-ciated volumes, dollars, and items—some of that was easy to get. Some of it, like looking at a float study, you've got to get some external information. So, some of this is harder to obtain than others.

If you look on the disbursement side, look for the same kinds of things. Do you have easy access to dollar amounts of disbursements, the type, claims, payroll? Again, look at drawing banks and the methods of funding. Some of this is pretty easy to get, some of it's a little more difficult. Certainly look at areas that are responsible for initiating payments and mapping that out and tracking that. It is very critical to understand what the new business is like.

In terms of short-term investments, as an insurance company looking at short-term portfolios, what is the philosophy? What are the types of things they invest in at the acquired company versus the one acquiring? And, cer-tainly, foreign exchange risk management was a reasonably big issue at the parent, the new parent company, not much of an issue for the other company. And yet, in terms of philosophy, how they invested and traded and benchmarked for foreign currency investments is something different than, say, manufacturing companies. So getting an idea of the policies and procedures and total exposure is important. Robin, what about these topics, were they easy or hard to get to?

Robin Speck:

Well, in terms of the short-term investing, we primarily use money markets as vehicles for cash. The St. Paul Companies have the St. Paul Investment Pool, which is an unregistered money market. So there were two very different philosophies from the two different sides of the table. USF&G didn't do a whole lot of foreign exchange, so it was relatively easy to streamline that over to the consultants and give them information on the transaction accounts.

Daniel Perkins:

Yes, I certainly wanted to emphasize the following point. The role of the consultants in a due diligence process is to gather information, to work with the company and establish the team. The most difficult part is what I'll call [the sensitivity of] the human factor, which is, in fact, the role that I really don't want. I don't want to judge individuals.

It's a role that we want to make sure that the company gets some synergy about who those individuals should be. So it's fairly important that our role is to define what the future treasury structure should look like, not to say who the people are that should fit it. It's entirely different and certainly a sensitive question. But as you're doing this and as you're either being acquired or in the process of acquiring, you should perform detailed interviews to understand the direct reports and see the potential of these people.

Certainly the CFO, or the treasurer of the company or the senior management, will ask me, "What do you think of these people? What do you think about the ones being acquired?"

So it's interesting because it's not a role most people like. I try to deal with it by thinking of it in terms of what roles need to be filled, what expertise do they need, not what individuals will fill them. But that does go on during this process. And I mention it because throughout this process they're thinking about who stays and who goes. It's an important element here, probably more important than all the data that's gathered. So transition discussions with potential candidates is going to happen real early in the process.

For that reason, I think, it's very critical to hear Robin's story, and I want to tell you a little bit about this experience. We found that dealing with Robin and the team made this exercise better for a lot of reasons—gathering information, but certainly this tough human element. Because we're sensitive to that issue and I think it's important for you to hear what it was like and what it's been like since the acquisition. So with that, I'll turn it over to Robin.

Robin Speck:

Thank you, Patrick. Just a little background on The St. Paul Companies. We're a 148-year-old insurance company. We're based in the Midwest and we serve the property liability insurance needs of customers around the world. In 1999, we had $7.6 billion in revenue. We're the fourth largest U.S. commercial insurer. We're the leading writer of Special G commercial insurance business. We lead in specialty niches, including health services, surety, technology, and financial and professional services. We have international operations in 14 countries, and USF&G merged with The St. Paul in 1998.

Prior to coming to USF&G in 1997, I had been on the bank side for 20 years. I decided to make the change because of all of the mergers and acquisitions I'd been through—four in 20 years. When I arrived at USF&G, one of the questions that I asked as part of the interview process was, "What are the strategic goals of USF&G in terms of merging, acquiring, or being acquired? Are you looking to acquire or do you consider yourself an acquisition target?"

At that time, they were acquiring. They were just in the process of acquiring a company out in Texas called the Titan Group. So I felt pretty comfortable taking my bag of skills, and going over on the corporate side. I started in September and before the end of October the grumbling started in terms of information that needed to be gathered for upper management. At that time you pretty much could read the writing on the wall. So I had a very short period of time to acclimate myself to the environment that I was currently working in, while preparing for what the future may bring to me.

Now, as part of your mergers and acquisitions, you always want to take a look at the human factor. At USF&G the employees were faced with many, many different things. Number one, you have to be flexible. You want to look at change as an opportunity and as a challenge. You want to be able to leave your comfort zone. There was a lot of longevity with the employees at USF&G. So, for them, any type of change was going to be monumental. It was going to be different, it was going to be difficult, it was going to be what they call "Tough Love." You need to keep a positive attitude. You need to understand that the acquisition decisions that are made are all business related, they're not personal. And always, always put your best foot forward at all times because, like Dan said, you're constantly in the limelight. You're being looked at. You're being seen as a possible candidate for the merged, combined entity.

Remember that attitude is one of the few things that is totally under your control. You need to turn the power of change into your advantage. You need to avoid placing blame on others. It's very easy to transfer to other people the problems that come up during this process. Also, you want to eliminate self-induced stress. Sometimes we're our worst enemies. We worry about things that are truly out of our control. By eliminating those things, you'll make the process much, much easier.

You want to look at a self-evaluation. Determine what are your strengths and weaknesses. Clearly define what your goals and objectives are, because you can be in control of this process 100 percent. Balance your personal and professional priorities. You have to look at how flexible you are. Can you relocate, can you not relocate? I was one of the fortunate ones within the treasury department because it was just me; I didn't have to worry about transferring children to a different state, timing of school seasons, all of those. So, always be prepared. You constantly want to be mindful that whatever education and training you're doing on an ongoing basis is a transferable skill set you can use in a variety of environments. And, remember, the best defense is a good offense.

What's important about this process is communication. It's vital. You want to make sure that you're communicating with your employees. You need to be as specific and candid as you can. You need to minimize surprises and keep your sense of humor. It's very important during this period of time that you continue to have fun. You can't view it as the end of the world; life goes on and you have to do the best that you can under the circumstances that you're operating [in].

Minimize ambiguity. Clarify the roles and responsibilities of each of your team members. You have to remember that during this period of time you're going to have integration activities that are constantly going on in addition to the day-to-day activities. And make sure that you're a good listener. Sometimes, all it takes is sitting down with an employee and listening to what their fears and concerns are—that can really show that you care about them and that you're going to be there for them during the transition period.

Make sure that your decisions are based on opportunity and challenge. What's going to make the most sense for you? What's going to make you happy? Think about what your plan B or your contingency plan would be if you were not to continue employment with the combined entity.

Since the merger, we have created one global treasury organization. Our locations are in St. Paul and London. We've built a highly talented and cohesive treasury team. We have a combination of USF&G and St. Paul treasury individuals. We've also brought individuals in from the outside of the financial services industry to offer a fresh and different perspective. And we have a blending of cultures. This has been good for the new treasury department. Now we see what both sides of the table were doing, as well as gain the advantage of outsiders' views from our other team members. What I tried to do was focus on business partnerships and adding value for St. Paul.

And we've definitely capitalized on lessons learned from our merger during consolidations of additional companies that we've done since. Since the 1998 merger of USF&G and St. Paul, we've done, probably, two—one major one just this past year with the MMI Companies located out in Deerfield, IL.

One point to remember: This may be a merger or an acquisition, you may be on the side of the table where you're acquiring someone else and you don't feel threatened. But keep in mind that you could be on the other side of the table in the future. So you always want to be respectful of the individuals that you're working with during this process.

Daniel Perkins:
Our emphasis on the human factor is critical because what you're really trying to do is expand your own horizon. I think Robin said it correctly. Make sure this is the kind of challenge for you.

Remember, there is no detail too small, because as we've found as part of our postmortem reviews, the devil's always in the detail. And it's normally the smaller details such as reconciliations, making sure that your unreconciled differences are documented so that when all of those staff members from the acquiring company are no longer there as your resources, you have something that can help you in resolving the difference. That's been a big, big issue for us. It's very important. Well, thank you all for joining us this afternoon and enjoy the rest of the conference.

AFTER THE MERGER: EASING THE TRANSITION

By Michael J. Major
From the *TMA Journal,* September–October 1999

Robin Speck left the banking industry, looking for something more stable. But after only three months at her new company, the dark cloud of "M&A" reared its daunting head.

After surviving two mergers while working as a banker, Robin Speck moved to the insurance business, thinking it was a more stable industry. After three months as the custody manager at USF&G in Baltimore, Maryland, the company merged with The St. Paul Companies, Inc., in St. Paul, MN. "I was afraid my luck had run out," Speck reflected.

It turns out that she survived this merger, too. But, in the process, Speck gained even more insight into the awkward and sometimes difficult task of merging two companies into one. Most often, the goal is not only integration, but instant integration, despite the fact that the two companies have entirely different histories. In addition, the two groups were formed and are run by people with distinct management styles and financial procedures. Moreover, consolidation invariably means downsizing, which is a polite way of saying that people will be put out of work. This obviously creates an environment of anxiety and turmoil.

At a time when management is asking for the biggest team effort, most employees are not sure whether they will even remain a part of the team.

Taking a Proactive Approach
So what can the treasury staff do to ease the transition during this difficult period? "Instead of simply waiting for what might come down from above, we took a proactive approach," noted Speck. "We focused on the collection of information for cash management and banking, short-term investing, bank debt, and foreign exchange. Being organized and focused on the task at hand helped throughout the integration process."

Seeking Help from a Consultant
In any transaction as complicated as a merger, it is helpful to have an outside consultant. In this case it was Arthur Andersen, LLP. "What Arthur Andersen did for this particular merger is help facilitate the integration of the treasury and cash management functions. The treasurer for St. Paul was promoted to senior vice president of investor relations prior to the merger being completed. Arthur Andersen kept the momentum going after the

acquisition, leading to the successful integration of treasury services between USF&G and St. Paul," Speck revealed.

"I feel my role as a consultant is to bring an objective evaluation to the transition," added Daniel Perkins, a partner and head of corporate treasury consulting at Arthur Andersen. "Sometimes you want a really fresh look from the outside. It might not be enough to look at only the acquirer's point of view. For example, if the acquirer has more experience in international cash management, that experience should be deferred to. But if the acquired has a very centralized treasury and the acquirer is very decentralized, the acquired may have the better practice. It might be wise to take the best out of both worlds and integrate."

Another important aspect in reviewing treasury operations is to line up all functions side-by-side, so they can be fully integrated. "Historically, each merger is a little different. So each one has to be thought through in terms of its specific financial areas," Perkins explained. Ideally the management and merger operating personnel should get together with specialists from treasury, legal, and maybe the accounting and human resources departments.

Perkins advised, "It's important to form a team with key representatives from both companies, so that people get comfortable with each other and can air out any problems early in the transition process."

Perkins stressed there are eight key areas for the treasurer to analyze during the transition process: cash management, bank relationships, short-term investments, bank debt, foreign-exchange requirements, other liabilities, pensions and savings plans, and risk management.

Cash Management   Treasurers should review the flow diagrams within the cash management system, evaluating how the system works on both a domestic and international basis, what the lockboxes look like, and how payrolls and disbursements are structured. The personnel with key responsibilities should be diagrammed, along with the flowcharts, to clarify who makes approvals and has sign-off authority. The calendar of payment dates for principals, interest, and lease-incurred costs also should be examined, along with the cash forecasting methodologies, customer payment terms, reconciliation of bank statements, petty cash, employee loans, treasury department audits, and foreign currency bank accounts.

Bank Relationships   Under this category, Perkins suggests that you examine copies of bank visit reports and account analyses. Pay special attention to the register of bank accounts, what the accounts are for, the types of accounts, authorized signers, documentation for each account, dollar limits, average account balances, and copies of corporate resolution terms and conditions. Study the documentation of depository and sweep arrangements and survey the banks' electronic services, including balance reporting, security proce- dures for wire transfers, cash accounting procedures, controlled disbursement processes, ACH multibank balance reporting, and treasury workstations provided by either the banks or other vendors. In addition, review the prices for services, compensating balance requirements, and the latest lockbox/ disbursement studies. "It's very important," added Perkins, "to understand any sweetheart deals or specialty arrangements with any bank or vendor."

Short-Term Investments   In this area, treasury should look at the various parts of the portfolio, such as marketability of the security, the cost at today's price, and the collateral held. Perkins also suggests that treasurers review the portfolio's supporting documentation, safekeeping or custody, and liq- uidity. Other things to consider are the arrangements with the broker and the depth of that relationship, the investment policy of the company, a schedule of the investments or rollovers, the portfolio return, and, again, the autho- rizations of who can invest, plus the sweep arrangements.

Bank Debt   Review all bank loan arrangements with the accompanying exhibits, contact names, amortization fee schedules, covenant agreements, embedded derivatives, default notification, and prepayment notices.

Foreign Exchange Requirements   The assessment of the foreign exchange con- tracts should include spot and forward contracts, plus options, futures, or other derivatives. Treasurers also should conduct a thorough analysis of the foreign exchange policy and any netting arrangements, authorized company traders, or confirmation procedures.

Other Liabilities   All leases are included under this category, terms and con- ditions, factors such as escalation and adjustment clauses, renewal and pur- chase options, plus default and change of control. Perkins advises that you should also look at letters of credit and understand their purpose, whether they are import, export, or standby letters of credit. Guarantees and comfort letters should be reviewed, as well as other liabilities such as purchase con- tracts that might have an embedded derivative. This is very important with the upcoming implementation of FAS 133 accounting regulations.

Pensions and Savings Plans   The characteristics of the pension plan, the date of the latest asset liability study, and the identities of investment managers, trustees and custodians are items to be considered here. "Also, determine the fee schedules." The audit and actuary reports, employee options plans and programs, communications to employees, as well as any reports and minutes of judiciary meetings also should be reviewed.

Risk Management   In this final area, look at global insurance policies. Locate the property insurance director and officers. Study various insurance policies, such as business interruption, fidelity, crime, employee practices, and entity and umbrella coverage. Also look at outstanding claims and the claims history, and locate brokers, both global and local.

Considering the Human Element

The checklist for the human factor is less clear-cut, but perhaps even more important during the transition process. Some of the critical questions that have to be answered are:

- Who goes and who stays?

- How will people perform if they are moving from one location to the other?

- How do you communicate the changes to senior management, employees, and the outside world, including vendors and investors?

- Will the transitional time be a few weeks or a few years?

- What plans are necessary to finalize the new structure?

Perhaps the biggest challenge is getting individuals from two different organizations to work together with a positive focus and a shared vision. "Since I had come from the banking side of the business and had been through some major acquisitions, I pretty much knew that what was expected was a positive attitude and putting your best foot forward," Speck remarked. "I also knew that decisions were made based on what was best for the business. They were not personal."

The merger process happened quickly for Speck. She started working at USF&G in September 1997, without any inkling of the impending change. In October, Speck's department received requests for information that intimated that the company was thinking about making an acquisition, or becoming one. In January 1998, the company announced it would become a part of St. Paul.

"Since I had come from the banking side of the business and had been through several acquisitions, I knew that what was expected was a positive attitude and looking at change as an opportunity and challenge," Speck recalled. "But I did know from my past experiences what I could do to make it easier for everyone else. And that was to make sure that everybody was totally aware of what was going on, who was playing what role in the integration, who the decision makers were, as well as how the various departments and positions were changing."

Communication is Key

Once St. Paul clearly communicated what its expectations were, employees had a pretty good idea whether or not they were on their way out. People who were considered as prospects for the move were interviewed to determine just how comfortable and willing they would be in making the transition to St. Paul. The interviews provided a level of clarity and relief for both the St. Paul and the USF&G employees.

"I don't think anyone was particularly surprised," Speck revealed. "If you know what's going on, you can mentally prepare. But if you're kept in the dark, that's when the anxiety develops, and people don't perform as well as they can if they are anxious."

Instead of passively waiting to see what fate would bring, the USF&G employees were very proactive. "My words of wisdom were that this was the time for people to look within, to assess their skills and see if they wanted to look for other opportunities, perhaps in other businesses or even starting their own. Some people who were used to being decision makers had to determine whether they were willing to accept a diminished role or take their skills and move to somewhere else."

For USF&G and St. Paul, the potential problems that can result from a merger were minimized, if not avoided. "The integration process was one of mutual respect, working toward a common goal. Positions were filled with quality individuals creating a treasury group that was bigger, better, and the best of both organizations," Speck concluded.

H

CORPORATE CULTURES PLAY BIG ROLE IN M&A INTEGRATION

For many corporate leaders involved in mergers and acquisitions (M&As), integration issues such as accounting methods, financial practices and operating systems often take precedence over the human aspect of blending two entities. But this often-neglected "soft side" is just as important as the technical end.

"Postclosing challenges raise a wide variety of human fears and uncertainties, which must be understood and addressed by both [the] buyer and seller," said Andrew J. Sherman, author of *M&A from A to Z* and capital partner of Katten, Muchin & Zavis. "The fear of the unknown experienced by the employees of the seller must be confronted and put to rest or the employees' stress and trauma will affect the seller's performance and the viability of the transaction."

Sensitivity Found Lacking

Many of the problems associated with mergers and acquisitions (M&As) are rooted in a lack of sensitivity to the cultures of the combining entities. Buyers and sellers each possess unique corporate cultures in which they operate, ranging from business philosophies, practices and ethics, down to dress codes and business hours. When these styles clash, attempting a merger can seem like blending oil and water.

So is it possible to merge companies at opposite ends of the cultural spectrum? The answer is yes, but the keys to successful cultural integration are good communication and due diligence in the early negotiation stages. For example, employees need to know why the merger took place, what its goals are, and how they will fit into the new company. Also important to employees is knowing whether the culture of the blended company will be different from the culture in which they currently work, and if so, how management plans to ease that transition.

In many cases, employees are unaware of their culture's strength and how it impacts their daily activities. It is therefore important for M&A administrators to follow four steps when attempting successful unions:

1.   Allow cultural differences to play a part in determining the deal's value.
2.   Realize that both companies' cultures are important.
3.   Admit that it is not in either company's interest to maintain both cultures.
4.   Combine the two cultures in a way that will prevent the deal from exploding.

Easier said than done? Perhaps, but if cultural differences remain unexplored and are not incorporated into the deal's terms, then buyers can anticipate disappointment in their return on investment. To avoid such distress, some companies place a conservative value on at least the first five years of earnings and cash flow. "Most companies experience up to a 15 percent drop in profitability in the first two years after the transaction is completed," said Barry R. Schimel, CPA, president of The Profit Advisors, Inc.

Due Diligence

So where does a cultural evaluation fit into the M&A process? According to Robert Rosen, founder and CEO of Healthy Companies International, it is vital to explore cultural issues during the due diligence stage. At this point, buyers must inquire about a seller's philosophies behind capital requirements, processes, and leadership methods, and determine what company values they share. "During mergers and acquistions, we spend a lot of time on the strategic possibilities and forget or undervalue the culture compatibility between the entities," said Rosen. "It's important to focus on the soft side *before* going into the deal."

Try to seek common ground on a philosophical level. Once you establish a primary goal for employees to focus on, the process of merging the two cultures can begin. "Combine old and new philosophies, and focus on what's good for the customer and for the company," Schimel added. "This has a bonding effect that has huge value."

By paying attention to the human side of the deal, buyers will be able to achieve more synergies and establish common goals that will go hand in hand with creating a new corporate culture. This encourages management and the employees to take a more proactive role in increasing the value of the company, which can only benefit shareholders. In the end, as cultural differences are resolved, it will be easier to focus on merging actual business practices. "No one likes change," Sherman concluded. "But failure to embrace the change inherent with acquisitions reduces the chances of success."

I

FASB'S RULE ON ACCOUNTING FOR BUSINESS COMBINATIONS: RESOLUTION OF AN IMPORTANT CONTROVERSY

The Financial Accounting Standards Board (FASB) has just adopted a new standard that will significantly affect the way companies account for business combinations. On June 29, 2001, Board members unanimously voted in favor of Statement 141, *Business Combinations,* and Statement 142, *Goodwill and Other Intangible Assets.* Both statements were published in July 2001.

Under accounting rules that existed prior to the adoption of this standard, there were two methods of accounting for business combinations, the purchase accounting method and the pooling-of-interests method. Companies had the option of choosing either one, although certain restrictions applied to the pooling method. FASB's proposed changes were first published in Exposure Draft 201-A in September 1999. Since that time the proposal has been subject to extensive comments, hearings, deliberations and evolution.

The new rule eliminates the pooling-of-interests method. In a pooling, combining companies simply add together the book values of assets and liabilities to create their new balance sheet. FASB will now require that all business combinations be accounted for by the purchase accounting method. Under this method an enterprise is identified as the acquirer in the combination and is required to record the firm it bought at the cost it actually paid. The excess of the purchase price over the fair value of the acquired company's net worth is recorded as goodwill. Exposure Draft 201-A, the original proposal, required that goodwill be written down over a period of not more than 20 years. Rules in effect prior to the adoption of the current standard called for goodwill to be amortized over a period not exceeding 40 years. Because there is no recognition of goodwill or amortization of it under the pooling method, companies that combine using this method of accounting generally report higher earnings after the combination than they would have if they had used purchase accounting.

1. Reasons for Proposal
Several arguments were given in support of Exposure Draft 201-A:

- Transactions in which the pooling method is applied are similar to those accounted for by the purchase method but investors are not provided with the same amount of information.

- When the pooling-of-interests method is used, values exchanged are not recorded and management is not held accountable for either the investment made in the business combination or the subsequent performance of that investment.

- Most foreign countries do not allow the pooling method and this makes comparisons between the performance of American and foreign companies more difficult.

- Twelve conditions must be met before companies can use the pooling method. Companies make uneconomic decisions to position themselves to meet these conditions.[1]

- Companies that can use the pooling method are willing to pay higher prices than they would if they had to use the purchase method because they do not have to account for the full cost of the resulting investment and the subsequent performance of that investment.

- Because actual cash flows generated after the combination are the same regardless of whether pooling or purchase accounting is used, the higher earnings reported under the use of the pooling method reflect artificial differences rather than real economic differences.[2]

2. Reasons for Objections

Opponents of FASB's proposal cited several objections:

- Goodwill is built up over a period of years by the actions of management yet it is put on the balance sheet only on the occasion of a merger. The result is a hybrid between historical accounting and mark-to-market accounting.

- Goodwill is the result of smart management decisions and new technologies. It does not decline in value. Requiring it to be amortized on a regular schedule gives an inaccurate picture of those companies that grow by merger relative to those that grow through internally generated retained earnings.

- Many of the mergers that are accounted for by the pooling method are in technology industries. Companies in these industries have been highly innovative and responsible for much of our country's favorable growth record in recent years. Forcing purchase accounting on mergers in these industries will inhibit these companies from growing and will diminish overall economic growth.

---

[1] The 12 conditions and the reasons they were required can be found in Financial Accounting Standards Board, *Current Text: Accounting Standards as of June 1, 2000* (Norwalk, Connecticut: Financial Accounting Standards Board, 2000), pp. 4803–4810.

[2] An elaboration of these arguments is given in "Viewpoints: Why Eliminate the Pooling Method?" FASB Status report, August 31, 1999, by L. Todd Johnson and Kimberly R. Petrone.

- While other countries do not allow pooling-of-interests accounting, they do not have the high economic growth record of the U.S. Neither do they have the innovative technology companies the U.S. has that have grown so much through mergers and acquisitions. We should not endanger economic growth in the U.S. merely to conform to other countries' accounting standards.[3]

3. AFP Survey

To see how the changes proposed in Exposure Draft 201-A would affect the companies that employ financial professionals, the Association for Financial Professionals (AFP) surveyed senior-level financial professionals on their views. The most important findings of the survey were:

- Two-thirds of the respondents' companies have experienced mergers in the past ten years and an even greater number will be considering mergers in the future.

- Of those respondents who anticipate future merger activity by their companies, one-third believe FASB's proposal would interfere with mergers and acquisitions.

- Financial professionals strongly prefer the option of having both the pooling-of-interests and purchase accounting methods for business combinations available to them.

- One-half of the respondents reported that purchase accounting would require reporting substantially lower earnings that they believe would be misinterpreted by investors.

- Forty-four percent said that lower reported earnings due to the purchase accounting method would pose difficulties in meeting loan covenants and bond indentures.

- Implementation of the FASB proposal would impact more heavily on those industries that have higher levels of intangible assets—mainly service industries such as finance, communications, and information technology—than on manufacturing firms. Concerns about the proposal are notably highest in those industries.

---

[3] For an elaboration of these arguments see the testimonies before the Senate Banking Committee on March 2, 2000, of Harvey Golub, Chairman and CEO, American Express, and Dennis Powell, Vice President and Corporate Controller, Cisco Systems.

4. Responses to Exposure Draft 201-A

AFP sent a comment letter and the survey report to FASB, the Chairman of the Securities and Exchange Commission (SEC), and all of the commissioners of the SEC, as well as to the members of the House and Senate Banking Committees. The AFP comment letter emphasized that the survey results support our view "that the preservation of the option of using pooling-of-interests accounting in business combinations is important to the continuation of economic growth in the most dynamic sectors of our economy."[4] The letter was signed by Patrick M. Montgomery, Chairman, AFP Government Relations committee, and James R. Haddad, Chairman, AFP Financial Accounting and Investor Relations task force. Both AFP's comment letter and the results of the survey can be found in the Government Relations section of AFP's Web site: http://www.AFPonline.org/Information_Center/Government_Relations/government_relations.html.

Many other companies, associations, and individuals submitted comments to the FASB on this proposal. Relevant committees of the Senate and House of Representatives held hearings. Key members of these committees expressed concern to the FASB and the SEC about the impact of Exposure Draft 201-A on economic growth. Although a variety of viewpoints were expressed in these communications, it became clear that there was a central core of concern focusing around the points demonstrated in the AFP survey. As a result of these concerns, FASB began a series of "redeliberations" of its entire proposal.

5. Subsequent Revisions

Although there were many technical issues considered in the redeliberations, the main focus was on two issues: (1) Was the pooling-of-interests method of accounting for business combinations to be maintained? and (2) How was goodwill to be defined and how would declines in its value be accounted for? It was clear that the FASB members believed these two issues were closely related. Although many opponents of FASB's proposal argued in favor of the pooling option per se, what concerned them most was the mandatory amortization of goodwill.

These concerns were concentrated among industries whose firms grew primarily by mergers and who would have had much larger amounts of goodwill on their balance sheets had they been forced to use purchase

---

[4] AFP letter to Edmund L. Jenkins, Chairman, Financial Accounting Standards Board, August 17, 2000.

accounting for past mergers. These firms were concentrated in technology and communications, financial services, and other service industries.

In its redeliberation phase, FASB made a twofold decision that accommodated its view that pooling-of-interests accounting should not be allowed and the views of its opponents that the mandatory amortization of goodwill was arbitrary. It decided that, under the new standard, all business combinations will be accounted for by purchase accounting, but there will not be mandatory amortization of goodwill. Rather than mandatory amortization of goodwill, there will be periodic tests for impairment of goodwill. If the results indicate that the value of goodwill has declined, a write-off will occur.

The impairment test will take place in two steps. First, the fair value of the reporting unit is to be compared to the book value of the net worth of the reporting unit.[5] If the fair value is substantially higher than the book value of the net worth of the reporting unit, nothing further needs to be done. If the fair value is close to or less than the book value of the reporting unit's net worth, a new assessment must be made of all the reporting unit's tangible and measurable but intangible assets and liabilities. The difference between the assessed value of the tangible and intangible but measurable assets and liabilities is then calculated. If this value is less than the book value of the reporting unit's net worth, a corresponding write-off is made of the recorded value of goodwill.

Thus, FASB stuck to its original goal of eliminating the pooling-of-interests method of accounting for business combinations. However, it also created a system of accounting for goodwill that could accommodate the views of those who opposed the proposal originally presented in Exposure Draft 201-A. The opponents of Exposure Draft 201-A believe goodwill is not necessarily an asset whose value automatically deteriorates and that if amortization were required it would present distorted financial pictures of those companies that grow through mergers and acquisitions.

6. Final Rule

Thus, the final rule entails elimination of the pooling-of-interests method of accounting for business combinations and a periodic test for impairment of goodwill. The elimination of the pooling-of-interests method of accounting

---

[5] For publicly traded firms, the fair value is generally considered to be the market value of all the firm's outstanding shares. If this is not available, then some other method, such as discounted cash flow, must be used to estimate fair value. A reporting unit is any unit for which financial statements are prepared. Examples would be the firm itself or any of its subsidiaries or business segments.

for business combinations took place on June 29, 2001. The other parts of FASB's proposal will be phased in over a six-month period. The details of this transition are given in the project summary on FASB's Web site: http://accounting.rutgers.edu/raw/fasb/.

7. Conclusions

By eliminating the pooling-of-interests method of accounting for business combinations, FASB has enforced what it considers to be a core accounting principle—that every business combination involves an exchange of assets that should be recorded on the balance sheet. However, by requiring periodic impairment testing of goodwill rather than amortization it has also given the proponents of the pooling option an opportunity to protect their interests within the constraints of generally accepted accounting principles (GAAP). The main concern of the opponents of the proposal in FASB's Exposure Draft 201-A was that the required amortization of goodwill was arbitrary and distorted a company's true financial picture. If goodwill is truly not an asset that declines in value, it will most likely not decline under periodic impairment testing.

J

CISCO SYSTEMS' S-3 FILING FOR THE KOMODO TECHNOLOGY DEAL

AS FILED WITH THE SECURITIES AND EXCHANGE COMMISSION ON OCTOBER 13, 2000

REGISTRATION NO.

SECURITIES AND EXCHANGE COMMISSION
WASHINGTON, D.C. 20549

FORM S-3
REGISTRATION STATEMENT
UNDER
THE SECURITIES ACT OF 1933

CISCO SYSTEMS, INC.
(EXACT NAME OF REGISTRANT AS SPECIFIED IN ITS CHARTER)

CALIFORNIA   77-0059951
(STATE OR OTHER JURISDICTION OF   IDENTIFICATION NUMBER)
(I.R.S. EMPLOYER INCORPORATION
OR ORGANIZATION)

170 WEST TASMAN DRIVE
SAN JOSE, CALIFORNIA 95134
(408) 526-4000
(ADDRESS, INCLUDING ZIP CODE, AND TELEPHONE NUMBER,
INCLUDING AREA CODE, OF REGISTRANT'S PRINCIPAL
EXECUTIVE OFFICES)

JOHN T. CHAMBERS
PRESIDENT AND CHIEF EXECUTIVE OFFICER

CISCO SYSTEMS, INC.
300 EAST TASMAN DRIVE
SAN JOSE, CALIFORNIA 95134
(408) 526-4000
(NAME AND ADDRESS, INCLUDING ZIP CODE, AND TELEPHONE
NUMBER, INCLUDING AREA CODE, OF AGENT FOR SERVICE)

COPY TO:
THERESE A. MROZEK, ESQ.
BROBECK, PHLEGER & HARRISON LLP
TWO EMBARCADERO PLACE
2200 GENG ROAD
PALO ALTO, CALIFORNIA 94303
(650) 424-0160

APPROXIMATE DATE OF COMMENCEMENT OF PROPOSED SALE TO THE PUBLIC:
From time to time after this registration statement becomes effective.

If the only securities being registered on this Form are being offered pursuant to dividend or interest reinvestment plans, please check the following box. [ ]

If any of the securities being registered on this Form are to be offered on a delayed or continuous basis pursuant to Rule 415 under the Securities Act of 1933, other than securities offered only in connection with dividend or interest reinvestment plans, check the following box. [X]

If this Form is filed to register additional securities for an offering pursuant to Rule 462(b) under the Securities Act, please check the following box and list the Securities Act registration statement number of the earlier effective registration statement for the same offering. [ ] _____

If this Form is a post-effective amendment filed pursuant to Rule 462(c) under the Securities Act, check the following box and list the Securities Act registration statement number of the earlier effective registration statement for the same offering. [ ] _____

If delivery of the prospectus is expected to be made pursuant to Rule 434, please check the following box. [ ]

CALCULATION OF REGISTRATION FEE

TITLE OF EACH CLASS OF SECURITIES TO BE REGISTERED	AMOUNT TO BE REGISTERED	PROPOSED MAXIMUM AGGREGATE OFFERING PRICE PER SHARE(1)	PROPOSED MAXIMUM AGGREGATE OFFERING PRICE(1)	AMOUNT OF REGISTRATION FEE
Common Stock, $0.001 par value per share	2,343,038	$50.80	$119,026,330.40	$31,422.95

(1) The price of $50.80, the average of the high and low prices of Cisco's common stock on The Nasdaq Stock Market's National Market on October 11, 2000, is set forth solely for the purpose of computing the registration fee pursuant to Rule 457(c).

THE REGISTRANT HEREBY AMENDS THIS REGISTRATION STATEMENT ON SUCH DATE OR DATES AS MAY BE NECESSARY TO DELAY ITS EFFECTIVE DATE UNTIL THE REGISTRANT SHALL FILE A FURTHER AMENDMENT WHICH SPECIFICALLY STATES THAT THIS REGISTRATION STATEMENT SHALL THEREAFTER BECOME EFFECTIVE IN ACCORDANCE WITH SECTION 8(A) OF THE SECURITIES ACT OF 1933, AS AMENDED, OR UNTIL THE REGISTRATION STATEMENT SHALL BECOME EFFECTIVE ON SUCH DATE AS THE SECURITIES AND EXCHANGE COMMISSION, ACTING PURSUANT TO SAID SECTION 8(A), MAY DETERMINE.

THE INFORMATION CONTAINED IN THIS PRELIMINARY PROSPECTUS IS NOT COMPLETE AND MAY BE CHANGED. THESE SECURITIES MAY NOT BE SOLD UNTIL THE REGISTRATION STATEMENT FILED WITH THE SECURITIES AND EXCHANGE COMMISSION IS EFFECTIVE. THIS PROSPECTUS IS NOT AN OFFER TO SELL THESE SECURITIES AND IT IS NOT SOLICITING AN OFFER TO BUY THESE SECURITIES IN ANY STATE WHERE THE OFFER OR SALE IS NOT PERMITTED.

SUBJECT TO COMPLETION, DATED OCTOBER 13, 2000

PRELIMINARY PROSPECTUS

2,343,038 Shares

CISCO SYSTEMS, INC.

Common Stock

The 2,343,038 shares of our common stock offered by this prospectus were originally issued by us in connection with our acquisition of Komodo Technology, Inc. All the shares of our common stock offered by this prospectus may be resold from time to time by us on behalf of certain of our shareholders. The shares were originally issued in a private offering made in reliance on Regulation D and/or Section 4(2) of the Securities Act of 1933.

The prices at which such shareholders may sell the shares will be determined by the prevailing market price for the shares or in negotiated transactions. We will not receive any of the proceeds from the sale of the shares.

Our common stock is quoted on The Nasdaq National Market under the symbol "CSCO." On October 6, 2000, the last sale price of our common stock as reported on The Nasdaq National Market was $51.188.

INVESTING IN OUR COMMON STOCK INVOLVES RISKS. SEE THE SECTIONS ENTITLED "RISK FACTORS" IN THE DOCUMENTS WE FILE WITH THE SECURITIES AND EXCHANGE COMMISSION THAT ARE INCORPORATED BY REFERENCES IN THIS PROSPECTUS FOR CERTAIN RISKS AND UNCERTAINTIES THAT YOU SHOULD CONSIDER.

NEITHER THE SECURITIES AND EXCHANGE COMMISSION NOR ANY STATE SECURITIES COMMISSION HAS APPROVED OR DISAPPROVED OF THESE SECURITIES OR PASSED UPON THE ADEQUACY OR ACCURACY OF THIS PROSPECTUS. ANY REPRESENTATION TO THE CONTRARY IS A CRIMINAL OFFENSE.

The date of this prospectus is OCTOBER __, 2000.

WHERE YOU CAN FIND MORE INFORMATION

We file annual, quarterly and special reports, proxy statements and other information with the Securities and Exchange Commission. You may read and copy any reports, statements, or other information that we file at the Securities and Exchange Commission's Public Reference Room at 450 Fifth Street, N.W., Washington, D.C. 20549. Please call the Securities and Exchange Commission at 1-800-SEC-0330 for further information on the operation of the Public Reference Room. Our Securities and Exchange Commission filings are also available to the public from our Web site at http://www.cisco.com or at the Securities and Exchange Commission's Web site at http://www.sec.gov.

INCORPORATION OF CERTAIN DOCUMENTS BY REFERENCE

The Securities and Exchange Commission allows us to "incorporate by reference" the information we file with them, which means that we can disclose important information to you by referring you to those documents. The information incorporated by reference is considered to be part of this prospectus except for any information superseded by information contained directly in this prospectus or in later filed documents incorporated by reference in this prospectus. We incorporate by reference the documents listed below and any future filings made with the Securities and Exchange Commission under Section 13a, 13(c), 14, or 15(d) of the Securities Exchange Act of 1934 after the date of this prospectus and prior to the time all of the securities offered by this prospectus are sold.

(a) Cisco's Annual Report on Form 10-K for the fiscal year ended July 29, 2000, filed September 29, 2000.

(b) The Registrant's Current Reports on Form 8-K filed on December 15, 1999 (as amended on Form 8-K/A filed on February 3, 2000 and on Form 8-K/A-1 filed on August 4, 2000), August 15, 2000, September 7, 2000, September 15, 2000, September 26, 2000, September 28, 2000 and September 29, 2000;

(c) The description of Cisco Common Stock contained in its registration statement on Form 8-A filed January 11, 1990, including any amendments or reports filed for the purpose of updating such descriptions; and

(d) The description of Cisco's Preferred Stock Purchase Rights, contained in its registration statement on Form 8-A filed on June 11, 1998, including any amendments or reports filed for the purpose of updating such description.

You may request a copy of these filings, at no cost, by writing or telephoning us at the following address:
Larry R. Carter
Senior Vice President, Chief Financial Officer and Secretary
Cisco Systems, Inc.
170 West Tasman Drive
San Jose, CA 95134-1706
408-526-4000

You should rely only on the information incorporated by reference or provided in this prospectus or any prospectus supplement. We have not authorized anyone to provide you with different information. We are not making an offer of these securities in any state where the offer is not permitted. You should not assume that the information in this prospectus or any prospectus supplement is accurate as of any date other than the date on the front of this Prospectus.

THE COMPANY

Our principal executive offices are located at 170 West Tasman Drive, San Jose, California 95134-1706. Our telephone number is (408) 526-4000.

PLAN OF DISTRIBUTION

We are registering all 2,343,038 shares on behalf of the selling shareholders. The selling shareholders named in the table below or pledgees, donees, transferees or other successors-in-interest selling shares received from a named selling shareholder as a gift, partnership distribution or other non-sale-related transfer after the date of this prospectus may sell the shares from time to time. The selling shareholders may also decide not to sell all the shares they are allowed to sell under this prospectus. The selling shareholders will act independently of us in making decisions with respect to the timing, manner and size of each sale. The sales may be made on one or more exchanges or in the over-the-counter market or otherwise, at prices and at terms then prevailing or at prices related to the then current market price, or in negotiated transactions. The selling shareholders may effect such transactions by selling the shares to or through broker-dealers. Our common stock may be sold by one or more of, or a combination of, the following:

- a block trade in which the broker-dealer so engaged will attempt to sell our common stock as agent but may position and resell a portion of the block as principal to facilitate the transaction,

- purchases by a broker-dealer as principal and resale by such broker-dealer for its account pursuant to this prospectus,

- an exchange distribution in accordance with the rules of such exchange,

- ordinary brokerage transactions and transactions in which the broker solicits purchasers, and

- in privately negotiated transactions.

To the extent required, this prospectus may be amended or supplemented from time to time to describe a specific plan of distribution. In effecting sales, broker-dealers engaged by the selling shareholders may arrange for other broker-dealers to participate in the resales.

The selling shareholders may enter into hedging transactions with broker-dealers in connection with distributions of our common stock or otherwise. In such transactions, broker-dealers may engage in short sales of the shares in the course of hedging the positions they assume with selling shareholders. The selling shareholders also may sell shares short and redeliver our common stock to close out such short positions. The selling shareholders may enter into option or other transactions with broker-dealers which require the delivery to the broker-dealer of our common stock. The broker-dealer may then resell or otherwise transfer such shares pursuant to this prospectus. The selling shareholders also may loan or pledge the shares to a broker-dealer. The broker-dealer may sell our common stock so loaned, or upon a default the broker-dealer may sell the pledged shares pursuant to this prospectus.

Broker-dealers or agents may receive compensation in the form of commissions, discounts or concessions from selling shareholders. Broker-dealers or agents may also receive compensation from the purchasers of our common stock for whom they act as agents or to whom they sell as principals, or both. Compensation as to a particular broker-dealer might be in excess of customary commissions and will be in amounts to be negotiated in connection with our common stock. Broker-dealers or agents and any other participating broker-dealers or the selling shareholders may be deemed to be "underwriters" within the meaning of Section 2(11) of the Securities Act of 1933 in connection with sales of the shares. Accordingly, any such commission, discount or concession received by them and any profit on the resale of our common stock purchased by them may be deemed to be underwriting discounts or commissions under the Securities Act of 1933. Because selling shareholders may be deemed to be "underwriters" within the meaning of Section 2(11) of the Securities Act of 1933, the selling shareholders will be subject to the prospectus delivery requirements of the Securities Act of 1933. In addition, any securities covered by this prospectus which qualify for sale pursuant to Rule 144 promulgated under the Securities Act of 1933 may be sold under Rule 144 rather than pursuant to this prospectus. The selling shareholders have advised us that they have not entered into any agreements, understandings or arrangements with any underwriters or broker-dealers regarding the sale of their securities. There is no underwriter or coordinating broker acting in connection with the proposed sale of shares by selling shareholders.

Our common stock will be sold only through registered or licensed brokers or dealers if required under applicable state securities laws. In addition, in certain states our common stock may not be sold unless they have been registered or qualified for sale in the applicable state or an exemption from the registration or qualification requirement is available and is complied with.

Under applicable rules and regulations under the Exchange Act of 1934, any person engaged in the distribution of our common stock may not simultaneously engage in market making activities with respect to our common stock for a period of two business days prior to the commencement of such distribution. In addition, each selling shareholder will be subject to applicable provisions of the Exchange Act of 1934 and the associated rules and regulations under the Exchange Act of 1934, including Regulation M, which provisions may limit the timing of purchases and sales of shares of our common stock by the selling shareholders. We will make copies of this prospectus available to the selling shareholders and have informed them of the need for delivery of copies of this prospectus to purchasers at or prior to the time of any sale of our common stock.

We will file a supplement to this prospectus, if required, pursuant to Rule 424(b) under the Securities Act of 1933 upon being notified by a selling shareholder that any material arrangement has been entered into with a broker-dealer for the sale of shares through a block trade, special offering, exchange distribution or secondary distribution or a purchase by a broker or dealer. Such supplement will disclose:

- the name of each such selling shareholder and of the participating broker-dealer(s),
- the number of shares involved,
- the price at which such shares were sold,

- the commissions paid or discounts or concessions allowed to such broker-dealer(s), where applicable,

- that such broker-dealer(s) did not conduct any investigation to verify the information set out or incorporated by reference in this prospectus, and

- other facts material to the transaction.

We will bear all costs, expenses and fees in connection with the registration of our common stock. The selling shareholders will bear all commissions and discounts, if any, attributable to the sales of the shares. The selling shareholders may agree to indemnify any broker-dealer or agent that participates in transactions involving sales of the shares against certain liabilities, including liabilities arising under the Securities Act.

SELLING SHAREHOLDERS

The following table sets forth the number of shares owned by each of the selling shareholders. None of the selling shareholders has had a material relationship with us within the past three years other than as a result of the ownership of our common stock or other securities of ours or as a result of their employment with us as of the date of the closing of the acquisition of Komodo Technology, Inc. No estimate can be given as to the amount of our common stock that will be held by the selling shareholders after completion of this offering because the selling shareholders may offer all or some of our common stock and because there currently are no agreements, arrangements or understandings with respect to the sale of any of our common stock. The shares offered by this prospectus may be offered from time to time by the selling shareholders named in the following text.

NAME OF SELLING SHAREHOLDER	NUMBER OF SHARES BENEFICIALLY OWNED	PERCENT OF OUTSTANDING SHARES	NUMBER OF SHARES REGISTERED FOR SALE HEREBY
Michael P. Sadikun	41,892	*	41,892
Denis Kar Man Mak	62,838	*	62,838
Ramah Sutardja	52,365	*	52,365
Chun-Chau Lin	73,311	*	73,311
Budi Sutardja	31,419	*	31,419
Michael C. Chen	39,274	*	39,274
Chang-Ho Chen	13,091	*	13,091
Andrew Fandrianto	83,785	*	83,785
Alex Fandrianto	83,785	*	83,785
Anthony Fandrianto	83,785	*	83,785
Jan Fandrianto	691,226	*	691,226
Wen-hsiung Chen	159,191	*	159,191
Caren H. Chen	16,757	*	16,757
Christina H. Chen	16,757	*	16,757
Colleen Y. Chen	16,757	*	16,757
Ming Hong Chan	20,946	*	20,946
Chorng Yeong Chu	20,946	*	20,946
Elim Huang	20,946	*	20,946
Sam K. Sin	31,419	*	31,419
Victoria H. Mah	10,473	*	10,473
Jen-Wen Tseng	4,189	*	4,189
Leila M. McGowan	10,473	*	10,473
Larry K. Lam	3,141	*	3,141
Raymond C. Hsu	20,946	*	20,946
Steven D. Toteda	83,785	*	83,785
Grace Hu-Morely	10,473	*	10,473
Emily J. Bates	10,473	*	10,473
ESS Technology	314,193	*	314,193
ESS Technology	314,193	*	314,193
Joel Porter	209	*	209
Totals	2,343,038		2,343,038

*Represents beneficial ownership of less than one percent.

(1) This registration statement also shall cover any additional shares of common stock which become issuable in connection with the shares registered for sale hereby by reason of any stock dividend, stock split, recapitalization or other similar transaction effected without the receipt of consideration which results in an increase in the number of our outstanding shares of common stock.

USE OF PROCEEDS

We will not receive any proceeds from the sale of the shares of common stock by the selling shareholders.

LEGAL MATTERS

The validity of our common stock offered hereby will be passed upon for us by Brobeck, Phleger & Harrison LLP, Palo Alto, California.

EXPERTS

Our consolidated financial statements incorporated in this prospectus by reference to the Annual Report on Form 10-K for the year ended July 29, 2000, have been so incorporated in reliance on the report of PricewaterhouseCoopers LLP, independent accountants, given on the authority of said firm as experts in accounting and auditing.

PricewaterhouseCoopers LLP ("PWC"), our independent accountants, has notified us that PWC is engaged in discussions with the Securities and Exchange Commission following an internal review by PWC, pursuant to an administrative settlement with the Securities and Exchange Commission, of PWC's compliance with auditor guidelines. PWC has advised us that we are one of the companies affected by such discussions. We are not involved in the discussions between the Securities and Exchange Commission and PWC and cannot predict the result of those discussions.

We have not authorized any person to make a statement that differs from what is in this prospectus. If any person does make a statement that differs from what is in this prospectus, you should not rely on it. This prospectus is not an offer to sell, nor is it seeking an offer to buy, these securities in any state in which the offer or sale is not permitted. The information in this prospectus is complete and accurate as of its date, but the information may change after that date.

CISCO SYSTEMS, INC.

2,343,038 SHARES
OF COMMON STOCK
PROSPECTUS

OCTOBER __, 2000

AGREEMENT OF MERGER
OF
CISCO SYSTEMS, INC.
AND
KOMODO TECHNOLOGY, INC.

This Agreement of Merger is dated as of the 25th day of September, 2000 ("Merger Agreement"), between Cisco Systems, Inc., a California corporation ("Acquirer"), and Komodo Technology, Inc., a California corporation ("Target").

RECITALS

A. Target was incorporated in the State of California and on the date hereof has outstanding 16,372,000 shares of Common Stock ("Target Common Stock"), 6,000,000 shares of Series A Preferred Stock (the "Target Series A Preferred Stock") and 2,648,170 shares of Series B Preferred Stock (the "Target Series B Preferred Stock"). The Target Series A Preferred Stock and the Target Series B Preferred Stock is hereinafter collectively referred to as the "Target Preferred Stock."

B. Acquiror and Target have entered into an Agreement and Plan of Merger and Reorganization (the "Agreement and Plan of Reorganization") providing for certain representations, warranties, covenants and agreements in connection with the transactions contemplated hereby. This Merger Agreement and the Agreement and Plan of Reorganization are intended to be construed together to effectuate their purpose.

C. The Boards of Directors of Target and Acquirer deem it advisable and in their mutual best interests and in the best interests of the shareholders of Target, that Target be acquired by Acquirer through a merger ("Merger") of Target with and into Acquirer.

D. The Boards of Directors of Acquirer and Target and the shareholders of Target have approved the Merger.

AGREEMENTS

The parties hereto hereby agree as follows:

1. Target shall be merged with and into Acquirer, and Acquirer shall be the surviving corporation.

2. The Merger shall become effective at such time (the "Effective Time") as this Merger Agreement and the officers' certificate of Target are filed with the Secretary of State of the State of California pursuant to Section 1103 of the Corporations Code of the State of California.

3. Immediately prior to the Effective Time of the Merger, each share of Target Preferred Stock shall convert into Target Common Stock. At the Effective Time of the Merger (i) all shares of Target Common Stock that are owned directly or indirectly by Target or any other direct or indirect wholly owned subsidiary of Target shall be cancelled, and no securities of Acquirer or other consideration shall be delivered in exchange therefor, and (ii) each of the issued and outstanding shares of Target Common Stock (other than shares, if any, held by persons who have not voted such shares for approval of the Merger and with respect to which such persons shall become entitled to exercise dissenters' rights in accordance with the Corporations Code of the State of California ("California Law"), referred to hereinafter as "Dissenting Shares") shall be converted automatically into and exchanged for 0.10473129 of a share of Acquirer Common Stock; provided, however, that no more than 2,635,790 shares of Common Stock of Acquirer shall be issued in such exchange (including Acquirer Common Stock reserved for issuance upon exercise of Target options and Target warrants assumed by Acquirer). Those shares of Acquirer Common Stock to be issued as a result of the Merger are referred to herein as the "Acquirer Shares."

4. Any Dissenting Shares shall not be converted into Acquirer Common Stock but shall be converted into the right to receive such consideration as may be determined to be due with respect to such Dissenting Shares pursuant to California Law. If after the Effective Time any Dissenting Shares shall lose their status as Dissenting Shares, then as of the occurrence of the event which causes the loss of such status, such shares shall be converted into Acquirer Common Stock in accordance with Section 3.

5. Notwithstanding any other term or provision hereof, no fractional shares of Acquirer Common Stock shall be issued, but in lieu thereof each holder of shares of Target Common Stock who would otherwise, but for rounding as provided herein, be entitled to receive a fraction of a share of Acquirer Common Stock shall receive from Acquirer an amount of cash equal to the per share market value of Acquirer Common Stock (deemed to be $66.39375) multiplied by the fraction of a share of Acquirer Common Stock to which such holder would otherwise be entitled. The fractional share interests of each Target shareholder shall be aggregated, so that no Target shareholder shall receive cash in an amount greater than the value of one full share of Acquirer Common Stock.

6. The conversion of Target Common Stock into Acquirer Common Stock as provided by this Merger Agreement shall occur automatically at the Effective Time of the Merger without action by the holders thereof. Each holder of Target Common Stock shall thereupon be entitled to receive shares of Acquirer Common Stock in accordance with the Agreement and Plan of Reorganization.

7. At the Effective Time of the Merger, the separate existence of Target shall cease, and Acquirer shall succeed, without other transfer, to all of the rights and properties of Target and shall be subject to all the debts and liabilities thereof in the same manner as if Acquirer had itself incurred them. All rights of creditors and all liens upon the property of each corporation shall be preserved unimpaired, provided that such liens upon property of Target shall be limited to the property affected thereby immediately prior to the Effective Time of the Merger.

8. This Merger Agreement is intended as a plan of reorganization within the meaning of Section 368(a) of the Internal Revenue Code of 1986, as amended.

9. (a) The Amended and Restated Articles of Incorporation of Acquirer in effect immediately prior to the Effective Time shall be the Amended and Restated Articles of Incorporation of the Surviving Corporation unless and until thereafter amended.

(b) The Bylaws of Acquirer in effect immediately prior to the Effective Time shall be the Bylaws of the Surviving Corporation unless and until amended or repealed as provided by applicable law, the Articles of Incorporation of the Surviving Corporation and such Bylaws.

(c) The directors and officers of Acquirer immediately prior to the Effective Time shall be the directors and officers of the Surviving Corporation.

10. (a) Notwithstanding the approval of this Merger Agreement by the shareholders of Target, this Merger Agreement shall terminate forthwith in the event that the Agreement and Plan of Reorganization shall be terminated as therein provided.

(b) In the event of the termination of this Merger Agreement as provided above, this Merger Agreement shall forthwith become void and there shall be no liability on the part of Target or Acquirer or their respective officers or directors, except as otherwise provided in the Agreement and Plan of Reorganization.

(c) This Merger Agreement may be signed in one or more counterparts, each of which shall be deemed an original and all of which shall constitute one agreement.

(d) This Merger Agreement may be amended by the parties hereto any time before or after approval hereof by the shareholders of Target, but, after such approval, no amendments shall be made which by law require the further approval of such shareholders without obtaining such approval. This Merger Agreement may not be amended except by an instrument in writing signed on behalf of each of the parties hereto.

IN WITNESS WHEREOF, the parties have executed this Merger Agreement as of the date first written above.

CISCO SYSTEMS, INC.

By: /s/ John T. Chambers
_____

John T. Chambers, President

By: /s/ David Rogan
_____

David Rogan, Assistant Secretary

KOMODO TECHNOLOGY, INC.

By: /s/ Jan Fandrianto

Jan Fandrianto, President and Secretary

[SIGNATURE PAGE TO AGREEMENT OF MERGER]

OFFICERS' CERTIFICATE
OF
TARGET

Jan Fandrianto, President and Secretary of Komodo Technology, Inc., a corporation duly organized and existing under the laws of the State of California (the "Corporation"), does hereby certify:

1. He is the duly elected, acting and qualified President and Secretary of the Corporation.

2. There are two authorized classes of shares, consisting of 29,000,000 shares of Common Stock, no par value, and 8,648,170 shares of Preferred Stock, no par value. On the record date for the vote on the Agreement of Merger, there were 16,372,000 shares of Common Stock, 6,000,000 shares of Series A Preferred Stock and 2,648,170 shares of Series B Preferred Stock outstanding and entitled to vote on the Agreement of Merger in the form attached.

3. The Agreement of Merger in the form attached was duly approved by the Board of Directors of the Corporation in accordance with the Corporations Code of the State of California.

4. Approval of the Agreement of Merger by the holders of at least 66-2/3 percent of the outstanding shares of Series A Preferred Stock, more than 50 percent of the outstanding shares of Series A Preferred Stock and Series B Preferred Stock, and more than 50 percent of the outstanding shares of Common Stock was required. The percentage of the

outstanding shares of each class of the Corporation's shares entitled to vote on the Agreement of Merger which voted to approve the Agreement of Merger equaled or exceeded the vote required.

The undersigned declares under penalty of perjury that the statements contained in the foregoing certificate are true of his own knowledge. Executed in Los Gatos, California, on September 25, 2000.

By: /s/ Jan Fandrianto
_____

Jan Fandrianto, President and Secretary

OFFICERS' CERTIFICATE
OF
ACQUIRER

The undersigned, John T. Chambers and David Rogan, hereby certify on behalf of Cisco Systems, Inc., a California corporation ("Acquirer"), that Mr. Chambers is the duly elected President and Chief Executive Officer and Mr. Rogan is the duly elected Assistant Secretary of Acquirer and they further certify on behalf of Acquirer that:

1. They are the duly elected, acting and qualified President and Assistant Secretary, respectively, of Acquirer.

2. There are two authorized classes of shares, consisting of 20,000,000,000 shares of Common Stock, of which 7,165,914,196 shares are issued and outstanding, and 5,000,000 shares of Preferred Stock, none of which are issued and outstanding.

3. The Agreement of Merger in the form attached was approved by the Board of Directors of Acquirer in accordance with the California Corporations Code.

4. No vote of the shareholders of Acquirer was required pursuant to Section 1201(b) of the California Corporations Code.

Each of the undersigned declares under penalty of perjury that the statements contained in the foregoing certificate are true of their own knowledge. Executed in San Jose, California on September 25, 2000.

By: /s/ John T. Chambers

John T. Chambers
President and Chief Executive Officer

By: /s/ David Rogan

David Rogan
Assistant Secretary

INDEX

Note to reader: Page references followed by *n.* refer to a specific footnote on that page.

ABOUT THE AUTHORS

ROBERT J. BORGHESE

Robert J. Borghese is principal of Borghese Law Firm, which provides legal and business advisory services to emerging growth companies. He has over 10 years of experience advising startup and emerging growth companies on legal, strategic, financial and business planning issues, and has cofounded several companies including a real estate merchant bank.

Mr. Borghese has been involved in numerous merger and acquisition transactions involving technology and health care companies where he has advised on strategic planning issues, target identification, and the structuring of transactions. In addition, Mr. Borghese has advised numerous emerging growth companies on legal and strategic planning issues including strategies for growth through strategic alliances, and mergers and acquisitions.

Mr. Borghese is a member of the faculty of the Wharton School of the University of Pennsylvania as a Lecturer in Law and Entrepreneurial Management. He teaches courses in the Wharton M.B.A., Executive M.B.A. and Executive Master's in Technology Management program on legal issues for emerging growth companies and on mergers and acquisitions. He has lectured extensively on strategic planning, mergers and acquisitions, strategic alliances, and legal issues for emerging growth companies.

Mr. Borghese is a graduate of the University of Pennsylvania Law School. He has an M.A. in Financial Economics from King's College, Cambridge

University, England, and holds a degree in finance from the Wharton School of the University of Pennsylvania.

PAUL F. BORGESE

Paul F. Borgese is an independent consultant who has worked on a wide variety of strategy initiatives for global corporations, emerging growth companies, financial institutions, professional service firms, government agencies, and professional associations. While working for the Federal Reserve System, he reviewed and advised bank holding companies and commercial banks on their operations, policies, and procedures. He lectures on mergers and acquisitions, corporate finance, leadership, entrepreneurship, marketing, business communications, and Internet strategy.

Mr. Borgese holds a B.S. in economics from the Wharton School; a B.A. in English from the University of Pennsylvania; an M.A. in literature from Trinity College, Cambridge University, England, where he was a British Marshall Scholar; a master's degree in governmental administration from the Fels Center of Government, University of Pennsylvania; and an M.B.A. in finance and marketing from the Stern School of Business, New York University.